ACCA
Paper F3

FIA
Diploma in Accounting and Business

Financial Accounting (FA/FFA)

EXAM KIT

PUBLISHING

British Library Cataloguing-in-Publication Data

A catalogue record for this book is available from the British Library.

Published by:

Kaplan Publishing UK
Unit 2 The Business Centre
Molly Millar's Lane
Wokingham
Berkshire
RG41 2QZ

ISBN: 978-1-78415-826-2

Acknowledgements

This Product includes propriety content of the International Accounting Standards Board which is overseen by the IFRS Foundation, and is used with the express permission of the IFRS Foundation under licence. All rights reserved. No part of this publication may be reproduced, stored in a retrieval system, or transmitted in any form or by any means, electronic, mechanical, photocopying, recording, or otherwise, without prior written permission of Kaplan Publishing and the IFRS Foundation.

The IFRS Foundation logo, the IASB logo, the IFRS for SMEs logo, the "Hexagon Device", "IFRS Foundation", "eIFRS", "IAS", "IASB", "IFRS for SMEs", "IFRS", "IASs", "IFRSs", "International Accounting Standards" and "International Financial Reporting Standards", "IFRIC" and "IFRS Taxonomy" are Trade Marks of the IFRS Foundation.

Trade Marks

The IFRS Foundation logo, the IASB logo, the IFRS for SMEs logo, the "Hexagon Device", "IFRS Foundation", "eIFRS", "IAS", "IASB", "IFRS for SMEs", "NIIF" IASs" "IFRS", "IFRSs", "International Accounting Standards", "International Financial Reporting Standards", "IFRIC", "SIC" and "IFRS Taxonomy".

Further details of the Trade Marks including details of countries where the Trade Marks are registered or applied for are available from the Foundation on request.

This product contains material that is ©Financial Reporting Council Ltd (FRC). Adapted and reproduced with the kind permission of the Financial Reporting Council. All rights reserved. For further information, please visit www.frc.org.uk or call +44 (0)20 7492 2300.

CONTENTS

Section

This document references IFRS® Standards and IAS® Standards, which are authored by the International Accounting Standards Board (the Board), and published in the 2016 IFRS Standards Red Book.

Features in this edition

In addition to providing a wide ranging bank of practice questions, we have also included in this edition:

- Details of the examination format.

- Examples of 'multi-task' questions that will form part of the examination format.

- Paper-specific information and advice on exam technique.

- Our recommended approach to make your revision for this particular subject as effective as possible.

    This includes step-by-step guidance on how best to use our Kaplan material (Study Text, Pocket Notes and Exam Kit) at this stage in your studies.

You will find a wealth of other resources to help you with your studies on the following sites:

www.MyKaplan.co.uk and www.accaglobal.com/students/

Quality and accuracy are of the utmost importance to us so if you spot an error in any of our products, please send an email to mykaplanreporting@kaplan.com with full details.

Our Quality Co-ordinator will work with our technical team to verify the error and take action to ensure it is corrected in future editions.

INDEX TO QUESTIONS AND ANSWERS

MULTIPLE CHOICE TEST QUESTIONS

MULTI-TASK QUESTIONS

KAPLAN PUBLISHING

EXAM TECHNIQUE

- **Do not skip any of the material** in the syllabus.

- **Read each question** *very* carefully.

- **Double-check your answer** before committing yourself to it.

- Answer **every** question – if you do not know an answer, you don't lose anything by guessing. Think carefully before you **guess**. The examiner has indicated that many candidates are still leaving blank answers in the paper-based exam.

- If you are answering a multiple-choice question, **eliminate first those answers that you know are wrong**. Then choose the most appropriate answer from those that are left.

- Remember that **only one answer to a multiple-choice question can be right**. After you have eliminated the ones that you know to be wrong, if you are still unsure, guess. Only guess after you have double-checked that you have only eliminated answers that are *definitely* wrong.

- Remember that the CBE resources available on ACCA's web site can still be used to support your learning, even if you intend to attempt the paper-based exam.

Computer-based exams – tips

- Do not attempt a CBE until you have **completed all study material** relating to it.

- On the ACCA website there is a CBE demonstration. It is **ESSENTIAL** that you attempt this before your real CBE. You will become familiar with how to move around the CBE screens and the way that questions are formatted, increasing your confidence and speed in the actual exam.

- Be sure you understand how to use the **software** before you start the exam. If in doubt, ask the assessment centre staff to explain it to you.

- Questions are **displayed on the screen** and answers are entered using keyboard and mouse. At the end of the exam, you are given a certificate showing the result you have achieved.

- In addition to the traditional multiple-choice question type, CBEs might also contain **other types of questions**, such as number entry questions, formula entry questions, and stem questions with multiple parts.

- Note that the CBE variant of the examination will not require you to input text, although you may be required to choose the correct text from options available.

- You need to be sure you **know how to answer questions** of this type before you sit the exam, through practice.

PAPER SPECIFIC INFORMATION

THE EXAM

FORMAT OF THE PAPER-BASED AND COMPUTER-BASED EXAM

	Number of marks
35 compulsory multiple-choice questions (2 marks each)	70
2 multi-task questions (15 marks each)	30

Total time allowed: 2 hours

- Two mark questions will usually comprise the following answer types:

    (i) Multiple choice with four options (A, B, C or D)

    (ii) Some MCQs may use a multiple response approach (e.g. identify which two of four available statements are correct, with four options to choose from, each option consisting of a combination of two of the available statements). Remember that only one of the four available options will be correct.

- The multi-task questions will test consolidations and preparation of financial statements. The consolidation question could include a small amount of interpretation.

- The examinations contain 100% compulsory questions and students must study across the breadth of the syllabus to prepare effectively for the examination

- The examination will be assessed by a two hour paper-based or computer-based examination. You should refer to the ACCA web site for information regarding the availability of the paper-based and computer-based examination.

PASS MARK

The pass mark for all ACCA Qualification examination papers is 50%.

DETAILED SYLLABUS

The detailed syllabus and study guide written by the ACCA can be found at:

www.accaglobal.com/students/

KAPLAN'S RECOMMENDED REVISION APPROACH

QUESTION PRACTICE IS THE KEY TO SUCCESS

Success in professional examinations relies upon you acquiring a firm grasp of the required knowledge at the tuition phase. In order to be able to do the questions, knowledge is essential.

However, the difference between success and failure often hinges on your exam technique on the day and making the most of the revision phase of your studies.

The **Kaplan study text** is the starting point, designed to provide the underpinning knowledge to tackle all questions. However, in the revision phase, poring over books is not the answer.

Kaplan online progress tests help you consolidate your knowledge and understanding and are a useful tool to check whether you can remember key topic areas.

Kaplan pocket notes are designed to help you quickly revise a topic area, however you then need to practice questions. There is a need to progress to full exam standard questions as soon as possible, and to tie your exam technique and technical knowledge together.

The importance of question practice cannot be over-emphasised.

The recommended approach below is designed by expert tutors in the field, in conjunction with their knowledge of the examiner.

The approach taken for the fundamental papers is to revise by topic area.

You need to practice as many questions as possible in the time you have left.

OUR AIM

Our aim is to get you to the stage where you can attempt exam standard questions confidently, to time, in a closed book environment, with no supplementary help (i.e. to simulate the real examination experience).

Practising your exam technique on real past examination questions, in timed conditions, is also vitally important for you to assess your progress and identify areas of weakness that may need more attention in the final run up to the examination.

The approach below shows you which questions you should use to build up to coping with exam standard question practice, and references to the sources of information available should you need to revisit a topic area in more detail.

Remember that in the real examination, all you have to do is:

- attempt all questions required by the exam
- only spend the allotted time on each question, and
- get them at least 50% right!

Try and practice this approach on every question you attempt from now to the real exam.

THE KAPLAN PAPER F3 REVISION PLAN

Stage 1: Assess areas of strengths and weaknesses

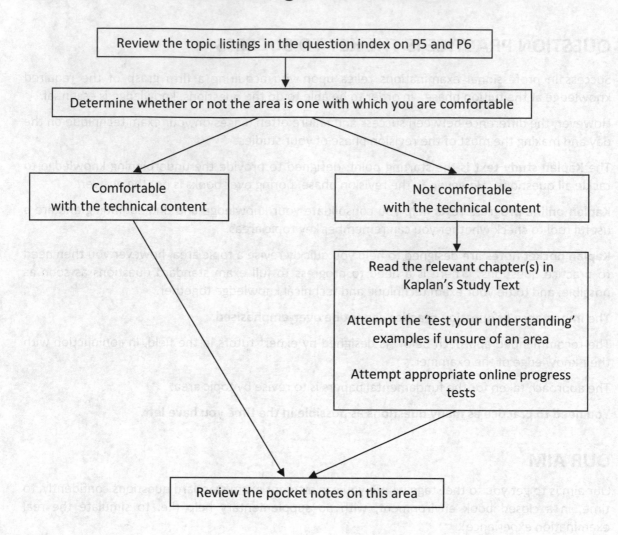

Review the topic listings in the question index on P5 and P6

Determine whether or not the area is one with which you are comfortable

Comfortable
with the technical content

Not comfortable
with the technical content

Read the relevant chapter(s) in
Kaplan's Study Text

Attempt the 'test your understanding'
examples if unsure of an area

Attempt appropriate online progress
tests

Review the pocket notes on this area

Stage 2: Practice questions

Ensure that you revise all syllabus areas as questions could be asked on anything.

Try to avoid referring to text books and notes and the model answer until you have completed your attempt.

Try to answer the question in the allotted time.

Review your attempt with the model answer. If you got the answer wrong, can you see why? Was the problem a lack of knowledge or a failure to understand the question fully?

Fill in the self-assessment box below and decide on your best course of action.

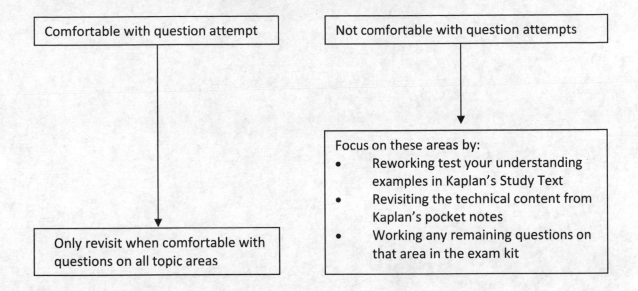

Comfortable with question attempt

Not comfortable with question attempts

Only revisit when comfortable with questions on all topic areas

Focus on these areas by:
- Reworking test your understanding examples in Kaplan's Study Text
- Revisiting the technical content from Kaplan's pocket notes
- Working any remaining questions on that area in the exam kit

Stage 3: Final pre-exam revision

We recommend that you **attempt at least one two hour mock examination** containing a set of previously unseen exam standard questions.

It is important that you get a feel for the breadth of coverage of a real exam without advanced knowledge of the topic areas covered – just as you will expect to see on the real exam day.

Ideally this mock should be sat in timed, closed book, real exam conditions and could be:

- a mock examination offered by your tuition provider, and/or

- the pilot paper in the back of this exam kit, and/or

- the practice simulation paper in this kit

Section 1

MULTIPLE CHOICE TEST QUESTIONS

THE CONTEXT AND PURPOSE OF FINANCIAL REPORTING

1 **Which of the following statements is true?**

A   The directors of a company are liable for any losses of the company

B   A sole trader business is owned by shareholders and operated by the proprietor

C   Partners are liable for losses in a partnership in proportion to their profit share ratio

D   A company is run by directors on behalf of its members

2 **Which of the following statements best defines a statement of financial position?**

A   It is a summary of income and expenditure for an accounting period

B   It is a summary of cash receipts and payments made during an accounting period

C   It is a summary of assets, liabilities and equity at a specified date

D   It is a summary of assets and expenses at a specified date

3 **Which of the following statements best defines a statement of profit or loss?**

A   It is a summary of assets and expenses at a specified date

B   It is a summary of cash receipts and payments made during an accounting period

C   It is a summary of assets, liabilities and equity at a specified date

D   It is a summary of income and expenditure for an accounting period

4 **Which one of the following user groups is likely to require the most detailed financial information?**

A   The management

B   Investors and potential investors

C   Government agencies

D   Employees

5 **Which of the following statements are true?**

(1) Accounting can be described as the recording and summarising of transactions.

(2) Financial accounting describes the production of a statement of financial position and statement of profit or loss for internal use.

A (1) only

B (2) only

C Both (1) and (2)

D None

6 **What is the main purpose of financial accounting?**

A To record all transactions in the books of account

B To provide management with detailed analyses of costs

C To enable preparation of financial statements that provides information about an entity's financial performance and position

D To calculate profit or loss for an accounting period

7 **Which one of the following sentences does NOT explain the distinction between financial statements and management accounts?**

A Financial statements are primarily for external users and management accounts are primarily for internal users.

B Financial statements are normally produced annually and management accounts are normally produced monthly.

C Financial statements are more accurate than management accounts.

D Financial statements are audited by an external auditor and management accounts do not normally have an external audit.

8 **Which of the following items is the IFRS Advisory Council is responsible for?**

(1) To give advice to the IASB or to the trustees.

(2) To give advice to the IASB on agenda decisions.

A (1) and (2)

B (1) only

C (2) only

D Neither (1) nor (2)

9 **Which one of the following statements best defines a liability?**

A   A liability is an obligation arising from a past transaction or event.

B   A liability is a legally binding amount owed to a third party.

C   A liability is an obligation arising from a past transaction or event which is expected to be settled by an outflow of economic benefits

D   A liability is anything which results in an outflow of economic benefits from an entity.

10 **Which, if any, of the following statements are true?**

(1)   International accounting standards are effective only if adopted by national regulatory bodies.

(2)   Accounting standards provide guidance on accounting for all types of transaction.

A   (1) only

B   (2) only

C   (1) and (2)

D   Neither

11 **Which one of the following statements best defines an expense?**

A   An expense is any outflow of economic benefits in an accounting period.

B   An expense is an outflow of economic benefits resulting from the purchase of resources in an accounting period.

C   An expense is an outflow of economic benefits resulting from a claim by a third party.

D   An expense is an outflow of economic benefits in an accounting period as a result of the using up of resources or a fall in the value of an asset.

12 **Which one of the following statements is true in relation to a partnership?**

A   A partnership is a separate legal entity

B   A partnership is jointly owned and managed by the partners

C   A partnership can raise capital by issuing shares to members of the public

D   A partnership is able to own property and other assets in its own name

13 **Which one of the following statements is true in relation to a sole trader?**

A   A sole trader cannot have any employees

B   A sole trader is able to introduce or withdraw capital from the business at any time

C   A sole trader has limited liability for the debts of the business

D   A sole trader can operate a business from only one location

14 Which of the following statements is true in relation to a limited liability company?

    A   A limited liability company can incur liabilities in its own name

    B   A limited liability company cannot acquire assets in its own name

    C   A limited liability company cannot incur liabilities in its own name

    D   A limited liability company can be formed on an informal basis by simple agreement between the first shareholders

15 Which one of the following items could be used to encourage executive directors to operate in the best interests of the company?

    A   They could be awarded a high salary

    B   They could receive bonuses based on both individual and company performance

    C   The could be entitled to large payment on resignation

    D   The could be asked to attend Annual General Meetings of the company

16 Which one statement relating to partnerships and limited liability companies is true?

    A   Both partnerships and limited liability companies are able to own assets in their own name.

    B   The members of a limited liability company have the right to participate in the management of that company, whereas partners do not have the right to participate in the management of their partnership.

    C   The partners have the right to participate in the management of the partnership, whereas members of a limited liability company do not have the right to participate in the management of that company.

    D   Partnerships are subject to the same regulations regarding introduction and withdrawal of capital from the business as a limited liability company.

17 Which one of the following items is the most obvious means of achieving public oversight of corporate governance?

    A   The company establishing a comprehensive web site

    B   Publication of the Annual Report and Accounts

    C   Press announcements of all significant developments

    D   Shareholder access to the Annual General Meeting

18 Which two items would you expect to see included within the financial statements of a sole trader?

    A   Issued share capital

    B   Revaluation surplus

    C   Personal drawings

    D   Capital account

19   Which two items would you expect to see included within the financial statements of a partnership?

   A   Dividends paid

   B   Capital accounts

   C   Profit appropriation account

   D   Share premium account

20   Which body is responsible for the issue of International Financial Reporting Standards?

   A   The IFRS Advisory Council

   B   The International Financial Reporting Interpretations Committee

   C   The International Accounting Standards Board

   D   The European Union

21   Which of the following statements relating to the IASB's Conceptual Framework for Financial Reporting 'the Framework' are true?

   (1)   The Framework is an accounting standard.

   (2)   The Framework assists in harmonising global accounting practices.

   (3)   The Framework assists national standard setters to develop national standards.

   (4)   The Framework assists users of financial information to interpret financial statements.

   A   (1) and (2)

   B   (2), (3) and (4)

   C   All four

   D   (1) and (3)

22   Which one of the following statements best defines an asset?

   A   An asset is a resource owned by the entity with a financial value.

   B   An asset is a resource controlled by an entity from which future economic benefits are expected to be generated.

   C   An asset is a resource controlled by an entity as a result of past events.

   D   An asset is a resource controlled by an entity as a result of past events from which future economic benefits are expected to be generated.

23   Which one of the following statements best defines the equity or capital of a business?

   A   Equity or capital of a business is represented by the net assets of the business

   B   Equity or capital of a business is equivalent to the value of the business

   C   Equity or capital of a business is equivalent to the value of the business assets

   D   Equity or capital of a business is represented by the total assets of the business

THE QUALITATIVE CHARACTERISTICS OF FINANCIAL INFORMATION

24 Which of the following items is not an enhancing qualitative characteristic of useful financial information as stated in the IASB Framework?

A   Comparability

B   Timeliness

C   Faithful representation

D   Understandability

25 Which one of the following statements is correct?

A   The going concern concept guarantees that a business will continue in operational existence for at least twelve months after the reporting date.

B   To comply with the law, the legal form of a transaction must always be reflected in financial statements.

C   If a non-current asset initially recognised at cost is revalued, the surplus must be credited in the statement of cash flows.

D   In times of rising prices, the use of historical cost accounting tends to understate assets and overstate profits.

26 Which two of the following items are enhancing qualitative characteristics of useful financial information as stated in the IASB Framework?

A   Relevance

B   Comparability

C   Faithful representation

D   Verifiability

27 Which of the following statements best explains the principle of faithful representation in relation preparation of the annual financial statements?

A   Transactions are presented any way that is considered appropriate.

B   Transactions are presented in such a way as to maximise profit for the year.

C   Transactions are presented in such a way to maximise asset values in the statement of financial position.

D   Transactions are presented to reflect their commercial substance of a transaction rather than their legal form.

28 The accounting concept which dictates that non-current assets should be valued at cost less accumulated depreciation, rather than at their enforced saleable value, is:

A   Understandability

B   Relevance

C   Comparability

D   Going concern

29 Which of the following pairs of items comprise the two fundamental qualitative characteristics of useful financial information?

A   Relevance and comparability

B   Relevance and faithful representation

C   Faithful representation and understandability

D   Faithful representation and comparability

30 Which of the following statements defines the business entity concept?

A   The business will continue to operate for the foreseeable future.

B   A business is always a separate legal entity, distinct from those who own or manage that business.

C   A business is never a separate legal entity from those who own or manage that business.

D   Financial transactions are recorded and presented from the perspective of the business, rather than from the perspective of the owners or managers of that business.

THE USE OF DOUBLE-ENTRY AND ACCOUNTING SYSTEMS

DOUBLE ENTRY BOOKKEEPING

31 Oscar runs a sole trader business selling computers. On 12 January 20X7, he employed his daughter as an administrator for the business and took a computer from the store room for her to use in the office.

What is the double entry for this transaction?

A	Dr Drawings	Cr Cost of sales
B	Dr Non-current assets	Cr Cost of sales
C	Dr Cost of sales	Cr Drawings
D	Dr Cost of sales	Cr Non-current assets

32 Which pair of the following items would appear on the same side of the trial balance?

A   Drawings and accruals

B   Carriage outwards and prepayments

C   Carriage inwards and rental income

D   Opening inventory and purchase returns

33 The double-entry system of bookkeeping normally results in which of the following balances on the ledger accounts?

	Debit balances:	Credit balances:
A	Assets and revenues	Liabilities, capital and expenses
B	Revenues, capital and liabilities	Assets and expenses
C	Assets and expenses	Liabilities, capital and revenues
D	Assets, expenses and capital	Liabilities and revenues

34 Which one of the following states the entries required to account for a reimbursement to the petty cash float of $125 from the bank account?

A	Dr Petty cash	Cr Cash and bank
B	Dr Cash and bank	Cr Petty cash
C	Dr Drawings	Cr Petty cash
D	Dr Drawings	Cr Cash and bank

35 Sasha has prepared a draft statement of profit or loss for her business as follows:

	$	$
Sales		256,800
Cost of sales		
Opening inventory	13,400	
Purchases	145,000	
Closing inventory	14,200	
		(144,200)
Gross profit		112,600
Expenses		(76,000)
Net profit		36,600

Sasha has not yet recorded the following items:

- Carriage in of $2,300
- Discounts received of $3,900
- Carriage out of $1,950

After these amounts are recorded, what are the revised values for gross and net profit of Sasha's business?

	Gross profit	Net profit
	$	$
A	108,350	36,250
B	108,350	28,450
C	110,300	28,450
D	110,300	36,250

36 Elijah started the month with cash at bank of $1,780.

What was the balance carried forward after accounting for the following transactions in June?

(1) Elijah withdrew $200 per week to cover living expenses.

(2) A customer paid for goods with a list price of $600, less trade discount of 5%.

(3) An amount of $400 was received from a credit customer.

(4) Bankings of $1,200 from canteen vending machines.

$ ☐

37 After corrections, what should be the balance on the following account?

Bank

	$		$
Overdraft at start of month	1,340	Returns of goods purchased for cash	50
Reimbursement of petty cash float	45	Payments to credit suppliers	990
Receipts from customers	4,400	Rental income	1,300
		Payment of electricity bill	700
		Balance c/f	2,745
	5,785		5,785

$ ☐

38 Andrea started a taxi business by transferring her car, at a value of $5,000, into the business.

What accounting entries are required to record this transaction?

A Dr Capital $5,000, Cr Car $5,000

B Dr Car $5,000, Cr Drawings $5,000

C Dr Car $5,000, Cr Capital $5,000

D Dr Drawing $5,000 Cr Car $5,000

39 Which one of the following statements best describes the purpose of a purchase order?

A It is issued to a supplier to request supply of goods from them on terms specified within the order.

B It is issued to a customer to confirm the supply of goods to them on terms specified in the order.

C It is issued to a supplier as notification of payment.

D It confirms the price that will be charged by a supplier for goods supplied.

40 Which one of the following statements best describes the purpose of a goods despatched note (delivery note)?

A   It is issued by a customer returning faulty goods to their supplier.

B   It is issued by a customer to their supplier and specifies the quantity and type of goods they require to be despatched.

C   It is issued by a supplier to their customer and specifies the quantity and type of goods delivered to that customer.

D   It is issued by a supplier to their customer and specifies what goods will be provided to them at a specified future date.

41 An invoice is best defined by which one of the following statements?

A   An invoice is raised by a business and confirms only the amount due to be paid for goods and services provided.

B   An invoice is raised by business and issued to a supplier as recognition of goods and services received from that supplier.

C   An invoice is raised by a business and issued to a customer to confirm amounts not yet paid.

D   An invoice is raised by a business and issued to a customer to request payment for goods and services provided.

42 With regard to the accounting equation, state whether each of the following statements is true or false.

A Business assets will always equal business liabilities	True/False
B Business assets will always exceed business liabilities	True/False
C Business assets include proprietor's capital	True/False
D Business liabilities include proprietor's capital	True/False

43 With regard to the journal, state whether each of the following statements is true or false?

A The journal records all bank and cash transactions	True/False
B The journal records all accounting transactions	True/False
C The journal is a book of prime entry	True/False
D The journal records all credit sales transactions	True/False

44 During the year, Ferguson made the following accounting entries to account for the depreciation charge relating to motor vehicles:

Debit Accumulated depreciation – motor vehicles $5,000

Credit Depreciation expense – motor vehicles $5,000

State the journal entries required to account correctly for the depreciation charge for motor vehicles for the year.

	Ledger account:	$
Debit		
Credit		

45 During the year, Redknapp made the following accounting entries to account for the increase in the allowance for receivables:

Debit Trade receivables $4,300

Credit Allowance for receivables $4,300

State the journal entries required to account correctly for the increase in the allowance for receivables for the year.

	Ledger Account:	$
Debit		
Credit		

46 During the year, Allardyce made the following accounting entries to account the cash proceeds received upon disposal of an item of machinery:

Debit Bank $2,500

Credit Sales revenue $2,500

State the journal entries required to account correctly for the disposal proceeds received upon disposal of the item of machinery.

	Ledger Account:	$
Debit		
Credit		

47 Pardew is unsure of the accounting entries required to account for a contra between the receivables ledger control and payables ledger control accounts for $1,250.

State the accounting entries required to account correctly for a contra between the receivables and payables ledger control accounts.

	Ledger Account:	$
Debit		
Credit		

48 State the accounting entries required to account for the depreciation charge for the year of $3,500 relating to buildings.

	Ledger Account:	$
Debit		
Credit		

49 State the accounting entries required to account for settlement discount received of $250 from a credit supplier.

	Ledger Account:	$
Debit		
Credit		

50 Pardew made the following accounting entries to account for the purchase of goods on credit from a supplier:

Debit Trade payables ledger control account $3,200

Credit Purchases $3,200

State the journal entries required to account correctly for the purchase of the goods on credit from a supplier.

	Ledger Account:	$
Debit		
Credit		

51 Bob used the following balances to prepare his financial statements as at 30 April 20X3.

	$	$
Receivables	6,000	
Bank loan		3,000
Bank overdraft		2,500
Drawings	4,100	
Capital 1 May 20X2		12,500
Revenue		22,000
Purchases	19,200	
Rent	5,400	
Bank interest	825	
Heat and light	4,475	
	40,000	40,000

The business does not hold inventory. No further adjustments were required.

What was the closing capital figure for Bob as at 30 April 20X3?

$

LEDGER ACCOUNTS, BOOKS OF PRIME ENTRY AND JOURNALS

52   **Which of the following are books of prime entry?**

    A   Sales day book and trial balance

    B   Petty cash book and accounts receivables ledger

    C   Petty cash book and journal

    D   Purchase day book and accounts payable ledger

53   The petty cash balance at 30 November 20X9 was $25. The following transactions occurred during November 20X9:

    (1)   Refreshments were purchased at a cost of $7.25.

    (2)   Travel expenses of $12.75 were reimbursed to an employee.

    (3)   The cleaner was paid $15.

    What was the petty cash float at 1 November 20X9?

    A $25

    B $60

    C $35

    D $50

54   **Which one of the following explains the imprest system of operating petty cash?**

    A   Weekly expenditure cannot exceed a set amount

    B   The exact amount of expenditure is reimbursed at intervals to maintain a fixed float

    C   All expenditure out of the petty cash must be properly authorised

    D   Regular equal amounts of cash are transferred into petty cash at intervals

55   You are given the following figures for sales and receivables:

	20X7	20X6
	$	$
Receivables at year end	74,963	69,472
Sales	697,104	
Total cash received from customers	686,912	
Specific allowance for receivables	2,014	1,578
Irrecoverable debts written off	1,697	

    What was the value of sales returns during 20X7?

    $ _____

56 Ignatius operates the imprest system for petty cash. At 1 July there was a float of $150, but it was decided to increase this to $200 from 31 July onwards. During July, the petty cashier received $25 from staff for using the photocopier and a cheque for $90 was cashed for an employee. In July, cheques were drawn for $500 for petty cash.

How much cash was paid out as cash expenses by the petty cashier in July?

$ [   ]

57 **Which ONE of the following might explain a debit balance on a payables ledger account?**

A   The business took a settlement discount to which it was not entitled and paid less than the amount due

B   The business mistakenly paid an invoice twice

C   The book-keeper failed to enter a contra with the receivables ledger

D   The book-keeper failed to post a cheque paid to the account

58 Allister's payables ledger control account has a balance at 1 October 20X8 of $34,500 credit. During October, credit purchases were $78,400, cash purchases were $2,400 and payments made to suppliers, excluding cash purchases, and after deducting settlement discounts of $1,200, were $68,900. Purchase returns were $4,700.

What was the closing balance on the purchase ledger control account?

$ [   ]

59 The entries in a receivables ledger control account for the first accounting period were:

Sales	$250,000
Bank	$225,000
Returns	$2,500
Irrecoverable debts	$3,000
Returned unpaid cheque	$3,500
Contra payables ledger account	$4,000

What is the balance on the receivables ledger control account at the end of the accounting period?

$ [   ]

60 **In which book of prime entry would a business record the part-exchange value received for a vehicle traded in when purchasing a new vehicle?**

A   The sales daybook

B   The cash payments book

C   The journal

D   The non-current asset register

61 Mike wrongly paid Norman $250 twice for goods purchased on credit. Norman subsequently reimbursed Mike for the overpayment of $250. How should Mike account for the reimbursement received from Norman?

A	Debit Cash received, and	Credit Sales
B	Debit Cash received, and	Credit Discount received
C	Debit Cash received, and	Credit Trade receivables control account
D	Debit Cash received, and	Credit Trade payables control account

62 State the accounting entries required if a business made sales on credit of $10,000, on which it must account for sales tax at the rate of 20%.

	Ledger Account:	$
Debit/Credit		
Debit/Credit		
Debit/Credit		

63 State the accounting entries required to record the purchase of goods for resale on credit with a gross invoice value of $1,541, which includes sales tax at the rate of 15%. The business is registered to account for sales tax.

	Ledger Account:	$
Debit/Credit		
Debit/Credit		
Debit/Credit		

64 Which one of the following best describes the purpose of a purchase invoice?

A   It is issued by a supplier as a request for payment

B   It is sent to supplier as a request for a supply

C   It is issued by supplier listing details of recent transactions

D   It is sent to the supplier as notification of payment

65 In which book of prime entry would discounts received be recorded?

A   Cash received book

B   Cash payments book

C   Sales day book

D   Purchases day book

66 Simran uses the imprest method of accounting for petty cash. She counted the petty cash and there was $66·00 in hand. There were also the following petty cash vouchers:

	$
Sundry purchases	22.00
Loan to sales manager	10.00
Purchase of staff drinks	19.00
Sundry sales receipts	47.00

What is Simran's imprest amount?

$ [   ]

RECORDING TRANSACTIONS AND EVENTS

SALES AND PURCHASES AND SALES TAX

67 Erin is registered for sales tax. During May, she sold goods with a list price of $600, excluding sales tax, to Kyle on credit. As Kyle was buying a large quantity of goods, Erin deducted trade discount of 5% of the normal list price.

If sales tax is charged at 15%, what will be the gross value of the sales invoice prepared by Erin?

$ [   ]

68 At 1 December 20X5, Laurel owes the sales tax authorities $23,778. During the month of December, she recorded the following transactions:

- Sales of $800,000 exclusive of 17.5% sales tax.
- Purchases of $590,790 inclusive of sales tax of 17.5%.

What is the balance on Laurel's sales tax account at the end of December?

$ [   ]

69 If sales (including sales tax) amounted to $27,612.50, and purchases (excluding sales tax) amounted to $18,000, what would be the balance on the sales tax account, assuming all transactions are subject to sales tax at 17.5%?

$ [   ]

70 In the quarter ended 31 March 20X2, Chas had taxable sales, net of sales tax, of $90,000 and taxable purchases, net of sales tax, of $72,000.

If the rate of sales tax is 10%, how much sales tax is payable to the tax authority?

A $1,800 receivable

B $2,000 receivable

C $1,800 payable

D $2,000 payable

71   A summary of the transactions of Ramsgate, who is registered to account for sales tax at 17.5% on all transactions, shows the following for the month of August 20X9:

Outputs $60,000 (exclusive of tax)

Inputs $40,286 (inclusive of tax)

At the beginning of the period Ramsgate owed $3,400 to the authorities, and during the period he paid $2,600 to them.

What is the amount due to the tax authorities at the end of the month?

$

72   **Which one of the following statements best explains the sales account?**

A   It is credited with the total of sales made, including sales tax

B   It is credited with the total of sales made, excluding sales tax

C   It is credited with the total purchases made, including sales tax

D   It is credited with the total expenses, excluding sales tax

73   A business sold goods that had a net value of $600 to Lucid.

What entries are required by the seller to record this transaction if sales tax is applied at 17.5%?

A   Dr Lucid $600, Dr Sales tax $105, Cr Sales $705

B   Dr Lucid $705, Cr Sales tax $105, Cr Sales $600

C   Dr Lucid $600, Cr Sales tax $105, Cr Sales $600

D   Dr Sales $600, Dr Sales tax $105, Cr Lucid $705

74   Laker, a customer, returned goods to Streamer that had a net value of $200.

What entries are required by Streamer to record this transaction if transactions are subject to sales tax is payable at 17.5%?

A   Dr Returns inward $200, Dr Sales tax $35, Cr Laker $235

B   Dr Returns inward $235, Cr Sales tax $35, Cr Laker $200

C   Dr Purchases $200, Dr Sales tax $35, Cr Laker $235

D   Dr Laker $235, Cr Returns inward $200, Cr Sales tax $35

75 Stung, which is registered to account for sales tax, purchased furniture on credit at a cost of $8,000, plus sales tax of $1,200.

What are the correct accounting entries to record this transaction?

		$		$
A	Debit Furniture	9,200	Credit Supplier	9,200
B	Debit Furniture	8,000	Credit Sales tax	1,200
			Credit Supplier	6,800
C	Debit Furniture	8,000	Credit Supplier	9,200
	Debit Sales tax	1,200		
D	Debit Furniture	8,000	Credit Supplier	8,000

76 **Which two of the following statements are true?**

(1) Sales tax is a form of indirect taxation.

(2) If input tax exceeds output tax the difference is payable to the authorities.

(3) Sales tax is included in the reported sales and purchases of the business.

(4) Sales tax cannot be recovered on some purchases.

A (1) and (4)

B (1) and (2)

C (2) and (3)

D (3) and (4)

77 **Based upon the following information, what was the cost of purchases?**

	$
Opening trade payables	142,600
Cash paid	542,300
Discounts received	13,200
Goods returned	27,500
Closing trade payables	137,800

$ _____

78 You are given the following information:

Receivables at 1 January 20X3	$10,000
Receivables at 31 December 20X3	$9,000
Total receipts during 20X3 (including cash sales of $5,000)	$85,000

Based upon the available information, what was the sales revenue figure for 20X3?

$ _____

79   P is a sole proprietor whose accounting records are incomplete. All the sales are cash sales and during the year $50,000 was banked, including $5,000 from the sale of a business car. He paid $12,000 wages in cash from the till and withdrew $2,000 per month as drawings. The cash in the till at the beginning and end of the year was $300 and $400 respectively.

What was the value of P's sales for the year?

A $80,900

B $81,000

C $81,100

D $86,100

80   The following transactions took place during Alan's first month of trading:

- Credit sales of $121,000 exclusive of sales tax
- Credit purchases of $157,110 inclusive of sales tax
- Cash payments to credit suppliers of $82,710 inclusive of sales tax

All transactions are subject to sales tax at 20%.

What was the balance on Alan's sales tax account at the end of his first month of trading?

A $1,985DR

B $1,985CR

C $15,770DR

D $15,770CR

81   **Which one of the following statements is correct?**

A   Carriage inwards and carriage outwards are both accounted for as an expense in the statement of profit or loss.

B   Carriage inwards and carriage outwards are both accounted for as income in the statement of profit or loss.

C   Carriage inwards is treated as an expense and carriage outwards is treated as income in the statement of profit or loss.

D   Carriage inwards is treated as income and carriage outwards is treated as an expense in the statement of profit or loss.

82   Jupiter returned unsatisfactory goods to Saturn. The goods had been sold on credit by Saturn at $100 plus sales tax of $20.

What accounting entries are required by Saturn to record the return of goods?

A   Dr Purchases $100, Dr Sales tax $20, Cr Jupiter $120

B   Dr Returns outward $100, Dr Sales tax $20, Cr Jupiter $120

C   Dr Returns inward $100, Dr Sales tax $20, Cr Jupiter $120

D   Dr Jupiter $120, Cr Returns outward $100, Cr Sales tax $20

83 Eric is registered for sales tax. During October, he sold goods with a tax exclusive price of $800 to Kevin on credit. As Kevin is buying a large quantity of goods, Eric reduced the price by 8%. Eric accounts for sales tax on all transactions at 25%.

What was the gross value of the sales invoice for Kevin prepared by Eric?

$\boxed{\$ \qquad\qquad\qquad}$

84 ABC Co sold goods with a list price of $1,000 to Smith which was subject to trade discount of 5% and early settlement discount of 4% if the invoice was paid within 7 days. The normal credit period available to credit customers is 30 days from invoice date. Smith has never taken advantage of early settlement terms and has always paid after 30 days.

If Smith subsequently pays within 7 days and is eligible for the settlement discount, what accounting entries should be made by ABC Co to record settlement of the amount outstanding?

A   Debit Cash $950, Debit Revenue $50 and Credit Trade receivables $1,000

B   Debit Cash $950, Credit Revenue $38 and Credit Trade receivables $912

C   Debit Cash $912, Debit Revenue $38 and Credit Trade receivables $950

D   Debit Cash $912, and Credit Trade receivables $912

85 ABC Co sold goods with a list price of $2,500 to Jones which was subject to trade discount of 5% and early settlement discount of 4% if the invoice was paid within 7 days. The normal credit period available to credit customers is 30 days from invoice date. Jones always takes advantage of early settlement terms.

If Jones subsequently pays within 7 days and is eligible for the settlement discount, what accounting entries should be made by ABC Co to record settlement of the amount outstanding?

A   Debit Cash $2,280, Debit Revenue $95 and Credit Trade receivables $2,375

B   Debit Cash $2,280 and Credit Trade receivables $2,280

C   Debit Cash $2,375, Debit Revenue $125 and Credit Trade receivables $2,500

D   Debit Cash $2,500, and Credit Trade receivables $2,500

86 ABC Co sold goods with a list price of $4,500 to Black which was subject to trade discount of 5% and early settlement discount of 4% if the invoice was paid within 7 days. The normal credit period available to credit customers is 30 days from invoice date. Black has always taken advantage of early settlement terms.

If, on this occasion, Black does not pay within 7 days and is not eligible for the settlement discount, what accounting entries should be made by ABC Co to record settlement of the amount outstanding?

A   Debit Cash $4,104, Debit Revenue $396 and Credit Trade receivables $4,500

B   Debit Cash $4,275, Debit Discount received $171 and Credit Trade receivables $4,104

C   Debit Cash $4,275 and Credit Trade receivables $4,275

D   Debit Cash $4,275, Credit Trade receivables $4,104 and Credit Revenue $171

87 ABC Co sold goods with a list price of $3,700 to White which was subject to trade discount of 5% and early settlement discount of 4% if the invoice was paid within 7 days. The normal credit period available to credit customers is 30 days from invoice date. White does not normally pay early to take advantage of early settlement terms.

If, as expected, White does not pay within the settlement discount period, what accounting entries should be made by ABC Co to record settlement of the amount outstanding?

A Debit Cash $3,515, and Credit Trade receivables $3,515

B Debit Cash $3,515, Credit Discount received $140.60 and Credit Trade receivables $3,374.40

C Debit Cash $3,374.40 and Credit Trade receivables $3,374.40

D Debit Cash $3,515, Debit Revenue $185 and Credit Trade receivables $3,700

88 ABC Co sold goods with a list price of $1,400 to Green which was subject to trade discount of 4% and early settlement discount of 5% if the invoice was paid within 7 days. The normal credit period available to credit customers is 30 days from invoice date. Green has always taken advantage of early settlement terms and has always paid within 7 days.

If, on this occasion, Green does not pay within the settlement discount period, what accounting entries should be made by ABC Co to record settlement of the amount outstanding?

A Debit Cash $1,400 Credit Trade receivables $1,400

B Debit Cash $1,344, Credit Trade receivables $1,276.80 and Credit Revenue $67.20

C Debit Cash $1,344 and Credit Trade receivables $1,344

D Debit Cash $1,276.80, and Credit Trade receivables $1,276.80

INVENTORY

89 An item of inventory was purchased for $500. It is expected to be sold for $1,200 although $250 will need to be spent on it in order to achieve the sale. To replace the same item of inventory would cost $650.

At what value should this item of inventory be included in the financial statements?

$

90 Appleby buys and sells inventory during the month of August as follows:

		No. of units	$
Opening inventory		100	2.52/unit
4 August	Sales	20	
8 August	Purchases	140	2.56/unit
10 August	Sales	90	
18 August	Purchases	200	2.78/unit
20 August	Sales	180	

Which one of the following statements is true?

A   Closing inventory is $19.50 higher when using the FIFO method instead of the periodic weighted average.

B   Closing inventory is $19.50 lower when using the FIFO method instead of the periodic weighted average.

C   Closing inventory is $17.50 higher when using the FIFO method instead of the periodic weighted average.

D   Closing inventory is $17.50 lower when using the FIFO method instead of the periodic weighted average.

91 In the year ended 31 August 20X4, Aplus' records show closing inventory of 1,000 units compared to 950 units of opening inventory.

Which of the following statements is true assuming that prices have fallen throughout the year?

A   Closing inventory and profit are higher using FIFO rather than AVCO

B   Closing inventory and profit are lower using FIFO rather than AVCO

C   Closing inventory is higher and profit lower using FIFO rather than AVCO

D   Closing inventory is lower and profit higher using FIFO rather than AVCO

92 David performs an inventory count on 30 December 20X6 ahead of the 31 December year end. He counts 1,200 identical units, each of which cost $50. On 31 December, David sold 20 of the units for $48 each.

What figure should be included in David's statement of financial position for inventory at 31 December 20X6?

$

93 **Which of the following statements about the treatment of inventory and work in progress in financial statements are correct?**

(1)   Inventory should be valued at the lower of cost, net realisable value and replacement cost.

(2)   In valuing work in progress, materials costs, labour costs and variable and fixed production overheads must be included.

(3)   Inventory items can be valued using either first in, first out (FIFO) or weighted average cost.

(4)   An entity's financial statements must disclose the accounting policies used in measuring inventories.

A   All four statements are correct

B   (1), (2) and (3) only are correct

C   (2), (3) and (4) only are correct

D   (1) and (4) only are correct

94 Kiera's interior design business received a delivery of fabric on 29 June 20X6 and was included in the inventory valuation at 30 June 20X6. As at 30 June 20X6, the invoice for the fabric had not been accounted for.

Based upon the available information, what effect(s) will this have on Kiera's profit for the year ended 30 June 20X6 and the inventory valuation at that date?

(1)   Profit for the year ended 30 June 20X6 will be overstated.

(2)   Inventory at 30 June 20X6 will be understated.

(3)   Profit for the year ended 30 June 20X7 will be overstated.

(4)   Inventory at 30 June 20X6 will be overstated.

A   (1) and (2)

B   (2) and (3)

C   (1) only

D   (1) and (4)

95 **What journal entry is required to record goods taken from inventory by the owner of a business for personal use?**

A   Dr Drawings   Cr Purchases

B   Dr Sales   Cr Drawings

C   Dr Drawings   Cr Inventory

D   Dr Inventory   Cr Drawings

96 A business had an opening inventory of $180,000 and a closing inventory of $220,000 in its financial statements for the year ended 31 December 20X5.

Which of the following accounting entries are required to account for opening and closing inventory when preparing the financial statements of the business?

		Debit	Credit
		$	$
A	Inventory account	180,000	
	Statement of P/L		180,000
	Statement P/L	220,000	
	Inventory account		220,000
B	Statement of P/L	180,000	
	Inventory account		180,000
	Inventory account	220,000	
	Statement of P/L		220,000
C	Inventory account	40,000	
	Purchases account		40,000
D	Purchases account	40,000	
	Inventory account		40,000

97 Ajay's annual inventory count took place on 7 July 20X6. The inventory value on this date was $38,950. During the period from 30 June 20X6 to 7 July 20X6, the following took place:

Sales $6,500

Purchases $4,250

The mark up is 25% on cost.

What is Ajay's inventory valuation at 30 June 20X6?

$ ☐

98 Inventory movements for product X during the last quarter were as follows:

Opening inventory at 1 January was 6 items valued at $15 each.

January	Purchases	10 items at $19.80 each
February	Sales	10 items at $30 each
March	Purchases	20 items at $24.50
	Sales	5 items at $30 each

What was gross profit for the quarter, if inventory is valued using the continuous weighted average cost method?

$ ☐

99 Your firm values inventory using the periodic weighted average cost method. At 1 October 20X8, there were 60 units in inventory valued at $12 each. On 8 October, 40 units were purchased for $15 each, and a further 50 units were purchased for $18 each on 14 October. On 21 October, 75 units were sold for $1,200.

What was the value of closing inventory at 31 October 20X8?

$$\boxed{\quad \$ \qquad\qquad\qquad }$$

100 Percy Pilbeam is a book wholesaler. On each sale, commission of 4% is payable to the selling agent. The following information is available in respect of total inventories of three of his most popular titles at his financial year-end:

	Cost $	Selling price $
Henry VII – Shakespeare	2,280	2,900
Dissuasion – Jane Armstrong-Siddeley	4,080	4,000
Pilgrim's Painful Progress – John Bunion	1,280	1,300

What is the value of these inventories in Percy's statement of financial position?

A $7,368

B $7,400

C $7,560

D $7,640

101 An organisation's inventory at 1 July was 15 units at a cost of $3.00 each. The following movements occur:

3 July 20X4   5 units sold at $3.30 each

8 July 20X4   10 units bought at $3.50 each

12 July 20X4   8 units sold at $4.00 each

What was the value of closing inventory at 31 July, if the FIFO method of inventory valuation is used?

A $31.50

B $36.00

C $39.00

D $41.00

102 What would be the effect on an entity's profit for the year of discovering that inventory with cost of $1,250 and a net realisable value of $1,000 had been omitted from the original inventory valuation?

A   An increase of $1,250

B   An increase of $1,000

C   A decrease of $250

D   No effect at all

103 S Co sells three products – Basic, Super and Luxury. The following information was available at the year-end:

	Basic	Super	Luxury
	$ per unit	$ per unit	$ per unit
Original cost	6	9	18
Estimated selling price	9	12	15
Selling and distribution costs	1	4	5
	units	units	units
Units in inventory	200	250	150

What was the valuation of inventory at the year-end?

$ [   ]

104 In times of rising prices, the valuation of inventory using the first in, first out method, as opposed to the weighted average cost method, will result in which ONE of the following combinations?

	Cost of sales	Profit	Closing inventory
A	Lower	Higher	Higher
B	Lower	Higher	Lower
C	Higher	Lower	Higher
D	Higher	Higher	Lower

105 If an entity uses the periodic weighted average cost method to value closing inventory, which of the following statements is true?

A Unit average cost is recalculated each time there is a purchase of inventory

B Unit average cost is recalculated each time there is a sale of goods

C Unit average cost is calculated once only at the end of an accounting period

D Unit average cost is recalculated each time there is a purchase or a sale

106 If an entity uses the continuous weighted average cost method to value closing inventory, which of the following statements is true?

A Unit average cost is recalculated each time there is a purchase of inventory

B Unit average cost is calculated once only at the end of an accounting period

C Unit average cost is recalculated each time there is a sale of goods

D Unit average cost is recalculated each time there is a purchase or a sale

107 If an entity uses the continuous weighted average cost method to value closing inventory, what is the value of closing inventory based upon the following information?

2 Feb   Purchased 10 units at a cost of $5.00 per unit

5 Feb   Sold 6 units at a price of $8 per unit

7 Feb   Purchased 10 units at a cost of $6.50 per unit

$ [   ]

108 If an entity uses the periodic weighted average cost method to value closing inventory, what is the value of closing inventory based upon the following information?

12 Apr   Purchased 10 units at a cost of $5.00 per unit

15 Apr   Sold 6 units at a price of $8 per unit

17 Apr   Purchased 10 units at a cost of $6.50 per unit

$ [   ]

109 Using the periodic weighted average cost method to value closing inventory, what is the value of cost of sales for April based upon the following information?

1 Apr   Opening inventory 4 units at a cost of $4.00 per unit

12 Apr   Purchased 10 units at a cost of $5.00 per unit

15 Apr   Sold 6 units at a price of $8 per unit

17 Apr   Purchased 10 units at a cost of $6.00 per unit

25 Apr   Sold 8 units at a price of $8.50 per unit

$ [   ]

110 Using the continuous weighted average cost method to value closing inventory, what is the value of cost of sales for April based upon the following information?

1 Apr   Opening inventory 4 units at a cost of $4.00 per unit

12 Apr   Purchased 10 units at a cost of $5.00 per unit

15 Apr   Sold 6 units at a price of $8 per unit

17 Apr   Purchased 10 units at a cost of $6.00 per unit

25 Apr   Sold 8 units at a price of $8.50 per unit

$ [   ]

TANGIBLE AND INTANGIBLE NON-CURRENT ASSETS

111 The non-current asset register shows a carrying amount for non-current assets of $85,600; the ledger accounts include a cost balance of $185,000 and an accumulated depreciation balance of $55,000.

Which one of the following statements may explain the discrepancy?

A The omission of an addition of land costing $30,000 from the ledger account and the omission of the disposal of an asset from the register (cost $25,600 and accumulated depreciation at disposal $11,200).

B The omission of the revaluation of an asset upwards by $16,600 and the depreciation charge of $20,000 from the ledger account and the omission of the disposal of an asset with a carrying amount of $41,000 from the register.

C The omission of the disposal of an asset from the ledger accounts (cost $25,600 and accumulated depreciation at disposal $11,200) and the omission of an addition of land costing $30,000 from the register.

D The omission of an upwards revaluation by $16,400 from the register and the accidental debiting of the depreciation charge of $28,000 to the accumulated depreciation ledger account.

112 Laurie bought an asset on the 1st January 20X4 for $235,000. He has depreciated it at 30% using the reducing balance method. On 1st January 20X7, Laurie revalued the asset to $300,000.

What accounting entries should Laurie post to record the revaluation?

		$		$
A	Dr Non-current assets – cost	65,000	Cr Revaluation surplus	219,395
	Dr Accumulated depreciation	154,395		
B	Dr Non-current assets – cost	65,000	Cr Revaluation surplus	276,500
	Dr Accumulated depreciation	211,500		
C	Dr Revaluation surplus	219,395	Dr Non-current assets – cost	65,000
			Dr Accumulated depreciation	154,395
D	Dr Revaluation surplus	276,500	Dr Non-current assets – cost	65,000
			Dr Accumulated depreciation	211,500

113 **Which one of the following statements is true in relation to the non-current asset register?**

A It is an alternative name for the non-current asset ledger account.

B It is a list of the physical non-current assets rather than their financial cost.

C It is a schedule of planned maintenance of non-current assets for use by the plant engineer.

D It is a schedule of the cost and other information about each individual non-current asset.

114 **Which one of the following four statements is correct?**

A   If all the conditions specified in IAS 38 Intangible assets are met, the directors can chose whether to capitalise the development expenditure or not.

B   Amortisation of capitalised development expenditure will appear as an item in an entity's statement of changes in equity.

C   Capitalised development costs are shown in the statement of financial position as non-current assets.

D   Capitalised development expenditure must be amortised over a period not exceeding five years.

115 The plant and equipment account in the records of C Co for the year ended 31 December 20X6 is shown below:

Plant and equipment – cost

	$		$
Balance b/f	960,000		
1 July Cash	48,000	30 Sept Disposals	84,000
		Balance c/f	924,000
	—————		—————
	1,008,000		1,008,000

C Co's policy is to charge straight line depreciation at 20% per year on a pro rata basis.

What should be the charge for depreciation in C Co's statement of profit or loss for the year ended 31 December 20X6?

$	

116 On 1 January 20X7, Z Co purchased an item of plant. The invoice showed:

	$
Cost of plant	48,000
Delivery to factory	400
One year warranty covering breakdown	800
	—————
	49,200

Modifications to the factory building costing $2,200 were necessary to enable the plant to be installed.

What amount should be capitalised for the plant in Z Co's accounting records?

$	

117 A non-current asset was purchased at the beginning of Year 1 for $2,400 and depreciated by 20% per annum using the reducing balance method. At the beginning of Year 4 it was sold for $1,200.

The result of this was:

A   a loss on disposal of $240.00

B   a loss on disposal of $28.80

C   a profit on disposal of $28.80

D   a profit on disposal of $240.00

118 A business' non-current assets had a carrying amount of $125,000. An asset which had cost $12,000 was sold for $9,000, at a profit of $2,000.

What is the revised carrying amount of non-current assets?

A $113,000

B $118,000

C $125,000

D $127,000

119 W Co bought a new printing machine from abroad. The cost of the machine was $80,000. The installation costs were $5,000 and the employees received training on how to use the machine, at a cost of $2,000. Before using the machine to print customers' orders, pre-production safety testing was undertaken at a cost of $1,000.

What should be the cost of the machine in W Co's statement of financial position?

$ _____

120 A non-current asset was disposed of for $2,200 during the last accounting year. It had been purchased exactly three years earlier for $5,000, with an expected residual value of $500, and had been depreciated on the reducing balance basis, at 20% per annum.

What was the profit or loss on disposal?

A $360 loss

B $150 loss

C $104 loss

D $200 profit

121 At the end of its financial year, Tanner Co had the following non-current assets:

Land and buildings at cost	$10.4 million
Land and buildings: accumulated depreciation	$0.12 million

Tanner Co decided to revalue its land and buildings at the year-end to $15 million.

What will be the value of the revaluation surplus if the revaluation is accounted for?

$ _____

122 Which one of the following items should be accounted for as capital expenditure?

    A   The cost of painting a building

    B   The replacement of broken windows in a building

    C   The purchase of a car by a car dealer for re-sale

    D   Legal fees incurred on the purchase of a building

123 F Co purchased a car for $12,000 on 1 April 20X1 which has been depreciated at 20% each year straight line, assuming no residual value. F Co's policy is to charge a full year's depreciation in the year of purchase and no depreciation in the year of sale. The car was traded in for a replacement vehicle on 1 August 20X4 for an agreed figure of $5,000.

What was the profit or loss on the disposal of the vehicle for the year ended 31 December 20X4?

    A   Loss $2,200

    B   Loss $1,400

    C   Loss $200

    D   Profit $200

124 At 30 September 20X2, the following balances existed in the records of Lambda Co:

Plant and equipment:

Cost $860,000

Accumulated depreciation $397,000

During the year ended 30 September 20X3, plant with a written down value of $37,000 was sold for $49,000. The plant had originally cost $80,000. Plant purchased during the year cost $180,000. It is the Lambda Co's policy to charge a full year's depreciation in the year of acquisition of an asset and none in the year of sale, using a rate of 10% on the straight line basis.

What is the carrying amount that should appear in Lambda Co's statement of financial position at 30 September 20X3 for plant and equipment?

$

125 Which of the following statements best describes depreciation?

    A   It is a means of spreading the payment for non-current assets over a period of years.

    B   It is a decline in the market value of the assets.

    C   It is a means of spreading the net cost of non-current assets over their estimated useful life.

    D   It is a means of estimating the amount of money needed to replace the assets.

126 On 1 January 20X8, Wootton has a building in its books which cost $380,000 with a carrying amount of $260,000. On 1 July 20X8, the asset was valued at $450,000 and Wootton wishes to include that valuation in its books. Wootton's accounting policy is to depreciate buildings at the rate of 3% on a straight-line basis.

What was depreciation charge included in the statement of profit or loss for the year ended 31 December 20X8?

$ [   ]

127 A car was purchased by a newsagent business in May 20X1 as follows:

	$
Cost	10,000
Vehicle tax – 1 year	150
	———
Total	10,150
	———

The business adopted a date of 31 December as its year-end.

The car was traded in for a replacement vehicle in August 20X5 at an agreed value of $5,000.

It was depreciated at 25 per cent per annum using the reducing-balance method, charging a full year's depreciation in the year of purchase and none in the year of sale.

What was the profit or loss on disposal of the vehicle during the year ended December 20X5?

A   Profit: $718

B   Profit: $781

C   Profit: $1,788

D   Profit: $1,836

128 **The reducing balance method of depreciating non-current assets is more appropriate than the straight-line method when:**

A   there is no expected residual value for the asset

B   the expected life of the asset is not capable of being estimated

C   the asset is expected to be replaced in a short period of time

D   the asset decreases in value less in later years than in the early years of use

129 SSG bought a machine at a cost of $40,000 on 1 January 20X1. The machine had an expected useful life of six years and an expected residual value of $10,000. The machine was depreciated using the straight-line basis on a monthly basis. At 31 December 20X4, the machine was sold for $15,000.

What was the profit or loss on disposal for inclusion in the financial statements for the year ended 31 December 20X4?

$ [   ]

130 Liza bought a guillotine for her framing business for $20,000 on 1 July 20X7. She expected the guillotine to have a useful life of ten years and a residual value of $500. On 1 July 20X8, Liza revised these estimates and now believes the guillotine to have a remaining useful life of 5 years and no residual value.

What was the depreciation charge for the year ended 30 June 20X9?

$ [   ]

131 Complete the following statement by selecting the appropriate wording from the choice available.

When accounting for intangible assets using the revaluation model, movements in the carrying amount are...

A accounted for in other comprehensive income and other components of equity

B accounted for in the statement of profit or loss only

C accounted for in other comprehensive income only

D accounted for on other components of equity only

132 What is the correct accounting treatment for an intangible asset with an indefinite useful life?

A It is recognised at cost for as long as the entity has the intangible asset.

B It is recognised at cost and is subject to an annual impairment review.

C It is recognised at cost and the entity must make an estimate of estimated useful life so that it can be amortised.

D It cannot be recognised as an intangible asset as it would not be possible to calculate an annual amortisation charge.

133 Identify whether or not each of the following items should be capitalised as intangible assets from the following list.

Capitalised?
Yes/No

Employment costs of staff conducting research activities

Cost of constructing a working model of a new product

Materials and consumables costs associated with conducting scientific experiments

Licence purchased to permit production and sale of a product for ten years

134 **Complete the following statement by selecting the appropriate wording from the choice available.**

When accounting for intangible assets using the cost model, annual impairment charges are:

A   accounted for in other comprehensive income and other components of equity

B   accounted for in the statement of profit or loss only

C   accounted for in other comprehensive income only

D   accounted for on other components of equity only

135 **Classify each of the following costs as either a research expense or as an intangible asset.**

	Research expense	Intangible asset
Market research costs		
Patented product design costs		
Product advertising		
Employee training costs		

136 **Which one of the following statements best defines an intangible asset?**

A   An intangible asset is an asset with no physical substance

B   An intangible asset is always generated internally by a business

C   An intangible asset is an asset which cannot be sold

D   An intangible asset is a purchased asset which has no physical substance

137 The following information of P Co is available for the year ended 31 October 20X2:

Property	$
Cost as at 1 November 2011	102,000
Accumulated depreciation as at 1 November 20X1	(20,400)
	81,600

On 1 November 20X1, P Co revalued the property to $150,000.

P Co's accounting policy is to charge depreciation on a straight-line basis over 50 years. On revaluation there was no change to the overall useful economic life. It has also chosen not to make an annual transfer of the excess depreciation on revaluation between the revaluation surplus and retained earnings.

What should be the balance on the revaluation surplus and the depreciation charge as shown in P Co's financial statements for the year ended 31 October 20X2?

	Depreciation charge $	Revaluation surplus $
A	3,750	68,400
B	3,750	48,000
C	3,000	68,400
D	3,000	48,000

138   **Which THREE of the following statements are correct in relation to application of IAS 38 Intangible Assets?**

(A)   Research costs should be expenses to the statement of profit or loss.

(B)   All types of goodwill can be capitalised.

(C)   Capitalised development costs that no longer meet the criteria specified by IAS 38 must be written off to the statement of profit or loss.

(D)   Capitalised development costs are amortised from the date the assets is available to use or sell.

(E)   Research costs written off can be re-capitalised when the developed asset is feasible.

(F)   Only purchased intangibles can be capitalised.

139   A business has an accounting year end of 31 March. It purchased a truck on 1 April 20X3 at a total cost of $21,000, including $1,000 for one year of insurance cover.

At the date of purchase, the truck had an estimated useful life to the business of eight years, and had an estimated residual value of $3,000. The truck was traded in for a replacement vehicle on 31 March 20X8 at an agreed valuation of $10,000. The truck was depreciated on a straight-line basis, with a pro-rated charge in the year of acquisition and disposal.

Calculate the profit or loss on disposal of the truck.

$ [   ]

140   **Complete the following statement by making one choice from each option available.**

When an entity has revalued a non-current asset, it is (Option 1)..............to account for excess depreciation arising on the revaluation. When excess depreciation is accounted for, the accounting adjustment is reflected in (Option 2)..........................

Option 1   compulsory/optional

Option 2   profit or loss/other comprehensive income/the statement of changes in equity

141   A business has an accounting year end of 30 June. It purchased an item of plant on 1 April 20X5 as follows:

	$
Cost	15,000
3 year maintenance agreement	450
Total	15,450

At the date of purchase, the item of plant and equipment had an estimated useful life to the business of five years and an estimated residual value of $2,000. This item of plant was traded in for a replacement item on 30 September 20X8 at an agreed valuation of $5,000.

It has been depreciated at 20 per cent per annum on a straight-line basis, with a pro-rated charge in the year of acquisition and disposal.

Calculate the profit or loss on disposal of the item of plant.

$ [   ]

142 Geranium is engaged in the following research and development projects:

Project 1   It is applying a new technology to the production of heat resistant fabric. The project is intended to last for a further 18 months after which the fabric will be used in the production of uniforms for the emergency services.

Project 2   It is considering whether a particular substance can be used as an appetite suppressant. If this is the case, it is expected be sold worldwide in chemists and pharmacies.

Project 3   It is developing a material for use in kitchens which is self-cleaning and germ resistant. A competitor is currently developing a similar material and for this reason Geranium are unsure whether their project will be completed.

The costs associated with which of these projects can be capitalised?

A   Projects 1, 2 and 3

B   Projects 1 and 2

C   Project 1 only

D   Projects 1 and 3

143 Merlot Co is engaged in a number of research and development projects:

Project A   A project to investigate the properties of a chemical compound.

Project B   A project to develop a new process which will save time in the production of widgets. This project was started on 1 January 20X5 and met the capitalisation criteria on 31 August 20X5.

Project C   A development project which was completed on 30 June 20X5. Related costs in the statement of financial position at the start of the year were $290,000.   Production and sales of the new product commenced on 1 September and are expected to last 36 months.

Costs for the year ended 31 December 20X5 were as follows:

	$
Project A	34,000
Project B costs to 31 August	78,870
Project B costs from 31 August	27,800
Project C costs to 30 June	19,800

What amount is expensed to the statement of profit or loss and other comprehensive income of Merlot Co in respect of these projects in the year ended 31 December 20X5?

$

ACCRUALS AND PREPAYMENTS

144 Leddley owns two properties which it rents to tenants. In the year ended 31 December 20X6, it received $280,000 in respect of property 1 and $160,000 in respect of property 2. Balances on the prepaid and accrued income accounts were as follows:

	31 December 20X6	31 December 20X5
Property 1	13,400 Dr	12,300 Cr
Property 2	6,700 Cr	5,400 Dr

What amount should be credited to the statement of profit or loss for the year ended 31 December 20X6 in respect of rental income?

$ _____

145 **Troy Co has a property rental business and received cash totalling $838,600 from tenants during the year ended 31 December 20X6.**

Figures for rent in advance and in arrears at the beginning and end of the year were:

	31 December 20X5	31 December 20X6
	$	$
Rent received in advance	102,600	88,700
Rent in arrears (all subsequently received)	42,300	48,400

What amount should appear in Troy Co's statement of profit or loss for the year ended 31 December 20X6 for rental income?

$ _____

146 Details of B Co's insurance policy are shown below:

Premium for year ended 31 March 20X6 paid April 20X5 $10,800

Premium for year ending 31 March 20X7 paid April 20X6 $12,000

What figures should be included in the B Co's financial statements for the year ended 30 June 20X6?

	Statement of profit or loss	Statement of financial position
	$	$
A	11,100	9,000 prepayment
B	11,700	9,000 prepayment
C	11,100	9,000 accrual
D	11,700	9,000 accrual

147 Vine Co sublets part of its office accommodation to earn rental income. The rent is received quarterly in advance on 1 January, 1 April, 1 July and 1 October. The annual rent has been $24,000 for some years, but it was increased to $30,000 from 1 July 20X5.

What amounts for rent should appear in Vine Co's financial statements for the year ended 31 January 20X6?

	Profit or loss	Statement of financial position
A	$27,500	$5,000 in accrued income
B	$27,000	$2,500 in accrued income
C	$27,000	$2,500 in prepaid income
D	$27,500	$5,000 in prepaid income

148 At 1 September, the motor expenses account showed 4 months' insurance prepaid of $80 and fuel costs accrued of $95. During September, the outstanding fuel bill was paid, plus further bills of $245. At 30 September there was a further outstanding fuel bill of $120.

What was the expense included in the statement of profit or loss for motor expenses for September?

$ [   ]

149 On 1 May 20X0, A commenced business and paid an annual rent charge of $1,800 for the period to 30 April 20X1.

What is the charge to the statement of profit or loss and the entry in the statement of financial position for the accounting period ended 30 November 20X0?

A $1,050 charge to statement of profit or loss and prepayment of $750 in the statement of financial position.

B $1,050 charge to statement of profit or loss and accrual of $750 in the statement of financial position.

C $1,800 charge to statement of profit or loss and no entry in the statement of financial position.

D $750 charge to statement of profit or loss and prepayment of $1,050 in the statement of financial position.

150 The electricity account for the year ended 30 June 20X3 was as follows:

	$
Opening balance for electricity accrued at 1 July 20X2	300
Payments made during the year:	
1 August 20X2 for three months to 31 July 20X2	600
1 November 20X2 for three months to 31 October 20X2	720
1 February 20X3 for three months to 31 January 20X3	900
30 June 20X3 for three months to 30 April 20X3	840

What was the expense charged to the statement of profit or loss for the year ended 30 June 20X3 and the accrual at 30 June 20X3?

Accrued at June 20X3	*Charged to statement of profit or loss, year ended 30 June 20X3*
$	$

151 The annual insurance premium for S for the period 1 July 20X3 to 30 June 20X4 was $13,200, which is 10% more than the previous year. Insurance premiums are paid on 1 July.

What is the statement of profit or loss charge for insurance for the year ended 31 December 20X3?

$

152 Farthing's year-end is 30 September. On 1 January 20X6 Farthing took out a loan of $100,000 with annual interest of 12%. The interest is payable in equal instalments on the first day of April, July, October and January in arrears.

How much should be charged to the statement of profit or loss account for the year ended 30 September 20X6, and how much should be accrued on the statement of financial position?

	Statement of profit or loss	*Statement of financial position*
A	$12,000	$3,000
B	$9,000	$3,000
C	$9,000	Nil
D	$6,000	$3,000

153 On 1 January 20X3, a business had prepaid insurance of $10,000. On 1 August 20X3, it paid, in full, the annual insurance invoice of $36,000, to cover the twelve months to 31 July 20X4.

What was the amount charged in the statement of profit or loss and the amount shown in the statement of financial position for the year ended 31 December 20X3?

	Statement of profit or loss	Statement of financial position
	$	$
A	5,000	24,000
B	22,000	23,000
C	25,000	21,000
D	36,000	15,000

154 **Which of the following statements is false?**

A Accruals decrease profit

B Accrued income decreases profit

C A prepayment is an asset

D An accrual is a liability

155 On 9 October, Parker paid his heat and power bill for the three months ended 30 September 20X4. The bill included a meter rental charge of $60 for the three months ending 31 December 20X4 and a usage charge of $135 for the three month period to 30 September 20X4. Parker has an accounting year end date of 31 October 20X4.

Which two of the following adjustments are required in relation to the heat and power expense as at 31 October 20X4?

A Accrual of $40

B Accrual of $45

C Prepayment of $40

D Prepayment of $45

IRRECOVERABLE DEBTS AND ALLOWANCES FOR RECEIVABLES

156 The following balances relate to Putney:

	$
Receivables at 1.1.X8	34,500
Cash received from credit customers	247,790
Contra with payables	1,200
Cash sales	24,000
Irrecoverable debts	18,600
Increase in allowance for receivables	12,500
Discounts received	15,670
Receivables at 31.12.X8	45,000

What is the revenue figure reported by Putney in the year ended 31 December 20X8?

A $275,690

B $278,090

C $320,690

D $302,090

157 The following account has been extracted from the general ledger of Purdey:

Receivables ledger control account

	$		$
Balance b/f	84,700	Irrecoverable debts	4,300
Contra with payables ledger control account	5,000	Increase in allowance for receivables	6,555
Discounts received	21,100	Cash received from credit customers	625,780
Credit sales	644,000		
Cash sales	13,500	Balance c/f	131,665
	768,300		768,300

After amendment, what is the correct receivables balance carried forward?

A $100,175

B $93,620

C $89,320

D $97,920

158 Newell's receivables ledger control account shows a balance at the end of the year of $58,200 before making the following adjustments:

(i) Newell decides to write off debts amounting to $8,900 as he believes they are irrecoverable.

(ii) He also decides to make specific allowance for Carroll's debt of $1,350, Juff's debt of $750 and Mary's debt of $1,416.

Newell's allowance for receivables at the previous year end was $5,650.

What is the charge to the statement of profit or loss in respect of the above information?

A $6,766

B $11,034

C $6,829

D $10,971

159 In the statement of financial position at 31 December 20X5, Boris reported net receivables of $12,000. During 20X6 he made sales on credit of $125,000 and received cash from credit customers amounting to $115,500. At 31 December 20X6, Boris decided to write off debts of $7,100 and increase the specific allowance for receivables by $950 to $2,100.

What was the net receivables figure reported in the statement of financial position at 31 December 20X6?

A $12,300

B $13,450

C $14,400

D $15,550

160 At 1 July 20X5, V Co's allowance for receivables was $48,000. At 30 June 20X6, trade receivables amounted to $838,000. It was decided to write off $72,000 of these debts and adjust the specific allowance for receivables to $60,000.

What are the final amounts for inclusion in V Co's statement of financial position at 30 June 20X6?

	Trade receivables	Allowance for receivables	Net balance
	$	$	$
A	838,000	60,000	778,000
B	766,000	60,000	706,000
C	766,000	108,000	658,000
D	838,000	108,000	730,000

161 In the year ended 30 September 20X8, Fauntleroy had sales of $7,000,000. The year-end receivables amounted to 5% of annual sales. At the year end, Fauntleroy's specific allowance for receivables equated to 4% of receivables. He also identified that this amount was 20% higher than at the previous year end.

During the year irrecoverable debts amounting to $3,200 were written off and debts amounting to $450 and previously written off were recovered.

What was the irrecoverable debt expense for the year?

A $5,083

B $5,550

C $5,583

D $16,750

162 On 1 January 20X3 Tipton's trade receivables were $10,000. The following relates to the year ended 31 December 20X3:

	$
Credit sales	100,000
Cash receipts	90,000
Contra with payables	800
Discounts received	700

Cash receipts include $1,000 in respect of a receivable previously written off.

What was the value of receivables at 31 December 20X3?

A $19,300

B $20,200

C $20,800

D $20,700

163 G Co has been notified that a customer has been declared bankrupt. G Co had previously made allowance for this receivable.

Which of the following is the correct double entry?

	Dr	Cr
A	Allowance for receivables	Receivables ledger control account
B	Receivables ledger control account	Irrecoverable debts account
C	Irrecoverable debts account	Receivables ledger control account
D	Receivables ledger control account	Allowance for receivables

164 Headington Co is owed $37,500 by its customers at the start, and $39,000 at the end, of its year ended 31 December 20X8.

During the period, cash sales of $263,500 and credit sales of $357,500 were made, contras with the payables ledger control account amounted to $15,750 and discounts received $21,400. Irrecoverable debts of $10,500 were written off. Headington Co also identified that the increase in the specific allowance for receivables required at 31 December 20X8 was $8,750.

How much cash was received from credit customers during the year ended 31 December 20X8?

A $329,750

B $593,175

C $593,250

D $614,650

165 The sales revenue of J Co was $2 million and its receivables were 5% of sales. J Co wishes to have a specific allowance for receivables of $4,000, which would make the allowance one-third higher than the current allowance.

How will the profit for the period be affected by the change in allowance?

A   Profit will be reduced by $1,000

B   Profit will be increased by $1,000

C   Profit will be reduced by $1,333

D   Profit will be increased by $1,333

166 Abacus Co started the year with total receivables of $87,000 and an allowance for receivables of $2,500.

During the year, two specific debts were written off, one for $800 and the other for $550. A debt of $350 that had been written off as irrecoverable in the previous year was paid during the year. At the year-end, total receivables were $90,000 and the allowance for receivables was $2,300.

What is the charge to the statement of profit or loss for the year in respect of irrecoverable debts and allowance for receivables?

A $800

B $1,000

C $1,150

D $1,550

167 **An increase in the allowance for receivables results in:**

A   an increase in net current assets

B   a decrease in net current assets

C   An increase in sales

D   A decrease in drawings

168 At the end of 20X7, Chester's receivable's balance is $230,000. He wishes to make specific allowance for Emily's debt of $450 and Lulu's debt of $980. Irrecoverable debts of $11,429 should be written off.

What amount should be charged or credited to the statement of profit or loss in respect of irrecoverable debts and the allowance for receivables if the allowance at the start of the year was $11,700?

A $1,159 Dr

B $1,230 Dr

C $200 Cr

D $12,930 Dr

169 **Which one of the following is not a benefit of providing credit to customers?**

A   It may result in increased sales

B   It may encourage customer loyalty

C   It may attract new customers

D   It may improve the cash flow of the business

170 **Which of the following best explains the purpose of an aged receivables analysis?**

A   To ensure that credit is not extended to unapproved customers

B   To ensure that credit customers regularly purchase goods from the business

C   To keep track of outstanding debts and identify overdue amounts to follow up

D   To keep track of customer addresses

171 On 31 March 20X4, the balance on the receivables control account of P Co was $425,700. The book-keeper has identified that the following adjustments for receivables are required:

Irrecoverable debt recovered $2,000

Specific allowance required $2,400

It was decided that amounts totalling $8,466 should be written off as irrecoverable. The allowance for receivables on 1 April 20X3 was $1,900.

What was the expense for irrecoverable debts and allowance for receivables for the year ended 31 March 20X4?

$ [   ]

PROVISIONS AND CONTINGENCIES

172 Which, if any, of the following items require a provision in accordance with IAS 37 Provisions, Contingent Liabilities and Contingent Assets?

(1) A retail outlet has a policy of providing refunds over and above the statutory requirement to do so. This policy is well publicised and customers have made use of this facility in the past.

(2) A customer has made a legal claim against an entity, claiming that faulty goods sold to them caused damage to their property. The entity's lawyers have advised that the claim will possibly succeed and, if it does, compensation of $10,000 will be payable.

A   (1) only

B   (2) only

C   (1) and (2)

D   Neither

173 Which of the following statements about the requirements relating to IAS 37 Provisions, Contingent Liabilities and Contingent Assets are correct?

(1) A contingent asset should be disclosed by note if an inflow of economic benefits is probable.

(2) No disclosure of a contingent liability is required if the possibility of a transfer of economic benefits arising is remote.

(3) Contingent assets must not be recognised in financial statements unless an inflow of economic benefits is virtually certain to arise.

A   All three statements are correct

B   (1) and (2) only

C   (1) and (3) only

D   (2) and (3) only

174 The following items need to be considered in finalising the financial statements of Q Co:

(1) Q Co gives warranties on its products. Q Co's statistics show that about 5% of sales give rise to a warranty claim.

(2) Q Co has guaranteed the overdraft of another entity. The likelihood of a liability arising under the guarantee is assessed as possible.

What is the correct action to be taken in the financial statements of Q Co for these items?

	Create a provision	Disclose by note only	No action
A	(1)	(2)	
B		(1)	(2)
C	(1) and (2)		
D		(1) and (2)	

175 Which one the following statements relating to the requirements of IAS 37 Provisions, Contingent Liabilities and Contingent Assets is correct?

    A   A contingent asset must always be recognised and accounted for in the financial statements.

    B   A contingent asset must always be disclosed in the notes to the financial statements.

    C   A contingent liability must always be disclosed in the notes to the financial statements if it is regarded as possible.

    D   A contingent liability must always be disclosed in the notes to the financial statements if it is regarded as probable.

176 Which one the following statements relating to the requirements of IAS 37 Provisions, Contingent Liabilities and Contingent Assets is correct?

    A   A contingent asset must be recognised and accounted for in the financial statements if it is regarded as probable.

    B   A contingent asset must never be recognised in the financial statements.

    C   A contingent liability must either be recognised and accounted for in the financial statements, or disclosed in the notes to the financial statements.

    D   A contingent liability may not be required to be accounted for or disclosed in the notes to the financial statements under certain circumstances.

177 Which of the following statements are correct in relation to provisions and liabilities?

    (1)   A provision will always be classified as falling due for payment within twelve months of the reporting date, whereas a liability may be classified as either current or non-current.

    (2)   A provision requires judgement and estimation to quantify the amount and/or the date of payment, whereas a liability is normally capable of precise calculation and the date of payment can be determined.

    (3)   A provision meets the definition of a liability, but is subject to uncertainty regarding the exact amount or date of the future outflow of economic benefits.

    A   (1) and (2)

    B   (2) and (3)

    C   (3) and (1)

    D   none of the above

178 Driller Co undertakes oil and gas exploration activities. One of the conditions of the operating licence is that Driller must make good any damage caused to the local environment as a result of its exploration activities. As at the year-end date of 31 August 20X4, Driller Co estimated that the cost of rectifying damage already caused at current exploration sites at $5 million. At that date Driller Co estimated that that the cost of rectifying expected future damage at current exploration sites at an additional $20 million. Driller Co also estimated that all current exploration sites will operate until 20X7 or beyond that date.

How should this information be reported in the financial statements of Driller Co for the year ended 31 August 20X4?

A   There should be a provision classified as a current liability for $5 million

B   There should be a provision classified as a current liability for $25 million

C   There should be a provision classified as a non-current liability for $5 million

D   There should be a provision classified as a non-current liability for $25 million

179 Recently, users of a new perfume have suffered blistering of the skin along with considerable pain and discomfort. Following investigation by the manufacturer, Fleur Co, it appears that product contamination occurred during the bottling process which was performed by Bottler. Fleur Co's legal representatives have advised it that it is probable that customers will make valid compensation claims totalling $3 million and that it is probable Fleur Co will be able to successfully counter-claim against Bottler for the same amount.

How should this information be reported in the financial statements of Fleur Co for the year ended 31 August 20X4?

A   There should be a provision for $3 million only recognised in the statement of financial position.

B   There should be a provision and an asset, each for $3 million, recognised in the statement of financial position.

C   No provision or asset should be recognised in the statement of financial position as the two amounts cancel each other.

D   There should be a provision for $3 million in the statement of financial position and a disclosure note only to deal with the contingent asset of the amount which may be recovered from Bottler.

180 Electrode manufactures vacuum cleaners and allows customers three months from the date of purchase to return cleaners if they are dissatisfied with the product for any reason. At 31 May 20X8, Electrode included a provision of $10,000 in the financial statements relating to the expected return of cleaners which had been sold before the year-end date. At 31 May 20X9, Electrode estimated that the amount of the provision should be changed to $13,000.

How should this information be accounted for in the financial statements for the year ended 31 May 20X9?

	Dr	Cr
A	Other comprehensive income $3,000	Provision $3,000
B	Provision $3,000	Other comprehensive income $3,000
C	Profit or loss $3,000	Provision $3,000
D	Provision $3,000	Profit or loss $3,000

181 During the year ended 30 April 20X7 Doolittle experienced a number of difficulties with employees. On 1 April 20X7 Doolittle dismissed an employee and subsequently received notice of a claim for unfair dismissal amounting to $50,000. Another employee suffered personal injury on 30 March 20X7 whilst operating machinery at work. On 30 May Doolittle received notice of a claim from that employee for compensation of $100,000. Doolittle's legal representatives have advised that the claim for unfair dismissal will probably be successful and result in a compensation award of $50,000 to the employee. They also advised that the compensation claim for injury suffered is regarded as possible, but not probable, that compensation will be payable. In the event that compensation was payable for personal injury suffered, an amount of $100,000 is a reliable estimate.

How should this information be accounted for in the financial statements of Doolittle for the year ended 30 April 20X7?

A   A provision should be recognised in the financial statement for $50,000 only.

B   A provision should be recognised in the financial statements for $50,000 plus a disclosure note included of the possible compensation payment relating to the personal injury claim.

C   A provision should be recognised in the financial statements for $150,000 only.

D   A provision should be recognised in the financial statements for $150,000 and a disclosure note included of the possible compensation payment relating to the personal injury claim.

CAPITAL STRUCTURE AND FINANCE COSTS

182 **Which of the following statements is/are correct in relation to a rights issue made by an entity?**

(1) A rights issue capitalises the entity's reserves, which can be a disadvantage, as this can reduce the amount of reserves available for future dividends.

(2) A rights issue is offered to the entity's existing shareholders and is usually at a discounted price compared to the nominal value of a share.

	Statement 1	Statement 2
A	Correct	Correct
B	Correct	Incorrect
C	Incorrect	Correct
D	Incorrect	Incorrect

183 **Which TWO items within the statement of financial position would change immediately following an issue of redeemable preference shares?**

(1) Cash

(2) Retained earnings

(3) Finance cost

(4) Equity

(5) Long-term debt

A (1) and (5)

B (1) and (4)

C (2) and (4)

D (3) and (5)

184 The statement of financial position of Cartwright Co shows closing retained earnings of $320,568. The statement of profit or loss showed profit of $79,285. Cartwright Co paid last year's dividend of $12,200 during the year and proposed a dividend of $13,500 at the year end. This had not been approved by the shareholders at the end of the year.

What is the opening retained earnings balance?

A $241,283

B $387,653

C $254,783

D $253,483

185   The following extract is from the statement of profit or loss of Gearing for the year ended 30 April 20X5:

	$
Profit before tax	68,000
Tax	(32,000)
Profit for the year	36,000

In addition to the profit above:

(1)   Gearing Co paid a dividend of $21,000 during the year.

(2)   A gain on revaluation of land resulted in a revaluation surplus of $18,000.

What total amount will be added to retained earnings at the end of the financial year?

$ [   ]

186   **Which of the following items would you exclude from the statement of changes in equity?**

A   Issued share capital

B   Bank loans

C   Revaluation surplus

D   Dividends paid

187   **Which TWO of the following statements are true?**

A   Redeemable preference shares are classified as a liability on the statement of financial position.

B   Irredeemable preference shares are classified as a liability on the statement of financial position.

C   Redeemable preference shares are classified as equity on the statement of financial position.

D   Irredeemable preference shares are classified as equity on the statement of financial position.

188   **Which one of the following statements is true in relation to a rights issue of shares by an entity?**

A   No cash is received by the entity as a result of making the rights issue

B   The entity issues shares for cash at market price of the shares

C   The entity issues shares for cash at a price less than the market price of the shares

D   None of the above

189 **Which one of the following statements is true in relation to a bonus issue of shares by an entity?**

A   The entity issues shares for cash at a price less than the market price of the shares

B   The entity issues shares for cash at market price of the shares

C   No cash is received by the entity as a result of making the bonus issue

D   None of the above

190 **Which two of the following statements are true?**

(1)   Dividends paid by an entity are excluded from the statement of changes in equity.

(2)   Dividends received by an entity are included in the statement of changes in equity.

(3)   Dividends received by an entity are excluded from the statement of changes in equity.

(4)   Dividends paid by an entity are included in the statement of changes in equity.

A   (1) and (2)

B   (3) and (4)

C   (1) and (4)

D   (2) and (3)

191 **When an entity pays a dividend, what accounting entries are required to account for the transaction?**

	Debit	*Credit*
A	Share capital	Bank
B	Share premium	Bank
C	Retained earnings	Bank
D	Profit or loss	Bank

192 An entity, Spark, makes an issue of 20,000 $1 equity shares at a price of $1.75.

What accounting entries are required to account for the transaction?

Debit or credit	Ledger account	$

193 An entity, Taylor, has issued equity share capital of 250,000 shares with a nominal value of $0.50 each and a share premium account balance of $100,000.

What accounting entries are required if Taylor was to make a bonus issue of one share for four held?

	Debit		Credit	
A	Share capital	$62,500	Share premium	$62,500
B	Share premium	$31,250	Share capital	$31,250
C	Share capital	$31,250	Share premium	$31,250
D	Share capital	$62,500	Share premium	$62,500

194 Which of the following would you exclude from the statement of changes in equity?

A Share premium

B Revaluation reserve

C Irredeemable preference shares

D Redeemable preference shares

195 Which of the following statements are correct?

(1) An limited company will always have both an issued share capital and a share premium account.

(2) An limited company will always have an issued share capital account, and may also have a share premium account.

(3) An limited company will always have ether a share premium account or a revaluation surplus account.

A (1) only

B (2) only

C (1) and (3) only

D (2) and (3) only

PREPARING A TRIAL BALANCE

FROM TRIAL BALANCE TO FINANCIAL STATEMENTS

196 Lord has extracted the following balances from his accounting records:

	$
Plant and machinery	89,000
Property	120,000
Inventory	4,600
Payables	6,300
Receivables	5,900
Bank overdraft	790
Loan	50,000
Capital	100,000
Drawings	23,000
Sales	330,000
Purchases	168,200
Sales returns	7,000
Discounts received	?
Sundry expenses	73,890

He has forgotten to extract the balance on the discounts received account.

What is the balance on the discounts received account?

A $1,900

B $9,500

C $4,500

D $15,900

197 **Which, if any, of the following statements are true?**

(1)   The trial balance provides a check that no errors exist in the accounting records of a business.

(2)   The trial balance is one of the financial statements prepared annually by an entity for its shareholders.

A   (1) only

B   (2) only

C   Both (1) and (2)

D   Neither (1) nor (2)

198 **Which of the following are limitations of the trial balance?**

(1) It does not include final figures to be included in the financial statements.

(2) It does not identify errors of commission.

(3) It does not identify in which accounts errors have been made.

A (1) and (2)

B (2) and (3) only

C All three

D None of the above

199 The following is an extract from the trial balance of Gardeners:

	Dr	Cr
	$	$
Non-current assets	50,000	
Inventory	2,600	
Capital		28,000
Receivables	4,500	
Allowance for receivables		320
Cash	290	
Payables		5,000
Sales		120,000
Purchases	78,900	
Rental expense	3,400	
Sundry expenses	13,900	
Bank interest		270
	153,590	153,590

- Rent of $200 has been prepaid.
- Inventory at the end of the year was $1,900.
- The allowance for receivables is to be $200.

What is the profit for the year?

A $23,690

B $23,610

C $23,100

D $25,500

200 The following is an extract from the trial balance of Ardvark Co:

	Dr $	Cr $
Premises	500,000	
Accumulated depreciation		120,000
Inventory		23,000
Share capital	200,000	
Retained earnings		105,000
Receivables	43,500	
Carriage in		1,500
Allowance for receivables		3,400
Bank overdraft	1,010	
Payables		35,900
Sales		500,080
Purchases	359,700	
Sales returns	10,300	
Sundry expenses	14,000	
Suspense		339,630
	1,128,510	1,128,510

After making corrections for errors in the list of balances, what is the revised balance on the suspense account?

A $15,710 Dr

B $14,730 Dr

C $13,390 Dr

D $33,630 Dr

201 The following year-end adjustments are required to a set of draft financial statements:

- Closing inventory of $45,700 to be recorded.

- Depreciation at 20% straight line to be charged on assets with a cost of $470,800.

- An Irrecoverable debt of $230 to be written off.

- Deferred income of $6,700 to be recorded.

What is the impact on net assets of these adjustments?

A $55,390 increase

B $55,390 decrease

C $41,990 decrease

D $41,990 increase

202 The following is the extract of Jordan's trial balance as at 31 December 20X7:

	DR
	$
Rent	22,000
Insurance	30,000

The following notes have been provided:

(i) The monthly rent charge is $2,000.

(ii) The annual insurance charge for the above year is $28,000.

What is the charge for rent and insurance for the year and the closing accrual and prepayment?

		Charge for the year		Closing
		$		$
A	Rent	22,000	Rent prepayment	2,000
	Insurance	28,000	Insurance prepayment	2,000
B	Rent	22,000	Rent accrual	2,000
	Insurance	30,000	Insurance prepayment	2,000
C	Rent	24,000	Rent accrual	2,000
	Insurance	28,000	Insurance prepayment	2,000
D	Rent	24,000	Rent accrual	2,000
	Insurance	30,000	Insurance accrual	2,000

203 The following is the extract of Jim's trial balance as at 31 December 20X7:

	DR	CR
	$	$
Receivables	29,600	
Allowance for receivables		3,100
Irrecoverable debts	1,600	

The following notes are provided.

(i) Additional irrecoverable debts of $3,000 were discovered at the year end.

(ii) It has been decided to make an allowance for receivables of $2,660 on the adjusted receivables at the year end.

What was the total irrecoverable debts expense (irrecoverable debts and allowances for receivables) for the year ended 31 December 20X7 and the closing net receivables balance as at 31 December 20X7?

	Irrecoverable debts expense	Net receivables
	$	$
A	4,160	23,940
B	5,040	23,940
C	2,560	21,830
D	4,000	19,800

204 The following is the extract of Jenny's trial balance as at 31 December 20X7:

The policy of the business is to charge depreciation at 10% per annum on a straight line basis.

	DR	CR
	$	$
Plant and machinery	50,000	
Plant and machinery accumulated depreciation		15,000

What is the depreciation charge to the statement of profit or loss for the year ended 31 December 20X7 and the closing carrying amount as at 31 December 20X7?

	Depreciation charge	Carrying amount
	$	$
A	3,500	31,500
B	5,000	30,000
C	5,000	45,000
D	3,500	30,000

205 The following is the extract of Julian's trial balance as at 31 December 20X7:

	DR	CR
	$	$
Motor vehicles	50,000	
Motor vehicles accumulated depreciation		21,875

The policy of the business is to charge depreciation at 25% per annum on a reducing balance basis.

What is the statement of profit or loss depreciation charge for the year ended 31 December 20X7 and the closing carrying amount as at 31 December 20X7?

Calculations to be rounded to the nearest $.

	Depreciation charge	Carrying amount
	$	$
A	12,500	15,625
B	7,031	42,969
C	12,500	37,500
D	7,031	21,094

206 **Which TWO of the following errors could cause the total of the debit column and the total of the credit column of the trial balance not to agree?**

A   A casting error of $300 made when totalling the sales day book.

B   A transposition error made when posting the total of cash payments into the general ledger.

C   Discount received was included in the trial balance as a debit balance.

D   A cheque paid to a supplier recorded was debited to cash and correctly recognised in trade payables.

CONTROL ACCOUNT RECONCILIATIONS

207 **What is the most important reason for producing a trial balance prior to preparing the financial statements?**

A   It confirms the accuracy of the ledger accounts

B   It provides all the figures necessary to prepare the financial statements

C   It shows that the ledger accounts contain debit and credit entries of an equal value

D   It enables the accountant to calculate any adjustments required

208 A payables ledger control account showed a credit balance of $768,420. The payables ledger totalled $781,200.

Which one of the following possible errors could account in full for the difference?

A   A contra against a receivables ledger debit balance of $6,390 has been entered on the credit side of the payables ledger control account.

B   Cash purchases cash purchases of $28,400 was entered to the debit side of the payables ledger control account instead of the correct figure for discounts received of $15,620.

C $12,780 cash paid to a supplier was entered on the credit side of the supplier's account on the payables ledger.

D   The total of discounts received $6,390 has been entered on the credit side of the payables ledger control account.

209 The payables ledger control account below contains a number of errors:

Payables ledger control account

	$		$
Balance b/f	318,600	Purchases	1,268,600
Cash paid to suppliers	1,367,000	Contras against debit balances in receivables ledger	48,000
Purchase returns	41,200	Discounts received	8,200
		Balance c/f	402,000
	1,726,800		1,726,800

All items relate to credit purchases.

What should be the closing balance on the payables ledger control account when all the errors are corrected?

A $122,800

B $139,200

C $205,200

D $218,500

210 Ordan received a statement from one of its suppliers, Alta, showing a balance due of $3,980. The amount due according to the payables ledger account of Ordan was only $230.

Comparison of the statement and the ledger account revealed the following differences:

(1)   A cheque sent by Ordan for $270 has not been recorded in Alta's statement.

(2)   Alta has not recorded goods returned by Ordan $180.

(3)   Ordan made a contra entry, reducing the amount due to Alta by $3,200, for a balance due from Alta in Ordan's receivables ledger. No such entry has been made in Alta's records.

What difference remains between the two entities' accounting records after adjusting for these items?

A $460

B $640

C $6,500

D $100

211 A business' receivables ledger control account did not agree with the total of the balances on the receivables ledger. An investigation revealed that the sales day book had been overcast by $10.

What effect will this have on the control account?

A   The control account should be credited with $10

B   The control account should be debited with $10

C   The control account should be credited with $20

D   The control account should be debited with $20

212 A supplier sent Lord a statement showing a balance outstanding of $14,350. Lord's records show a balance outstanding of $14,500.

The reason for this difference could be that:

A   The supplier sent an invoice for $150 which Lord has not yet received

B   The supplier has allowed Lord $150 cash discount which you had omitted to enter in your ledgers

C   Lord has paid the supplier $150 which he has not yet accounted for

D   Lord has returned goods worth $150 which the supplier has not yet accounted for

213 **Which of the following items would NOT lead to a difference between the total of the balances on the receivables ledger and the balance on the receivables ledger control account?**

A   An error in totalling the sales day book

B   An error in totalling the receipts column of the cash book

C   An overstatement of an entry in a customer's account

D   An entry posted to the wrong customer's account

214 A receivables ledger control account showed a debit balance of $37,642. The individual customers' accounts in the receivables ledger showed a total of $35,840.

The difference could be due to:

A   Undercasting the sales day book by $1,802

B   Overcasting the sales returns day book by $1,802

C   Entering cash receipts of $1,802 on the debit side of a customer's account

D   Entering a contra with the payables ledger control account of $901 on the debit side of the receivables ledger control account

215 Tarbuck has received a statement of account from one of its suppliers, showing an outstanding balance due to it of $1,350. On comparison with the ledger account, the following was identified:

• The ledger account shows a credit balance of $260.

• The supplier has disallowed a cash discount of $80 due to late payment of an invoice.

• The supplier has not yet allowed for goods returned at the end of the period of $270.

• Cash in transit of $830 has not been received by the supplier.

Following consideration of these items, what was the unreconciled difference between the statement of account from the supplier and Tarbuck's ledger account?

A $70

B $90

C $430

D $590

216 The purchases day book of Arbroath has been undercast by $500, and the sales day book has been overcast by $700. Arbroath maintains payables and receivables ledger control accounts as part of the double-entry bookkeeping system.

The effect of correcting these errors will be to:

A   Make adjustments to the ledger balances of the individual customers and suppliers, with no effect on profit

B   Make adjustments to the ledger balances of the individual customers and suppliers, with a decrease in profit of $1,200

C   Make adjustments to the control accounts, with no effect on profit

D   Make adjustments to the control accounts, with a decrease in profit of $1,200

217 For the month of November 20X0 Figgin's purchases totalled $225,600 plus sales tax of $33,840. A total of $259,440 was credited to the payables ledger control account as $254,940.

Which of the following adjustments is correct?

	Control account	List of suppliers' balances
A	$4,500 Cr	No adjustment
B	$4,500 Cr	Increase by $4,500
C	$29,340 Dr	No effect
D	$33,840 Dr	Increase by $4,500

218 In reconciling the receivables ledger control account with the list of receivables ledger balances of SK, the following errors were found:

(1) The sales day book had been overcast by $370.

(2) A total of $940 from the cash receipts book had been recorded in the receivables ledger control account as $490.

What adjustments must be made to correct the errors?

A Credit sales control account $820. Decrease total of receivables ledger balances by $820

B Credit sales control account $820. No change in total of receivables ledger balances.

C Debit sales control account $80. No change in total of receivables ledger balances

D Debit sales control account $80. Increase total of receivables ledger balances by $80

219 Mark is a sole trader who has provided the following information relating to transactions with credit customers and suppliers for the year ended 30 April 20X5:

	$
Trade receivables 1 May 20X4	200,000
Trade payables 1 May 20X4	130,000
Cash received form customers	576,800
Cash paid to suppliers	340,000
Discount received	3,500
Contra between payables and receivables	3,800
Trade receivables 30 April 20X5	240,000
Trade payables 30 April 20X5	150,000

What was the cost of Mark's purchases for the year ended 30 April 20X5?

$ _____

BANK RECONCILIATIONS

220 The cash book of Worcester shows a credit balance of $1,350. Cheques of $56 have been written to suppliers but not yet cleared the bank; uncleared lodgements amount to $128. The bank has accidentally credited Worcester's account with interest of $15 due to another customer. A standing order of $300 has not been accounted for in the general ledger.

What is the balance on the bank statement?

A $993 Cr

B $993 Dr

C $1,707 Cr

D $1,707 Dr

221 Jo's bank ledger account shows a balance of $190 credit. Her bank statement reports a balance of $250 credit.

Which of the following will explain the difference in full?

A Unpresented cheques of $100 and an uncleared lodgement of $30

B Unpresented cheques of $150, the misposting of a cash receipt of $130 to the wrong side of the cash account and unrecorded bank interest received of $30

C An unrecorded direct debit of $30, a dishonoured cheque of $70 and an uncleared lodgement of $40

D An unrecorded standing order of $60, an unpresented cheque of $110 and a bank error whereby Jo's account was accidentally credited with $110

222 **Which of the following statements about bank reconciliations are correct?**

(1) In preparing a bank reconciliation, unpresented cheques must be deducted from a balance of cash at bank shown in the bank statement.

(2) A cheque from a customer paid into the bank but dishonoured must be corrected by making a debit entry in the cash book.

(3) An error by the bank must be corrected by an entry in the cash book.

(4) An overdraft is a debit balance in the bank statement.

A (1) and (3)

B (2) and (3)

C (1) and (4)

D (2) and (4)

223 The following bank reconciliation statement has been prepared by an inexperienced bookkeeper at 31 December 20X5:

	$
Balance per bank statement (overdrawn)	38,640
Add: Lodgements not credited	19,270
	———
	57,910
Less: Unpresented cheques	14,260
	———
Balance per cash book	43,650
	———

What should the final cash book balance be when all the above items have been properly accounted for?

A $43,650 overdrawn

B $33,630 overdrawn

C $5,110 overdrawn

D $72,170 overdrawn

224 A bank reconciliation statement for Dallas at 30 June 20X5 is being prepared. The following information is available:

(1) Bank charges of $2,340 have not been entered in the cash book.

(2) The bank statement shows a balance of $200 Dr.

(3) Unpresented cheques amount to $1,250.

(4) A direct debit of $250 has not been recorded in the ledger accounts.

(5) A bank error has resulted in a cheque for $97 being debited to Dallas' account instead of Dynasty's account.

(6) Cheques received but not yet banked amounted to $890.

The final balance in the cash book after all necessary adjustments should be:

A $463 Dr

B $463 Cr

C $63 Cr

D $63 Dr

225 The following information relates to a bank reconciliation:

(1) The bank balance in the cash book before taking the items below into account was $8,970 overdrawn.

(2) Bank charges of $550 on the bank statement have not been entered in the cash book.

(3) The bank has credited the account in error with $425 which belongs to another customer.

(4) Cheque payments totalling $3,275 have been entered in the cash book but have not been presented for payment.

(5) Cheques totalling $5,380 have been correctly entered on the debit side of the cash book but have not been paid in at the bank.

What was the balance as shown by the bank statement before taking the items above into account?

A $8,970 overdrawn

B $11,200 overdrawn

C $12,050 overdrawn

D $17,750 overdrawn

226 Sharmin's bank statement at 31 October 20X8 shows a balance of $13,400. She subsequently discovers that the bank has dishonoured a customer's cheque for $300 and has charged bank charges of $50, neither of which is recorded in the cash book.

There are unpresented cheques totalling $1,400 and an automatic receipt from a customer of $195 has been recorded as a credit in Sharmin's cash book.

Sharmin's cash balance, prior to correcting the errors and omissions, was:

A $11,455

B $11,960

C $12,000

D $12,155

227 Wimborne's bank statement shows a balance of $715 overdrawn. The statement includes bank charges of $74 which have not been entered in the cash book. There are also unpresented cheques totalling $824 and lodgements not yet credited of $337. In addition the bank statement erroneously includes a dividend receipt of $25 belonging to another customer.

The bank overdraft in the statement of financial position should be:

A $253

B $1,177

C $1,202

D $1,227

228 The cash book shows a bank balance of $5,675 overdrawn at 31 August 20X5. It is subsequently discovered that a standing order for $125 has been entered twice, and that a dishonoured cheque for $450 has been debited in the cash book instead of credited.

The correct bank balance should be:

A $5,100 overdrawn

B $6,000 overdrawn

C $6,250 overdrawn

D $6,450 overdrawn

229 An organisation's cash book had an opening balance of $485 credit. During the following week, the following transactions took place:

Cash sales $1,450 including sales tax of $150.

Receipts from credit customers of $2,400.

Payments to suppliers of debts of $1,800 less 5% cash discount.

Dishonoured cheques from customers amounting to $250.

What was the resulting balance in the cash book after the transactions had been recorded?

A $1,255 debit

B $1,405 debit

C $1,905 credit

D $2,375 credit

230 The bank statement at 31 October 20X7 showed an overdraft of $800. On reconciling the bank statement, it was discovered that a cheque drawn in favour of Smith for $80 had not been presented for payment, and that a cheque for $130 from a customer had been dishonoured on 30 October 20X7, but that this had not yet been notified to you by the bank.

The correct bank balance to be shown in the statement of financial position at 31 October 20X7 is:

A $1,010 overdrawn

B $880 overdrawn

C $750 overdrawn

D $720 overdrawn

231 Your firm's cash book at 30 April 20X8 showed a balance at the bank of $2,490. Comparison with the bank statement at the same date revealed the following differences:

	$
Unpresented cheques	840
Bank charges not in cash book	50
Receipts not yet credited by the bank	470
Dishonoured cheque not in cash book	140

The correct bank balance at 30 April 20X8 was:

A $1,460

B $2,300

C $2,580

D $3,140

232 Your firm's cash book shows a credit bank balance of $1,240 at 30 April 20X9. On comparison with the bank statement, you determine that there are unpresented cheques totalling $450, and a receipt of $140 which has not yet been passed through the bank account. The bank statement shows bank charges of $75 which have not been entered in the cash book.

The balance on the bank statement is:

A $1,005 overdrawn

B $930 overdrawn

C $1,475 in credit

D $1,550 in credit

233 Which of the following is not an 'unrecorded difference' when reconciling the balance on the cash book to the amount shown in the bank statement?

A   A standing order

B   Bank interest

C   An uncleared lodgement

D   A BACS receipt

234 An entity has prepared its bank reconciliation at 31 March 2014 taking the following information into account:

	$		$
Outstanding lodgements	5,000	Unpresented cheques	2,800

Bank charges included in the bank statement but not recorded in the cash book were $125.

The adjusted cash book balance per the bank reconciliation was a debit balance of $1,060.

What was the balance as shown on the bank statement at 31 March 2014?

A $1,140 debit

B $1,140 credit

C $1,265 debit

D $1,265 credit

CORRECTION OF ERRORS AND SUSPENSE ACCOUNTS

235 A trial balance shows a total of debits of $347,800 and a total of credits of $362,350.

(1)   A credit sale of $3,670 was incorrectly entered in the sales day book as $3,760.

(2)   A non-current asset with a carrying amount of $7,890 was disposed of for $9,000. The only accounting entry was to debit cash.

(3)   The allowance for receivables was increased from $8,900 to $10,200. The allowance account was debited in error.

After adjusting for the errors above, what is the balance on the suspense account?

A $26,150 debit

B $26,060 debit

C $26,240 debit

D $2,950 credit

236 The trial balance of Kelvin does not balance.

Which TWO of the following errors could explain this, assuming that Kelvin maintains control accounts for its receivables and payables within the double entry system?

(1)   The sales day book was undercast by $100.

(2)   Discounts received were credited to sales revenue account.

(3)   An opening accrual was omitted from the rent account.

(4)   The debit side of the cash account was undercast.

A   (1) and (2)

B   (2) and (3)

C   (3) and (4)

D   (1) and (4)

237   The trial balance of MHSB does not balance at the year end.

What type of error may explain this?

A   Extraction error

B   Error of commission

C   Compensating error

D   An error of principle

238   The trial balance of Butler Co shows total debts of $125,819 and total credits of $118,251.

Which of the following explains the difference in full?

A   Carriage inwards of $3,784 has been shown on the wrong side of the trial balance.

B   Discounts received of $3,784 have been credited to the payables ledger control account.

C   The sales day book has been undercast by $7,568.

D   An opening accrual of $7,568 has been omitted from the rental expense account.

239   **Which one of the following journals is correct according to its narrative?**

		Debit	Credit
		$	$
A	Mr Smith personal account	100,000	
	Directors' remuneration		100,000
	Bonus allocated to account of managing director (Mr Smith)		
B	Purchases	14,000	
	Wages	24,000	
	Repairs to buildings		38,000
	Transfer of costs of repairs to buildings carried out by employees using materials from inventory		
C	Sales commission paid	2,800	
	Wages and salaries		2,800
	Correction of error: sales commission paid incorrectly debited to wages and salaries account.		
D	Suspense account	20,000	
	Rent receivable		10,000
	Rent payable		10,000
	Correction of error: rent received credited in error to rent payable account.		

240 The trial balance of Koi did not balance, and a suspense account was opened for the difference.

Which of the following errors would require an entry to the suspense account to correct them?

(1)   A cash payment to purchase a motor van had been correctly entered in the cash book but had been debited to the motor expenses account.

(2)   The debit side of the wages account had been undercast.

(3)   The total of the discounts received column in the cash book had been posted to the payables ledger control account correctly and debited to the purchases account.

(4)   A refund to a credit customer had been recorded by debiting the cash book and crediting the customer's account.

A   (1) and (2)

B   (2) and (3)

C   (3) and (4)

D   (2) and (4)

241 An entity's trial balance failed to agree, and a suspense account was opened for the difference.

Subsequent investigation revealed that cash sales of $13,000 had been debited to the purchases account and an entry on the credit side of the cash book for the purchase of some machinery costing $18,000 had not been posted to the plant and machinery account.

Which two of the following journal entries would correct the errors?

		Debit	Credit
		$	$
(1)	Purchases	13,000	
	Sales revenue		13,000
(2)	Purchases	13,000	
	Sales revenue	13,000	
	Suspense account		26,000
(3)	Suspense account	26,000	
	Purchases		13,000
	Sales revenue		13,000
(4)	Plant and machinery	18,000	
	Suspense account		18,000
(5)	Suspense account	18,000	
	Plant and machinery		18,000

A   (1) and (4)

B   (2) and (5)

C   (3) and (4)

D   (3) and (5)

This information is relevant to questions 242 and 243.

K Co's draft financial statements for 20X5 showed a profit of $630,000. However, the trial balance did not agree, and a suspense account appeared in the company's financial statements.

Subsequent checking revealed the following errors:

(1) The cost of an item of plant $48,000 had been entered in the cash book and in the plant account as $4,800. Depreciation at the rate of 10% per year ($480) had been charged.

(2) Bank charges of $440 appeared in the bank statement in December 20X5 but had not been entered in the company's records.

(3) One of the directors paid $800 due to a supplier in K Co's payables ledger by a personal cheque. The bookkeeper recorded a debit in the supplier's ledger account but did not complete the double entry for the transaction (K Co does not maintain a payables ledger control account).

(4) The payments side of the cash book had been understated by $10,000.

242 **Which of the above items would require an entry to the suspense account to correct them?**

    A   All four items

    B   (3) and (4) only

    C   (2) and (3) only

    D   (1), (2) and (4) only

243 **What would the K Co's profit be after the correction of the above errors?**

    A $634,760

    B $624,760

    C $624,440

    D $625,240

244 The draft financial statements of Galahad's business for the year ended 31 July 20X0 show a profit of $54,250 prior to the correction of the following errors:

    (1)   Cash drawings of $250 have not been accounted for.

    (2)   Debts amounting to $420, which were provided against in full during the year, should have been written off as irrecoverable.

    (3)   Rental income of $300 has been classified as interest receivable.

    (4)   On the last day of the accounting period, $200 in cash was received from a customer, but no bookkeeping entries have been made.

What is the correct profit of Galahad for the year ended 31 July 20X2?

    A $53,580

    B $53,830

    C $54,250

    D $55,830

245 The trial balance of Flo Co does not agree and a suspense account has been opened.

Inventory bought at a sales tax inclusive cost of $4,700 has been credited to the payables ledger control account. The sales tax, at 17.5%, has been recorded in the sales tax account and the total $4,700 has been recorded in the purchases account.

What entry is required to correct the error?

A	Dr Payables ledger control account $700	Cr Suspense account $700
B	Dr Payables ledger control account $822.50	Cr Suspense account $822.50
C	Dr Suspense account $700	Cr Purchases $700
D	Dr Suspense account $822.50	Cr Purchases $822.50

246 Weagan's trial balance at 31 October 20X9 is out of agreement, with the debit side totalling $500 less than the credit side. During November, the following errors are discovered:

- The credit side of the sales account for October had been undercast by $150.

- Rent received of $240 had been credited to the rent payable account.

- The allowance for receivables, which decreased by $420, had been recorded in the allowance for receivables account as an increase.

Following the correction of these errors, the balance on the suspense account would be:

A $190 Cr

B $670 Cr

C $1,190 Cr

D $1,490 Dr

247 Which ONE of the following is an error of principle?

A   A gas bill credited to the gas account and debited to the bank account.

B   The purchase of a non-current asset credited to the asset at cost account and debited to the supplier's account.

C   The purchase of a non-current asset debited to the purchases account and credited to the supplier's account.

D   The payment of wages debited and credited to the correct accounts, but using the wrong amount.

248 The trial balance of C did not agree, and a suspense account was opened for the difference. Checking in the bookkeeping system revealed a number of errors:

Error

(1) $4,600 paid for motor van repairs was correctly treated in the cash book but was credited to motor vehicles asset account.

(2) $360 received from Brown, a customer, was credited in error to the account of Green.

(3) $9,500 paid for rent was debited to the rent account as $5,900.

(4) The total of the discount received column in the cash book, $325, had been credited in error to the purchases account.

(5) No entries had been made to record a cash sale of $100.

Which of the errors above would require an entry to the suspense account as part of the process of correcting them?

A   Errors (3) and (4) only

B   Errors (1) and (3) only

C   Errors (2) and (5) only

D   Errors (2) and (3) only

249 Drive incurred bank charges of $40, which was then credited to the bank interest receivable account.

What was the effect upon profit for the year of recording the bank charges in this way?

A   Profit will be unchanged

B   Profit will be overstated by $80

C   Profit will be understated by $80

D   Profit will be understated by $40

250 A suspense account was opened when a trial balance failed to agree. The following errors were subsequently discovered:

Error

(1) A gas bill of $420 had been recorded in the Gas account as $240.

(2) A payment of $50 for stationery of $50 had been credited to Discounts received.

(3) Interest received of $70 had been entered in the bank account only.

If the errors when corrected clear the suspense account, what was the original balance on the suspense account?

A   debit $210

B   credit $210

C   debit $160

D   credit $160

251 The book-keeper of High Hurdles was instructed to make a contra entry for $270 between the supplier account and the customer account for Greyfold. He recorded the transaction by debiting the customer account and crediting the supplier account with $270. The business accounts do not include control accounts.

Which of the following statements is correct?

A   Unless the error is corrected, profit will be over-stated by $540

B   Unless the error is corrected, net assets will be over-stated by $270

C   Unless the error is corrected, net assets will be over-stated by $540

D   The errors should be corrected, but neither the profit nor the net assets are over-stated

252 **Which one of the following errors would lead to creation of a suspense account?**

A   Sales returns were credited to the Purchase returns account and debited to Receivables.

B   The total of the sales day book has been totalled incorrectly before being posted to the ledger accounts.

C   Discounts received have been dealt with correctly in the Payables ledger control account, but credited to the Purchases account.

D   Purchases from the purchases day book have been credited to Sales and dealt with correctly in the Payables ledger control account.

253 Pelle had a balance on his suspense account of $1,820 credit. He discovered the following errors:

(1)   Sundry income of $1,750 has been recorded in the sundry income account as $1,570.

(2)   Sales of $2,800 from the sales day book have been posted to the receivables ledger control account, but no other entry has been made.

(3)   The purchases day book was undercast by $950.

What was the balance on the suspense account after Pelle has corrected the above errors?

$ ⬚

254 Marlon created a suspense account with a debit balance of $1,250 in order to balance his trial balance. He subsequently investigated and found the following errors:

(1)   The closing balance of the purchase ledger control account at the year-end had been undercast by $160.

(2)   Cash received of $450 from customers has only been entered into the cash account.

(3)   The purchase returns day book has been overcast by $300.

What is the remaining debit balance on the suspense account after the errors have been corrected?

$ ⬚

255 At 30 September 20X8, the following require items inclusion in MCD Co's financial statements:

(1) On 1 September 20X8, MCD Co received $5,000 as a deposit for goods which were despatched to the customer on 15 October 20X8.

(2) On 1 August 20X8, MCD Co paid an insurance premium of $5,000 for the six month period commencing 1 July 20X8.

(3) On 1 April 20X8, MCD Co raised a five-year bank loan of $12,000 which is repayable in a single capital sum at the end of the loan term. Interest is payable on the loan annually in arrears at 5% per annum.

For these items, what was the effect of these transactions total figures included in the MCD Co's statement of financial position at 30 September 20X8?

A	Current assets	$17,000	Current liabilities	$2,800
B	Current assets	$19,500	Current liabilities	$10,300
C	Current assets	$14,500	Current liabilities	$5,300
D	Current assets	$7,500	Current liabilities	$5,300

256 The statement of profit or loss for a business for the year ended 31 July 20X8 showed a net profit of $57,400. It was later discovered that a suite of office furniture had been purchased on 1 February 20X8 at a cost of $15,500 had been charged to the office expenses account. The suite of office furniture had an estimated useful life of ten years with an estimated residual value of $1,500. Depreciation is charged on a monthly basis, commencing with the month of purchase.

What was the net profit for the year ended 31 July 20X8 after adjusting for this error?

$ [   ]

PREPARING BASIC FINANCIAL STATEMENTS

STATEMENT OF FINANCIAL POSITION AND STATEMENT OF PROFIT OR LOSS AND OTHER COMPREHENSIVE INCOME

257 The following information relates to Minnie's hairdressing business in the year ended 31 August 20X7:

	$
Expenses	7,100
Opening inventory	1,500
Closing inventory	900
Purchases	12,950
Gross profit	12,125
Inventory drawings of shampoo	75

What is the sales figure for the business?

A $32,700

B $25,600

C $25,675

D $25,750

258 Astral Co has a debit balance relating to income tax of $500 included in its trial balance extracted on 30 June 20X4. Astral estimated that its income tax liability for the year ended 30 June 20X4 was $8,000.

What amounts should be included in Astral Co's financial statements for the year ended 30 June 20X4?

	Statement of profit or loss	Statement of financial position
A	$8,000	$8,000
B	$8,500	$8,000
C	$7,500	$8,500
D	$8,000	$7,500

259 Arthur had net assets of $19,000 at 30 April 20X7. During the year to 30 April 20X7, he introduced $9,800 additional capital into the business and his profit for the year was $8,000. During the year ended 30 April 20X7 he withdrew $4,200.

What was the balance on Arthur's capital account at 1 May 20X6?

A $5,400

B $13,000

C $16,600

D $32,600

260 The capital of a business would change as a result of:

A   a supplier being paid by cheque

B   raw materials being purchased on credit

C   non-current assets being purchased on credit

D   wages being paid in cash

261 A draft statement of financial position has been prepared for Lollipop, a sole trader. It is now discovered that a loan due for repayment by Lollipop fourteen months after the reporting date has been included in trade payables.

The necessary adjustment will:

A   have no effect on net current assets

B   increase net current assets

C   reduce net current assets

D   increase current assets but reduce net current assets

262 The profit of a business may be calculated by using which one of the following formulae?

A   Opening capital – drawings + capital introduced – closing capital

B   Closing capital + drawings – capital introduced – opening capital

C   Opening capital + drawings – capital introduced – closing capital

D   Closing capital – drawings + capital introduced – opening capital

263 Which accounting concept requires that amounts of goods taken from inventory by the proprietor of a business are treated as drawings?

A   Accruals

B   Prudence

C   Separate entity

D   Substance over form

264 The following information is available about Andrew's business at 30 September 20X6:

	$
Motor van	14,000
Loan (repayable in 4 equal annual instalments starting 1 January 20X7)	100,000
Receivables	23,800
Bank balance (a debit on the bank statement)	3,250
Accumulated depreciation	7,000
Payables	31,050
Inventory	12,560
Petty cash	150
Rent due	1,200
Allowance for receivables	1,500

What are the correct figures for current liabilities and current assets?

	Current liabilities	Current assets
	$	$
A	34,300	35,010
B	32,250	38,260
C	57,250	38,260
D	60,500	35,010

265 The following transactions relate to Max's business:

1 May	Purchase of goods for resale on credit	$300
2 May	Max injects long term capital into the business	$1,400
3 May	Payment of rent made	$750
5 May	Max withdraws cash from the business	$400
7 May	Goods which had cost $600 were sold on credit	1,200

At the start of the week, the assets of the business were $15,700 and liabilities amounted to $11,200.

At the end of the week, what was the amount of Max's capital?

A $5,350

B $1,400

C $850

D $1,000

266 State the amount that will be included in other comprehensive income of Zappa Co for the year ended 30 June 20X4 based upon the following information.

There was a revaluation surplus of $70,000 arising on revaluation of land and buildings during the year.

The depreciation charge for the year relating to buildings was $20,000. Zappa Co does not make an annual transfer of 'excess depreciation' between revaluation surplus and retained earnings.

During the year, there was a gain on disposal on disposal of motor vehicles of $1,000.

$

267 State the total amount that will be charged as an expense in the statement of profit or loss of Clapton Co or the year ended 30 September 20X6 based upon the following information.

Clapton Co incurred development expenditure during the year of $50,000.

The amortisation charge on intangible assets for the year was $15,000.

During the year, there was a loss on disposal on disposal of plant and equipment of $3,000.

$

268 On 1 January 20X8 Baker Co revalued its property to $100,000. At the date of the revaluation, the asset was accounted for at a cost of $80,000, and had accumulated depreciation $16,000. The property had an expected useful life of fifty years from the date of purchase and nil residual value.

What was the amount of the 'excess depreciation' transfer required from revaluation surplus to retained earnings at 31 December 20X8 as a result of accounting for the revaluation?

$

269 On 1 January 20X8 Hendrix Co revalued its property to $200,000. Up to the date of the revaluation, the asset had been accounted for at a cost of $160,000, and had accumulated depreciation $40,000. The property had an expected useful life of fifty years from the date of purchase and nil residual value.

State the accounting entries required to account for the revaluation in the financial statements of Hendrix Co.

Debit or Credit	Account title	$

270 **The following information is relevant to Wimbledon:**

	$
Opening inventory	12,500
Closing inventory	17,900
Purchases	199,000
Distribution costs	35,600
Administrative expenses	78,800
Audit fee	15,200
Carriage in	3,500
Carriage out	7,700
Depreciation	40,000

Depreciation is to be split in the ratio 70:30 between the factory and the office. All office expenses are classified as administrative expenses.

Based upon the available information, what was Wimbledon's cost of sales?

A $233,600

B $221,600

C $225,100

D $237,100

271 Brown Co had $100,000 50c shares and $400,000 8% irredeemable preference shares in issue. A dividend of 3c per ordinary share and half of the preference dividend was paid during the year.

Which of the following statements is/are true?

(1)   An ordinary dividend of $3,000 was paid during the year.

(2)   A preference dividend of $16,000 was accrued at the year end.

A   (1) only

B   (2) only

C   Neither (1) nor (2)

D   Both (1) and (2)

272 At 1 October 20X6, Ozber Co's capital structure was as follows:

	$
Ordinary shares of 25c	100,000
Share premium	30,000

On 10 January 20X7, in order to raise finance for expansion, Ozber Co made a 1 for 4 rights issue at $1.15. The issue was fully taken up. This was followed by a 1 for 10 bonus issue on 1 June 20X7.

What was the balance on the share premium account after these transactions?

A $17,500

B $21,250

C $107,500

D $120,000

273 Where, in a set of financial statements complied in accordance with international accounting standards, would you expect to find dividends paid?

(1)   Statement of profit or loss and other comprehensive income.

(2)   Statement of financial position.

(3)   Statement of cash flows.

(4)   Statement of changes in equity.

A   (1) and (3)

B   (2) and (3)

C   (1) and (4)

D   (3) and (4)

274 Where in the financial statements should tax on profit for the current period, and unrealised surplus on revaluation of properties in the year, be separately disclosed?

	Tax on profit for the current period	*Unrealised surplus on revaluation of properties*
A	Statement of profit or loss and other comprehensive income	Statement of cash flows
B	Statement of changes in equity	Statement of profit or loss and other comprehensive income
C	Statement of profit or loss and other comprehensive income	Statement of profit or loss and other comprehensive income
D	Statement of cash flows	Statement of cash flows

275 The following information is available about L Co's dividends:

Sept 20X5	Final dividend for the year ended 30 June 20X5 paid (declared August 20X5)	$100,000
March 20X6	Interim dividend for the year ended 30 June 20X6 paid	$40,000
Sept 20X6	Final dividend for the year ended 30 June 20X6 paid (declared August 20X6)	$120,000

What figures, if any, should be disclosed in L Co's statement of profit or loss and other comprehensive income for the year ended 30 June 20X6 and its statement of financial position at that date?

	Statement of profit or loss and other comprehensive income	Statement of financial position
A	$160,000 deduction	$120,000
B	$140,000 deduction	Nil
C	Nil	$120,000
D	Nil	Nil

276 **Which two of the following statements are correct?**

(1) An entity may make a rights issue if it wished to raise more equity capital.

(2) A rights issue might increase the share premium account whereas a bonus issue is likely to reduce it.

(3) A rights issue will always increase the number of shareholders in an entity whereas a bonus issue will not.

(4) A bonus issue will result in an increase in the market value of each share

A (1) and (2)

B (1) and (3)

C (2) and (3)

D (2) and (4)

277 Florabundi Co's trial balance at 31 December 20X8 included a credit balance of $3,400 on its tax liability account, having already settled the tax liability for the year ended 31 December 20X7 during the year. Florabundi Co estimated that its income tax charge arising on its profits for the year ended 31 December 20X8 at $67,900.

What amounts should be included in Florabundi Co's financial statements for the year ended 31 December 20X8 in respect of tax?

	Statement of profit or loss	Statement of financial position
A	$67,900 tax charge	$67,900 tax payable
B	$64,500 tax charge	$64,500 tax payable
C	$64,500 tax charge	$67,900 tax payable
D	$71,300 tax charge	$67,900 tax payable

278 Classify the following assets and liabilities as current or non-current in Albatross Co's financial statements:

(1) A sale has been made on credit to a customer. They have agreed to terms stating that payment is due in 12 months' time.

(2) A bank overdraft facility of $30,000 is available under an agreement with the bank which extends 2 years.

(3) Albatros Co purchases a small number of shares in another entity which it intends to trade.

(4) A bank loan has been taken out with a repayment date 5 years hence.

	Current	Non-current
A	(2) and (3)	(1) and (4)
B	(3) only	(1), (2) and (4)
C	(1), (2) and (3)	(4)
D	(1) and (3)	(2) and (4)

279 Extracts from the accounting records of Andratx Co relating to the year ended 31 December 20X6 are as follows:

Revaluation surplus	$230,000
Ordinary interim dividend paid	$12,000
Profit before tax	$178,000
Estimated tax liability for year	$45,000
8% $1 Preference shares	$100,000
Under provision for tax in previous year	$5,600
Proceeds of issue of 2,000 $1 ordinary Shares	$5,000
Final ordinary dividend proposed	$30,000

What was the total of equity reported in the statement of changes in equity at 31 December 20X6?

A $312,400

B $356,000

C $348,000

D $342,400

280 Which of the following statements is/are true in relation to a preference share?

(1) They carry voting rights.

(2) Their dividend is paid out in priority to an ordinary dividend.

(3) Their dividend is related to profits.

A   All three statements

B   (1) and (2)

C   (2) and (3)

D   (2) only

281 Bangeroo Co, issues 100,000 3% $1 redeemable preference shares during the year ended 30 September 20X8 at 98c per share.

What is the correct entry to account for this transaction?

		Debit		Credit
		$		$
A	Cash	$98,000	Liability	$98,000
B	Cash	$98,000	Share capital	$100,000
	Share premium	$2,000		
C	Cash	$98,000	Share capital	$98,000
D	Cash	$98,000	Share capital	$100,000
	Statement of profit or loss	$2,000		

282 The nominal value paid by the shareholder plus further amounts that they have agreed to pay in the future' best describes:

A   Paid up share capital

B   Called up share capital

C   Authorised share capital

D   Issued share capital

283 Argonaut Co issued $400,000 12% loan notes for $380,000 on 1 August 20X6.

What accounting entries are required in the year ended 30 September 20X6?

A		
	Dr Cash	$400,000
Cr Non-current liabilities	$400,000	
And		
Dr Interest	$7,600	
Cr Current liabilities	$7,600	
B	Dr Cash	$380,000
Cr Non-current liabilities	$380,000	
And		
Dr Interest	$8,000	
Cr Current liabilities	$8,000	
C	Dr Cash	$400,000
Cr Non-current liabilities	$400,000	
And		
Dr Interest	$8,000	
Cr Current liabilities	$8,000	
D	Dr Cash	$380,000
Cr Non-current liabilities	$380,000	
And		
Dr Interest	$7,600	
Cr Current liabilities	$7,600	

284 **Which of the following are advantages of a bonus issue?**

(1)   It is the cheapest way for an entity to raise finance through the issuing of shares.

(2)   It makes the shares in the entity more marketable.

(3)   The total reserves of the entity will increase.

(4)   Issued share capital is brought more into line with assets employed in the entity.

A   (2) and (4)

B   (1) and (2)

C   (3) and (4)

D   (1) and (3)

285 **Revenue reserves would decrease if an entity:**

A   Sets aside profits to pay future dividends

B   Transfers amounts into 'general reserves'

C   Issues shares at a premium

D   Pays dividends

286 Radar Co has accounted for the revaluation of buildings in its financial statements for the year ended 31 December 20X4. The increase in carrying amount of the property was $50,000, with a depreciation charge for the year of $13,000. Radar Co accounts for excess depreciation and this has been calculated at $2,000.

For each of the following items, state where in the statement of profit or loss and other comprehensive income each item would be included, or if it would be omitted completely from that statement.

A   Profit or loss

B   Other comprehensive income

C   Omitted from the statement of profit or loss and other comprehensive income

Choice: A, B or C

Excess depreciation on revaluation

Increase in carrying amount of the property

Depreciation charge

287 Saturn Co disposed of a property that had been revalued in an earlier accounting period. The details relating to this property are as follows:

	$000
Carrying amount at disposal date	150
Disposal proceeds	165
Revaluation surplus at disposal date	15

How should the property disposal be accounted for in Saturn's financial statements?

A   Gain on disposal of $15,000 included in profit or loss for the year only.

B   Gain on disposal of $30,000 included in profit or loss for the year only.

C   Gain on disposal of $15,000 included in profit or loss for the year and revaluation gain of $15,000 included in other comprehensive income for the year.

D   Gain on disposal of $15,000 included in profit or loss for the year and a transfer within the statement of changes in equity of $15,000 from revaluation surplus to retained earnings.

288 Starstruck Co estimated that its income tax liability for the year ended 30 September 20X6 was $15,000. The income tax charge disclosed in the statement of profit or loss for the year ended 30 September 20X6 was $14,200.

Which of the following statements is true?

A   The difference between the statement of profit or loss charge and the liability in the statement of financial position is the result of an adjustment relating to an under provision in an earlier year.

B   The difference between the statement of profit or loss charge and the liability in the statement of financial position is the result of an adjustment relating to an overprovision in an earlier year.

C   It is not possible to state whether the difference between the statement of profit or loss charge and the liability in the statement of financial position is due to an underprovision or overprovision in an earlier year.

D   There is no relationship between the amounts included in the statement of financial position and statement of profit or loss relating to income tax.

289 Details of two of Clooney's transactions in the year ended 31 August 20X7 were as follows:

(1)   Clooney sold a machine to a customer, Pitt, on 28 August 20X7. Pitt is responsible for installation and operation of the machine following delivery.

(2)   Clooney sold a number of food mixers to Damon, on credit. Damon collected the food mixers from Clooney on 26 August 20X7. Damon has not yet paid for the goods purchased.

For which of the transactions should sales revenue be recognised?

A   (1) only

B   (2) only

C   Both (1) and (2)

D   Neither (1) nor (2)

290 Kaplin publishes study materials and runs courses for students studying for professional accountancy examinations. Details of two transactions that occurred in December 20X8 were as follows:

(1) Ten students enrolled on a course due to commence in January 20X9 at a price of $1,000 per student and each student paid their fees in advance. If sold separately, the study materials would be sold for $200 and the course of ten lectures would be sold for a total of $800. The study materials are issued on the first day of the course.

(2) Kaplin sold study materials to forty self-study students at a price of $400 per student who will receive no further support with their studies, which were delivered to students prior to 31 December 20X8.

What sales revenue should Kaplin recognise in the financial statements for the year ended 31 December 20X8?

$ ☐

291 Vostok sells computer games and is the sole distributor of a new game 'Avalanche'. Customer demand for the new game has resulted in lots of advance orders pending release of the game later in the year. As at 31 July 20X2, Vostok had received customer orders and deposits received amounting to $500,000. Vostok anticipates that all orders will be despatched to customers by 1 December 20X2.

What sales revenue can Vostok recognise in the financial statements for the year ended 31 July 20X2?

$ ☐

292 Scrubber provides contract cleaning services in commercial office premises. Scrubber charges each business an annual fee of $1,200, based upon providing an agreed level of service each month. In one office block there are twelve businesses which use Scrubber to provide cleaning services. At 1 April 20X5 four businesses had paid one month in advance and two customers were in one month in arrears. With effect from 31 August 20X5, one customer terminated their agreement with Scrubber, whilst two additional contracts were signed to take effect from 1 December 20X5. At 31 March 20X6, the same four businesses had paid one month in advance and two customers were in arrears by one month. Each annual service contract is regarded as a contract which gives rise to obligations which are satisfied over a period of time.

What sales revenue can Scrubber recognise in the financial statements for the year ended 31 March 20X6?

$ ☐

293 Hamilton provides internet and website support services to its customers. On 1 September 20X7, Hamilton agreed a three-year support service agreement with a customer at a total price of $2,250.

How much revenue can be recognised from this transaction for the year ended 31 March 20X8?

$ ☐

294 At 1 January 20X8, Clarinet Co had an estimated income tax liability of $2,350. This liability was settled by a payment of $2,050 made In March 20X8. Due to challenging trading conditions, Clarinet Co made a loss for the year ended 31 December 20X8 and expects to recover a repayment of income tax of $2,120 during 20X9.

What amounts should be included in Clarinet Co's financial statements for the year ended 31 December 20X8 for income tax?

	Statement of profit or loss	*Statement of financial position*
A	$2,420 tax charge	$1,820 tax recoverable asset
B	$2,120 tax credit	$2,120 tax payable
C	$2,420 tax credit	$2,120 tax recoverable asset
D	$1,820 tax charge	$2,120 tax recoverable asset

295 Banjo Co estimated that its income tax liability on the profit for the year ended 30 June 20X5 was $16,940. This liability was settled in February 20X6 by a payment of $17,500. Having made a trading loss for the year ended 30 June 20X6, Banjo Co estimated that it would receive repayment of income tax of $4,500 during the following accounting period.

What amounts should be included in Banjo Co's financial statements for the year ended 30 June 20X6 for income tax?

	Statement of profit or loss	*Statement of financial position*
A	$3,940 tax credit	$4,500 tax recoverable asset
B	$4,500 tax credit	$4,500 tax payable
C	$3,940 tax charge	$4,500 tax payable
D	$5,060 tax credit	$4,500 tax recoverable asset

DISCLOSURE NOTES

296 **Which of the following should be disclosed in the notes to the financial statements relating to intangible assets?**

(1) Accumulated amortisation charges at the start and at the end of the reporting period.

(2) A reconciliation of the movement in the net carrying amount of intangible assets for the reporting period.

(3) A statement from the directors, explaining whether or not they believe that capitalised development costs will be recovered at some future date.

A (1) only

B (2) only

C (1) and (2)

D (2) and (3)

297 **Which of the following would be a suitable accounting policy note for disclosure in the financial statements relating to intangible assets?**

A   The entity has some intangible assets accounted for using the cost model and other intangible assets accounted for using the valuation model, based upon the judgement of the directors. All intangible assets are written off over their expected useful lives to the business.

B   The entity accounts for intangible assets using the cost model. All intangible assets are amortised over their expected useful lives to the business, between five and fifteen years, on a straight-line basis.

C   The entity accounts for intangible assets using the valuation model, based upon a valuation estimated by the directors. All changes in the carrying valuation from one reporting date to the next are accounted for in the statement of profit or loss.

D   The entity uses the same accounting policy for tangible and intangible non-current assets.

298 **Which of the following would be a suitable accounting policy note for disclosure in the financial statements relating to land and buildings?**

A   Land and buildings are accounted for at cost and are written off over their expected useful life of fifty years on a straight-line basis.

B   Land and buildings are accounted for at cost and are not depreciated as the directors believe that the market value of land and buildings will increase over time.

C   Land and buildings are accounted for at cost, and the buildings are written off over their expected useful life of fifty years on a straight-line basis.

D   The entity uses the same accounting policy for land and buildings as it does for intangible assets.

299 **Which of the following would be a suitable accounting policy note for disclosure in the financial statements relating to inventory?**

A   Inventory is valued at the lower of total cost and total net realisable value.

B   Inventory is valued at the lower of cost and net realisable value for each separate product or item.

C   Inventory is valued at the higher of cost and net realisable value for each separate product or item.

D   Inventory is valued at cost for each separate product or item.

300 **Is the following statement true or false?**

Non-adjusting events can be ignored when preparing the annual financial statements and supporting disclosure notes.

A   True

B   False

301 **When dealing with non-adjusting events what information should be disclosed in the notes to the financial statements?**

(1)   The nature of the event.

(2)   The names of those with responsibility for the event.

(3)   The geographical location of the event.

(4)   An estimate of the financial effect of the event.

A   (1) and (2)

B   (1), (3) and (4)

C   (2), (3) and (4)

D   (1) and (4)

302 **In relation to non-current assets, which of the following items should be disclosed in the notes to the financial statements?**

(1)   Reconciliation of carrying amounts of non-current assets at the beginning and end of period.

(2)   Useful lives of assets or depreciation rates used.

(3)   Increases in asset values as a result of revaluations in the period.

(4)   Depreciation expense for the period.

A   (1) and (2) only

B   (1) and (3) only

C   (2), (3) and (4) only

D   (1), (2), (3) and (4)

303 IAS 1 Presentation of Financial Statements requires certain items to be presented on the face of the statement of profit or loss for the year.

Which THREE of the following items must be disclosed on the face of the statement of profit or loss for the year?

(1)   Revenue

(2)   Closing inventory

(3)   Finance costs

(4)   Dividends paid

(5)   Tax expense

(6)   Depreciation charge for the year

304 **Which one of the following statements is true in relation to disclosure requirements?**

    A   Disclosure requirements consist only of monetary disclosures

    B   Disclosure requirements consist only of narrative disclosures

    C   Disclosure requirements consist of both monetary and narrative disclosures

    D   Disclosure notes do not form part of the annual financial statements

305 **When considering disclosures required in the financial statements relating to property, plant and equipment, is the following statement true or false?**

The estimated useful lives of the property plant and equipment and the depreciation rates used must be disclosed.

    A   True

    B   False

306 **When making disclosures required in the financial statements relating to provisions, which of the following needs to be disclosed?**

    (1)   The nature of the obligation.

    (2)   Expected timing of any payment.

    (3)   The name of the party to whom the obligation is owed.

    (4)   The nature of any uncertainties which may affect the amount to be paid.

    A   (1), (2) and (3)

    B   (2), (3) and (4)

    C   (1), (3) and (4)

    D   (1), (2), and (4)

307 **When considering disclosures required in the financial statements in relation to provisions, is the following statement true or false?**

An entity need only state the carrying amount of the obligation at the beginning and end of the accounting period, without providing a reconciliation of the movement in the provision during the year.

    A   True

    B   False

308 In relation to non-current assets, which of the following items must be disclosed in the notes to the financial statements of an entity which complies with international accounting standards?

(1) The depreciation charge on property, plant and equipment for the year.

(2) The amortisation charge on intangible assets for the year.

(3) The date of any revaluation of property plant and equipment made during the accounting year.

(4) Whether an independent valuer was used in the revaluation of property, plant and equipment during the accounting year.

A (1), (2) and (3) only

B (2), (3) and (4) only

C (1), (3) and (4) only

D (1), (2), (3) and (4)

309 How are intangible assets disclosed in the statement of financial position?

A Cost only without any recognition of amortisation or impairment

B Cost or valuation – amortisation – impairment = Carrying amount

C The amortisation amount only

D At the disposal proceeds value

EVENTS AFTER THE REPORTING PERIOD

310 Ribblesdale Co has prepared financial statements for the year ended 30 September 20X8. The financial statements were approved by the directors on 12 January 20X9 and issued to the shareholders on 20 February 20X9.

Which of the following are adjusting events after the reporting period?

(1) A flood on 3 October 20X8 that destroyed a relatively small quantity of inventory which had cost $1,700.

(2) A credit customer with a balance outstanding at 30 September 20X8 was declared insolvent on 20 December 20X8.

(3) Inventory valued at a cost of $800 at 30 September 20X8 was sold for $650 on 11 November 20X8.

(4) A dividend on ordinary shares of 4c per share was declared on 1 December 20X8.

A (1) and (2) only

B (1), (3) and (4) only

C (2) and (3) only

D (2), (3) and (4) only

311 Which of the following statements are correct based upon the requirements of IAS 10 Events after the Reporting Period?

    (1)   Details of all adjusting events must be disclosed by note to the financial statements.

    (2)   A material loss arising from the sale, after the reporting date of inventory valued at cost at the statement of financial position date must be reflected in the financial statements.

    (3)   If the market value of property, plant and equipment falls materially after the reporting date, the details must be disclosed by note.

    (4)   Events after the reporting period are those that occur between the statement of financial position date and the date on which the financial statements are approved.

    A   (1) and (2) only

    B   (1), (3) and (4) only

    C   (2) and (3) only

    D   (2), (3) and (4) only

312 Brakes Co had a reporting date of 30 September 20X8. The financial statements for that year were approved by the directors on 14 December 20X8 and issued to the shareholders on 17 January 20X9. Details of several events which occurred after the reporting date of 30 September 20X8 are as follows:

    (1)   On 3 October 20X8 a fire destroyed all inventory on the premises with the consequence that it was unlikely Brakes would be able to continue as a going concern.

    (2)   A credit customer with an outstanding balance at 30 September 20X8 was declared bankrupt on 12 December 20X8.

    (3)   An ordinary dividend of 6c per share was declared on 1 December 20X8.

    (4)   Inventory valued at a cost of $800 at the year-end was sold for $650 on 11 November 20X8.

Which of the above are non-adjusting events?

    A   All are non-adjusting events

    B   (3) only is a non-adjusting event

    C   (3) and (4) only are non-adjusting events

    D   (1) and (3) only are non-adjusting events

313 Where there are material non-adjusting events, a note to the financial statements should disclose:

    A   The nature of the event and the estimated financial effect

    B   A letter from the solicitor

    C   Nothing

    D   Where the event took place

314 Viola has an accounting year-end of 31 January 20X4. Which of the following events, if they occurred before the financial statements were approved, would be classified as adjusting events in accordance with IAS 10 Events after the Reporting Period?

(1)   Viola paid an equity dividend of $10,000 on 28 February 20X4. The dividend had been proposed by the directors on 20 January 20X4.

(2)   Notification of a compensation claim from a customer was received on 15 February 20X4 which related to a faulty product sold by Viola in January 20X4.

(3)   Viola received notification on 5 February 20X4 that a major credit customer was insolvent.

A   (1), (2) and (3) are adjusting events

B   (2) and (3) are adjusting events

C   (1) and (3) are adjusting events

D   (2) only is an adjusting event

REVENUE FROM CONTRACTS WITH CUSTOMERS

315 Rep Co is preparing its financial statements for the year ended 30 September 20X4. During that year, Rep Co entered acted as an agent on behalf of Zip Co and arranged a sale of goods on 1 August 20X4 at a price of $80,000. Rep Co is entitled to 10% commission upon receipt of cash from the customer. The customer paid for the goods on 28 September 20X4.

How much revenue can be recognised by Rep Co in its statement of profit or loss for the year ended 30 September 20X4?

$ _____

316 Loc Co sells machines, and also offers installation and technical support services. The selling price of each product is shown below.

Sale price of machine	$750
Installation	$100
One year service support agreement	$120

Cox Co purchased a machine, along with the installation service and the service agreement on 1 October 20X5. The machine was delivered and installed on 1 October 20X5 and the service support agreement also commenced from that date.

How much can Loc Co recognise as revenue for the year ended 31 December 20X5?

$ _____

317 **Which one of the following items has been included correctly in Hat Co's revenue for the year ended 31 March 20X5?**

A Hat Co negotiated a sale at a value of $200,000 on behalf of a client, Res Co, one of its clients. Hat Co is entitled to 10% commission on the agreed sale price and has recognised revenue of $200,000 in its financial statements.

B Hat Co entered into a contract to supply consultancy services to Cap Co for a three year term for a total fee of $300,000. The contract commenced on 1 July 20X4, and Hat Co recognised revenue of $100,000 on this transaction in its financial statements.

C On 1 November 20X4 Hat Co purchased goods at a cost of $50,000 and sold those goods to Far Co for $75,000 on 20 January 20X5. Hat Co recognised revenue of $75,000 on this contract in its financial statements.

D On 1 December 20X4 Hat Co purchased goods at a cost of $25,000 and sold those goods to Ber Co for $50,000 on 10 January 20X5. Hat Co recognised revenue of $25,000 on this contract in its financial statements.

318 **Which one of the following items is not part of the 'five step' approach for revenue recognition as outlined in IFRS 15 Revenue from Contracts with Customers?**

A Allocate the total price between the separate performance obligations in the contract

B All contracts must be in writing

C Recognise revenue when a performance obligation is satisfied

D Identify the contract

319 **Which of the following items is an acceptable basis for recognition of revenue in the financial statements of an entity?**

(1) On any reasonable basis

(2) At a point in time

(3) Annually

(4) Over a period of time

A All four items

B (1), (3) and (4) only

C (2) and (4) only

D (3) only

STATEMENTS OF CASH FLOWS

320 Extracts from the financial statements of Deuce Co showed balances as follows:

	20X9	20X8
$1 Share capital	300,000	120,000
Share premium	260,000	100,000

A bonus issue of 1 share for every 12 held at the 20X8 year-end occurred during the year and loan notes of $300,000 were issued at par. Interest of $12,000 was paid during the year.

What is the net cash inflow from financing activities?

A $480,000

B $605,000

C $617,000

D $640,000

321 Nobus Co is producing its statement of cash flows for the year ended 31 December 20X5. The accountant has identified the following balances in the financial statements:

	$
Interest accrual b/f	4,900
Interest accrual c/f	1,200
Interest payable	20,000
Interest receivable	13,000
Preference dividend payable b/f	120,000
Preference dividends payable c/f	140,000
Dividends (statement of changes in equity)	600,000

What is the net cash flow from investing activities?

A   ($10,700)

B $13,000

C   ($603,700)

D   ($590,700)

322 **Which of the following items could appear as items in an entity's statement of cash flows?**

(1)   A bonus issue of shares.

(2)   A rights issue of shares.

(3)   The revaluation of non-current assets.

(4)   Dividends paid.

A   All four items

B   (1), (3) and (4) only

C   (2) and (4) only

D   (3) only

323 A draft statement of cash flows contains the following:

	$m
Profit before tax	22
Depreciation	8
Increase in inventories	(4)
Decrease in receivables	(3)
Increase in payables	(2)
Net cash inflow from operating activities	21

Which of the following corrections need to be made to the calculations?

(1)   Depreciation should be deducted, not added.

(2)   Increase in inventories should be added, not deducted.

(3)   Decrease in receivables should be added, not deducted.

(4)   Increase in payables should be added, not deducted.

A   (1) and (2)

B   (1) and (3)

C   (2) and (4)

D   (3) and (4)

324 **Where, in an entity's financial statements, complying with International accounting standards, should you find the proceeds of non-current assets sold during the period?**

A   Statement of cash flows and statement of financial position

B   Statement of changes in equity and statement of financial position

C   Statement of profit or loss and other comprehensive income and cash flow statement

D   Statement of cash flows only

325 The figures below have been prepared for inclusion in the statement of cash flows of Bamboo.

Tax and dividends paid	$87,566
Increase in payables	$13,899
Decrease in inventory	$8,900
Redemption of loans	$300,000
Increase in receivables	$6,555
Reduction in cash and cash equivalents	$3,211
Depreciation charge	$10,600
Payments to acquire non-current assets	$47,999
Proceeds from sale of non-current assets	$13,100

What is the cash generated from operations?

A $331,688

B $338,110

C $425,676

D $419,254

326 A business's bank balance increased by $750,000 during its last financial year. During the same period it issued shares, raising $1 million and repaid a loan of $750,000. It purchased non-current assets for $200,000 and charged depreciation of $100,000. Receivables and inventory increased by $575,000.

What was the profit for the year?

A $1,175,000

B $1,275,000

C $1,325,000

D $1,375,000

327 A business had non-current assets with a carrying amount of $50,000 at the start of the financial year. During the year the business sold assets that had cost $4,000 and had been depreciated by $1,500. Depreciation for the year was $9,000. The carrying amount of assets at the end of the financial year was $46,000.

How much cash has been invested in non-current assets during the year?

A $4,000

B $7,500

C $9,000

D $10,000

328 A business has made a profit of $8,000 but its bank balance has fallen by $5,000.

Which one of the following statements could be a possible explanation for this situation?

A Depreciation charge of $3,000 and an increase in inventories of $10,000

B Depreciation charge of $6,000 and the repayment of a loan of $7,000

C Depreciation charge of $12,000 and the purchase of new non-current assets for $25,000

D The disposal of a non-current asset for $13,000 less than its carrying amount

329 A Co made a profit for the year of $18,750, after accounting for depreciation of $1,250. During the year, non-current assets were purchased for $8,000, receivables increased by $1,000, inventories decreased by $1,800 and payables increased by $350.

What was A Co's increase in cash and bank balances during the year?

A $10,650

B $10,850

C $12,450

D $13,150

330 A statement of cash flows prepared in accordance with the indirect method reconciles profit before tax to cash generated from operations.

Which of the following lists of items consists only of items that would be ADDED to profit before tax?

A Decrease in inventory, depreciation charge, profit on sale of non-current assets

B Increase in payables, decrease in receivables, profit on sale of non-current assets

C Loss on sale of non-current assets, depreciation charge, increase in receivables

D Decrease in receivables, increase in payables, loss on sale of non-current assets

331 **In relation to statements of cash flows, which, if any, of the following statements are correct?**

(1) The direct method of calculating net cash from operating activities leads to a different figure from that produced by the indirect method, but this is balanced elsewhere in the statement of cash flows.

(2) An entity making high profits must necessarily have a net cash inflow from operating activities.

(3) Profits and losses on disposals of non-current assets appear as items under investing activities in the statement of cash flows.

A Statement (1) only

B Statement (2) only

C Statement (3) only

D None of the statements

332 The movement on the plant and machinery account for X is shown below:

Cost b/f	$10,000
Additions	$2,000
Disposals	($3,000)
Cost c/f	$9,000
Depreciation b/f	$2,000
Charge for the year	$1,000
Disposals	($1,500)
Depreciation c/f	$1,500
Carrying amount b/f	$8,000
Carrying amount c/f	$7,500

The profit on the sale of the machine was $500. What figures would appear in the statement of cash flows of X under the heading of 'Investing activities'?

A Movement on plant account $500 and profit on disposal of $500

B Movement on plant account $500 and proceeds on sale of plant $2,000

C Purchase of plant $2,000 and profit on disposal of $500

D Purchase of plant $2,000 and proceeds on sale of plant $2,000

333 Which one of the following is not an advantage of the statement of cash flows?

A It highlights the effect of non-cash transactions

B It helps an assessment of the liquidity off a business

C The numbers within it cannot be manipulated through the adoption of beneficial accounting policies

D It helps users to estimate future cash flows

334 Grainger makes all sales for cash and is preparing its statement of cash flows using the direct method. Grainger has compiled the following information:

Cash sales		$212,500
Cash purchases		$4,600
Cash expenses		$11,200
Payables at start and at the end of the year	$12,300	and $14,300
Credit purchases		$123,780
Wages and salaries due at start and at the end of the year	$1,500	and $2,300
Wages and salaries expense		$34,600
Inventory at start and ay the end of the year	$23,000	and $$17,800

What is the cash generated from operations by Grainger?

A $35,520

B $46,320

C $74,920

D $41,120

335 Howard Co provided the following extracts from the statement of financial position for the years ended 31 December:

	20X6	20X7
	$000	$000
Accumulated profits	72,000	82,000
10% Loan notes	30,000	40,000
Tax payable	12,000	15,000
Dividends payable	1,200	1,600

All dividends were declared and proposed **before** the year end. There was no adjustment for under/over provision for tax in the year ended 31 December 20X7. No interim dividends were paid during the year. The additional 10% loan notes were issued on 1 January 20X7.

What is Howard Co's operating profit (profit before interest and tax) for the year ended 31 December 20X7?

A $29,600

B $27,200

C $30,600

D $102,600

336 In the year ended 31 May 20X2, Galleon purchased non-current assets at a cost of $140,000, financing them partly with a new loan of $120,000. Galleon also disposed of non-current assets with a carrying amount of $50,000, making a loss of $3,000. Cash of $18,000 was received from the disposal of investments during the year.

What is Galleons net cash inflow or outflow from investing activities to include in the statement of cash flows?

$ [   ]

337 The following is an extract from the financial statements of Pompeii at 31 October:

	20X7	20X6
	$000	$000
Equity and liabilities:		
Share capital	120	80
Share premium	60	40
Retained earnings	85	68
	265	188
Non-current liabilities:		
Bank loan	100	150
	365	338

What was Pompeii's net cash inflow or outflow from financing activities to include in the statement of cash flows for the year ended 31 October 20X7?

$ [   ]

338 Carter Co has non-current assets with a carrying amount of $2,500,000 on 1 December 20X7. During the year ended 20 November 20X8, the following occurred:

(1)   Depreciation of $75,000 was charged to the statement of profit or loss.

(2)   Land and buildings with a carrying amount of $1,200,000 were revalued to $1,700,000.

(3)   An asset with a carrying amount of $120,000 was disposed of for $150,000.

The carrying amount of non-current assets at 30 November 20X8 was $4,200,000.

What amount should be shown for the purchase of non-current assets in the statement of cash flows of Carter Co for the year ended 30 November 20X8?

$ [   ]

339 Which **THREE** of the following items would you expect to see included within the operating activities section of a statement of cash flows prepared using the direct method?

(1)   Payments made to suppliers

(2)   Increase or decrease in receivables

(3)   Receipts from customers

(4)   Increase or decrease in inventories

(5)   Increase or decrease in payables

(6)   Finance costs paid

340 When comparing two statements of cash flows, one prepared using the direct method and the other prepared using the indirect method, the only differences between the two statements relate to the presentation of items within 'cash flows from operating activities'.

Is the above statement true or false?

A   True

B   False

341 When preparing a statement of cash flows using the direct method in accordance with IAS 7, the depreciation charge for the year is disclosed as an adjustment to reported profit for the year within 'cash flows from operating activities'.

Is the above statement true or false?

A   True

B   False

INCOMPLETE RECORDS

342 The following information is available about the transactions of Razil, a sole trader who does not keep proper accounting records:

	$
Opening inventory	77,000
Closing inventory	84,000
Purchases	763,000
Gross profit margin	30%

Based on this information, what was Razil's sales revenue for the year?

A $982,800

B $1,090,000

C $2,520,000

D $1,080,000

343 You have been provided with the following incomplete and incorrect extract from the statement of profit or loss of a business that trades at a mark-up of 25% on cost:

	$	$
Sales		174,258
Less: Cost of goods sold:		
Opening inventory	12,274	
Purchases	136,527	
Closing inventory	X	
		(X)
Gross profit		X

Having discovered that the sales revenue figure should have been $174,825 and that purchase returns of $1,084 and sales returns of $1,146 have been omitted, what should be the amount for closing inventory?

A $8,662

B $8,774

C $17,349

D $17,458

344 On 1 September 20X8, Winston had inventory of $380,000. During the month, sales totalled $650,000 and purchases $480,000. On 30 September 20X8 a fire destroyed some of the inventory. The undamaged goods were valued at $220,000. The business operates with a standard gross profit margin of 30%.

Based on this information, what is the cost of the inventory destroyed in the fire?

A $185,000

B $140,000

C $405,000

D $360,000

345 A fire in the offices of Lewis has destroyed most of the accounting records. The following information has been retrieved:

	$
Sales	630,000
Opening inventory	24,300
Closing inventory	32,750
Opening payables	29,780
Closing payables	34,600

Gross profit for the period should represent a mark-up of 40%.

What was the total cash paid to suppliers in the year?

A $463,270

B $381,630

C $391,270

D $453,630

346 Pioneer's annual inventory count took place on 6 January 20X6. The value of inventory on this date was $32,780. During the period from 31 December 20X5 to 6 January 20X6, the following events occurred:

Sales	$8,600
Purchases	$4,200

The value of inventory at 31 December 20X5 was $34,600.

What is the gross margin of Pioneer?

A   70%

B   72%

C   30%

D   43%

347 Harry has a mark-up of 25% on cost of sales. The following information is also available:

	$
Receivables at start of year	6,340
Receivables at end of year	5,200
Cash at start of year	620
Cash at end of year	500
Total cash payments	16,780

The only receipts during the year consisted of cash and cheques received from customers.

What is the gross profit for the year?

A $3,880

B $3,152

C $3,560

D $3,104

348 During September, Edel had sales of $148,000, which made a gross profit of $40,000. Purchases amounted to $100,000 and opening inventory was $34,000.

The value of closing inventory was:

A $24,000

B $26,000

C $42,000

D $54,000

349 **The gross profit mark-up is 40% if:**

A   sales are $120,000 and gross profit is $48,000

B   sales are $120,000 and cost of sales is $72,000

C   sales are $100,800 and cost of sales is $72,000

D   sales are $100,800 and cost of sales is $60,480

350 Many of the records of G have been destroyed by fire. The following information is available for the period under review.

(1)   Sales totalled $480,000.

(2)   Inventory at cost was opening $36,420, closing $40,680.

(3)   Trade payables were opening $29,590, closing $33,875.

(4)   Gross profit for the period should represent a mark-up on cost of 50%.

What was the total of cash paid to suppliers for the period under review?

A $239,975

B $315,715

C $319,975

D $328,545

351 Pike runs an angling shop in the south of Spain. He spends all of his spare time fishing and consequently has kept no accounting records in the year ended 31 August 20X5. He knows that he has taken $6,800 cash out of his business during the year plus bait which cost the business $250. He can also remember putting his $20,000 winnings on the Spanish lottery into the business in March.

Pike knows that at the last year end his business had assets of $40,000 and liabilities of $14,600. He has also calculated that the assets of the business at 31 August 20X5 are worth $56,000, and the liabilities $18,750.

What profit or loss has Pike made in the year?

A $1,100 profit

B $1,100 loss

C $1,350 profit

D $1,350 loss

352 Ives makes and sells handmade pottery. He keeps all finished items in a storeroom at the back of his workshop on the banks of the River Flow. In August 20X5, freak weather conditions led to extensive flooding, and Ives lost pottery which had cost $3,400 and had a retail value of $5,750.

Ives was insured for loss of inventory due to flooding.

What double entry is required to record the loss of inventory?

	Dr	Cr
A	Expense (P/L) $5,750	Cost of sales (P/L) $5,750
B	Current asset (SFP) $5,750	Cost of sales (P/L) $5,750
C	Expense (P/L) $3,400	Cost of sales (P/L) $3,400
D	Current asset (SFP) $3,400	Cost of sales (P/L) $3,400

PREPARING SIMPLE CONSOLIDATED FINANCIAL STATEMENTS

353 At 1 January 20X4 Yogi acquired 80% of the share capital of Bear for $1,400,000. At that date the share capital of Bear consisted of 600,000 ordinary shares of 50c each and its reserves were $50,000. The fair value of the non-controlling interest was valued at $525,000 at the date of acquisition.

In the consolidated statement of financial position of Yogi and its subsidiary Bear at 31 December 20X8, what amount should appear for goodwill?

A $1,575,000

B $630,000

C $1,050,000

D $450,000

354 At 1 January 20X8 Tom acquired 80% of the share capital of Jerry for $100,000. At that date the share capital of Jerry consisted of 50,000 ordinary shares of $1 each and its reserves were $30,000. At 31 December 20X9 the reserves of Tom and Jerry were as follows:

Tom $400,000

Jerry $50,000

In the consolidated statement of financial position of Tom and its subsidiary Jerry at 31 December 20X9, what amount should appear for group reserves?

A $400,000

B $438,000

C $416,000

D $404,000

355 At 1 January 20X6 Fred acquired 75% of the share capital of Barney for $750,000. At that date the share capital of Barney consisted of 20,000 ordinary shares of $1 each and its reserves were $10,000. The fair value of the non-controlling interest was valued at $150,000 at 1 January 20X6.

In the consolidated statement of financial position of Fred and its subsidiary Barney at 31 December 20X9, what amount should appear for goodwill?

A $150,000

B $720,000

C $870,000

D $750,000

356 At 1 January 20X6 Gary acquired 60% of the share capital of Barlow for $35,000. At that date the share capital of Barlow consisted of 20,000 ordinary shares of $1 each and its reserves were $10,000. At 31 December 20X9 the reserves of Gary and Barlow were as follows:

Gary $40,000

Barlow $15,000

At the date of acquisition the fair value of the non-controlling interest was valued at $25,000.

In the consolidated statement of financial position of Gary and its subsidiary Barlow at 31 December 20X9, what amount should appear for non-controlling interest?

A $25,000

B $27,000

C $28,000

D $31,000

357 At 1 January 20X8 Williams acquired 65% of the share capital of Barlow for $300,000. At that date the share capital of Barlow consisted of 400,000 ordinary shares of 50c each and its reserves were $60,000. At 31 December 20X9 the reserves of Williams and Barlow were as follows:

Williams $200,000

Barlow $75,000

The fair value of the non-controlling interest was valued at $50,000 at the date of acquisition.

In the consolidated statement of financial position of Williams and its subsidiary Barlow at 31 December 20X9, what amount should appear for non-controlling interest?

A $55,250

B $50,000

C $76,250

D $5,250

358 The following extracts are provided from the statements of financial position of Dora and Diego at the year-end:

	Dora	Diego
	$000	£000
Current assets		
Inventory	200	100
Receivables	540	160
Cash	240	80
Current liabilities		
Payables	320	180

Dora's statement of financial position includes a receivable of $40,000 due from Diego.

In the consolidated statement of financial position what will be the correct amounts for receivables and payables?

	Payables	Receivables
A	$460,000	$660,000
B	$306,000	$660,000
C	$294,000	$694,000
D	$294,000	$654,000

359 Salt owns 70% of Pepper and sells goods to Pepper valued at $1,044 at a mark-up of 20%. 40% of these goods were sold on by Pepper to external parties at the year end.

What is the provision for unrealised profit (PURP) adjustment in the group financial statements?

A $69.60

B $104.40

C $125.28

D $83.52

360 Stress acquired 100% of the ordinary share capital of Full on 1 October 20X7 when Full's retained earnings stood at $300,000. Full's statement of financial position at 30 September 20X9 was as follows:

	$000
Assets	
Property, plant and equipment	1,800
Current assets	1,000
	2,800
Equity and reserves	
Share capital	1,600
Retained earnings	500
Current liabilities	700
	2,800

On 1 October 20X7 the fair value of land included within Full's non-current assets was $400,000 greater than the carrying amount. Stress had non-current assets at 30 September 20X9 at a carrying amount of $2.2m.

What is the total amount for non-current assets that will appear on the consolidated statement of financial position at 30 September 20X9?

A $4,320,000

B $4,400,000

C $4,380,000

D $4,000,000

The following data relate to questions 361 to 363.

Hard acquired 80% of the ordinary share capital of Work on 1 April 20X8. The summarised statement of profit or loss for the year-ended 31 March 20X9 is as follows:

	Hard	Work
	$000	$000
Revenue	120,000	48,000
Cost of sales	84,000	40,000
Gross profit	36,000	8,000
Distribution costs	5,000	100
Administration expenses	7,000	300
Profit from operations	24,000	7,600
Investment income	150	–
Finance costs	–	400
Profit before tax	24,150	7,200
Tax	6,000	1,200
Profit for the year	18,150	6,000

During the year Hard sold Work some goods for $24m, these had originally cost $18m. At the year-end Work had sold half of these goods to third parties.

361 **What is the provision for unrealised profit (PURP) adjustment for the year-ended 31 March 20X9?**

 A $1,000,000

 B $6,000,000

 C $3,000,000

 D $7,000,000

362 **What is the total amount for revenue and cost of sales to be shown in the consolidated statement of profit or loss for the year-ended 31 March 20X9?**

	Sales	Cost of sales
A	$144,000,000	$100,000,000
B	$168,000,000	$97,400,000
C	$192,000,000	$100,600,000
D	$144,000,000	$103,000,000

363 **What is the total share of group profit attributable to non-controlling interest?**

    A $1,200,000

    B $4,800,000

    C $3,630,000

    D $1,440,000

The following data relate to questions 364 to 365

Really acquired 75% of the ordinary share capital of Hard on 1 January 20X9 when Hard had retained losses of $112,000. Also on that date, Really acquired 30% of the ordinary share capital of Work when Work had retained earnings of $280,000. The summarised statement of financial position for the year-ended 31 December 20X9 is as follows:

	Really	Hard
Non-current assets	$000	$000
Property, plant and equipment	1,918	1,960
Investment in Hard	1,610	
Investment in Work	448	
	3,976	1,960
Current assets		
Inventory	760	1,280
Receivables	380	620
Cash	70	116
	5,186	3,976
Equity and reserves		
$1 ordinary shares	2,240	1,680
Retained earnings	2,464	1,204
	4,704	2,884
Current liabilities		
Payables	300	960
Taxation	182	132
	5,186	3976

364 **What is the amount for property, plant and equipment to be included in the consolidated statement of financial position?**

    A $3,878,000

    B $5,558,000

    C $5,552,400

    D $3,872,400

365 What is the amount for retained earnings to be included in the consolidated statement of financial position?

A $3,959,200

B $3,451,800

C $3,735,200

D $3,740,800

366 Which of the following statements is most likely to indicate an investment by one entity in another which should be recognised and accounted for as an associate?

A Ownership of 100% of the ordinary shares of another entity

B Ownership of over 50% and less than 100% of the ordinary shares of another entity

C Ownership of between 20% and 50% of the ordinary shares of another entity

D Ownership of less than 20% of the ordinary shares in another entity

367 IFRS 10 Consolidated Financial Statements specify three necessary elements to determine whether or not one company controls another.

Which one of the following is not one of the three necessary elements to determine whether one entity has control of another?

A Power over the other entity

B Exposure or rights to variable returns from involvement in the other entity

C The ability to use power over the other entity to affect the amount of investor returns

D The ability to exercise significant influence over another entity

368 Which of the following would normally indicate that one entity has significant influence over the activities of another?

A Ability to appoint the majority of the board of directors of that other entity

B Ability to appoint at least one person to the board of directors of that other entity

C Ability to request that a director is appointed to the board of directors of that other entity

D Ability to submit requests regarding corporate policy to the board of directors of that other entity

369 Which of the following would normally indicate that one entity has control over the activities of another?

A Ownership of some equity shares in another entity

B Ownership of up to twenty per cent of the equity shares of another entity

C Ownership of over fifty per cent of the equity shares of another entity

D Ownership of between twenty per cent and fifty per cent of the equity shares of another entity

370 **Which of the following would normally indicate that one entity has control of another?**

    A   Ownership of the majority of the equity share capital of that other entity

    B   Ownership of between twenty per cent and fifty per cent of the equity share capital of that other entity

    C   Ownership of less than twenty per cent of the equity shares of that other entity

    D   Ownership of some of the shares of that other entity – the precise percentage of shares held is not relevant

371 **Which of the following would normally indicate that one entity has significant influence over the activities of another entity?**

    A   Ownership of some equity shares in another entity

    B   Ownership of up to twenty per cent of the equity shares of another entity

    C   Ownership of over fifty per cent of the equity shares of another entity

    D   Ownership of between twenty per cent and fifty per cent of the equity shares of another entity

372 Entity A acquired sixty per cent of the issued equity shares of entity B by exchanging three shares in entity A for every two shares acquired in entity B. At that date, entity B had issued equity capital of one hundred thousand shares. At the date of acquisition, the fair value of an equity share in entity A was $3.50 and the fair value of an equity share in entity B was $2.00. The nominal value per share of both entities was $1.00 per share.

What was the fair value of consideration paid by entity A to gain control of entity B?

    A $80,000

    B $90,000

    C $180,000

    D $315,000

373 Entity C acquired eighty per cent of the issued equity shares of entity D by paying cash of $3.00 per share plus exchanging three shares in entity C for every five shares acquired in entity D. At that date, entity D had issued equity capital of two hundred and fifty thousand shares. At the date of acquisition, the fair value of an equity share in entity C was $3.50 and the fair value of an equity share in entity D was $2.00. The nominal value per share of both entities was $1.00 per share.

What was the fair value of consideration paid by entity C to gain control of entity D?

$ [   ]

374 Entity X acquired sixty per cent of the issued equity shares of entity Z on 1 October 20X3. During the year ended 31 December 20X3, X and Z had sales revenue of $2 million and $1.5 million respectively. During the post-acquisition period, X made sales to Z of $0.1 million.

What is the group sales revenue figure for the year ended 31 December 20X3?

   A $2.275 million

   B $2.375 million

   C $3.4 million

   D $3.5 million

375 Entity T acquired eighty per cent of the issued equity shares of entity S on 1 July 20X6. The sales revenue for the year ended 31 March 20X7 for entity T and entity S was $5 million and $3 million respectively. During the post-acquisition period, S made sales to T of $0.5 million.

What is the group sales revenue figure for the year ended 31 March 20X7?

   A $6.75 million

   B $7.25 million

   C $7.5 million

   D $8.0 million

376 Entity F acquired eighty per cent of the issued equity shares of entity G on 1 July 20X6. The cost of sales for the year ended 31 March 20X7 for entity F and entity G were $10 million and $4 million respectively. During the post-acquisition period, F made sales to G of $1.6 million. The intra-group sales were made at a mark-up of twenty-five per cent. At the year end, one quarter of the goods sold by F to G remained within G's inventory.

What was the group cost of sales figure for the year ended 31 March 20X7?

   A $12.480 million

   B $12.320 million

   C $11.480 million

   D $11.320 million

377 On 1 June 20X5 Hightown acquired control of Southport. During the year ended 30 September 20X5, Hightown and Southport had cost of sales of $10 million and $6 million respectively. During the post-acquisition period, Hightown had sales to Southport of $1.8 million. These sales had been made at a mark-up of twenty per cent and at the year end, one third of the goods remained within Southport's inventory.

What was the group cost of sales figure for the year ended 30 September 20X5?

   $ [   ]

378 On 1 July 20X4 Lion paid $20 million to acquire seventy per cent of the issued equity capital of Tiger. For the year ended 31 December 20X4, Tiger had earned profit after tax of $2 million. Tiger had retained earnings of $10 million at 1 January 20X4. At the date of acquisition, Tiger had issued equity capital of $8 million and the fair value of the non-controlling interest at that date was $6 million.

Based upon the available information, what was goodwill on acquisition of Tiger for inclusion in the Lion consolidated financial statements for the year ended 31 December 20X4?

$

379 Pole acquired eighty per cent of the issued equity shares of Rod for $43 million on 1 March 20X8. Rod had retained earnings of $15 million at 1 July 20X7 and made a profit after tax of $6 million for the year ended 30 June 20X8. At the date of acquisition, Rod had issued share capital of $25 million and the fair value of the non-controlling interest was $10 million. On 1 March 20X8 the fair value of freehold land and buildings owned by Rod was $1 million in excess of their carrying amount.

Based upon the available information, what was goodwill an acquisition of Rod for inclusion in the Pole consolidated financial statements for the year ended 30 June 20X8?

A $4.0 million

B $8.0 million

C $16.0 million

D $20.0 million

380 Plank acquired sixty per cent of the issued equity share capital of Splinter on 1 January 20X2. On that date, Plank paid $3 cash per share acquired and also issued two shares (nominal value $1 per share) in exchange for each Splinter share acquired. At the date of acquisition, Splinter had ten million equity shares of $1 nominal value in issue, plus a share premium account balance of $10 million and had retained earnings of $50 million. The fair value of the non-controlling interest in Splinter at the date of acquisition was $14 million. The fair value of an equity share in Plank and Splinter were $4.50 and $1.50 respectively at 1 January 20X2.

What was goodwill on acquisition of Splinter for inclusion in the consolidated financial statements of Plank for the year ended 31 December 20X2?

A $2 million

B $4 million

C $16 million

D $26 million

381 On 1 October 20X5, Luton acquired seventy-five per cent of the issued equity capital of Bedford. In exchange for gaining control of Bedford, Luton made immediate cash payment of $4.50 per share acquired and also issued one new share for each share acquired. At the date of acquisition, Bedford had issued share capital of fifteen million shares of $1 nominal value and a share premium account balance of $5 million. On 1 October 20X5, Bedford had retained earnings of $76.875 million and the fair value of the non-controlling interest in Bedford was $27 million. Bedford had a freehold factory that had a fair value of $2 million in excess of its carrying amount at the date of acquisition. The fair value of a $1 equity share of Luton at the date of acquisition was $5.00 per share.

What was goodwill on acquisition of Bedford for inclusion in the consolidated financial statements of Luton for the year ended 30 September 20X6?

A $35 million

B $37 million

C $39 million

D $40 million

382 On 1 January 20X6, Hyndland acquired ninety per cent of the issued equity capital of Shawfield. In exchange for gaining control of Shawfield, Hyndland made immediate cash payment of $3 per share acquired and also issued one new share of $0.5 nominal value per share for each share acquired. At the date of acquisition, Shawfield had issued share capital of 200,000 shares of $1 nominal value, a share premium account balance of $100,000 and retained earnings of $590,000. On 1 January 20X6, the fair value of the non-controlling interest in Shawfield was $75,000. In addition, at the date of acquisition, Shawfield had several items of property plant and equipment which together had a fair value of $90,000 and a carrying amount of $70,000. The fair value of a $0.5 equity share of Hyndland at 1 January 20X3 was $2.00 per share. There has been no impairment of goodwill.

What was goodwill on acquisition of Shawfield for inclusion in the consolidated financial statements of Hyndland for the year ended 30 September 20X6?

$ [   ]

383 On 1 July 20X5 Huyton acquired sixty per cent of the equity shares of Speke. For the year ended 31 December 20X5, Huyton made a profit after tax of $600,000 and Speke had a profit after tax of $400,000. During the post-acquisition period, Huyton sold goods to Speke which included a profit element of $20,000. At the year-end, one quarter of the goods sold by Huyton to Speke remained within the inventory of Speke.

What was the non-controlling interest share of the group profit after tax for the year ended 31 December 20X5?

A $75,000

B $80,000

C $120,000

D $160,000

384 Honey Co acquired 75% of Bee Co on 1 April 20X3, paying $2 for each ordinary share acquired. The fair value of the non-controlling interest at 1 April 20X3 was $300. Bee Co's individual financial statements as at 30 September 20X3 included:

Statement of financial position:	$
Ordinary share capital ($1 each)	1,000
Retained earnings	710
	1,710

Statement of profit or loss:	
Profit after tax for the year	250

Profit accrued evenly throughout the year.

What was goodwill on acquisition at 1 April 20X3?

A $715

B $90

C $517

D $215

385 Panther acquired 80% of the equity shares in Seal on 31 August 20X2. The statements of profit or loss for Panther and Seal for the year ended 31 December 20X2 were as follows:

	Panther	Seal
	$	$
Revenue	100,000	62,000
Cost of sales	25,000	16,000

During October 20X2, sales of $6,000 were made by Panther to Seal. None of these items remained in inventory at the year-end.

What is the consolidated revenue for Panther Group or the year ended 31 December 20X2?

$

386 Tulip acquired 70% of the equity shares of Daffodil on 1 March 20X2. The following extracts are from the individual financial statements of profit and loss for each entity for the year ended 31 August 20X2:

	Tulip	Daffodil
	$	$
Revenue	61,000	23,000
Cost of sales	(42,700)	(13,800)
Gross profit	18,300	9,200

What should be the consolidated gross profit for the year ended 31 August 20X2?

$

387 Venus acquired 75% of Mercury's 100,000 $1 ordinary shares on 1 November 20X4. The consideration comprised $2 cash per share plus one share in Venus for every share acquired in Mercury.

Shares in Venus have a nominal value of $1 and a fair value of $1.75. The fair value of the non-controlling interest was $82,000 and the fair value of the net assets acquired was $215,500.

What should be recorded as goodwill on acquisition of Mercury in the consolidated Mercury Group financial statements?

> $ _____

388 **Which of the following investments of Coffee should be equity accounted in the consolidated financial statements?**

(1) 40% of the non-voting preference share capital in Tea Co

(2) 18% of the ordinary share capital in Café Co with two of the five directors of Coffee Co on the board of Café Co

(3) 50% of the ordinary share capital of Choc Co, with five of the seven directors of Coffee Co on the board of Choc Co

A (1) and (2)

B (2) only

C (1) and (3) only

D (2) and (3) only

389 **Which of the following statements, if any, are correct in relation to accounting for associates?**

(1) Equity accounting will always be used when an investing entity holds between 20% – 50% of the equity shares in another entity.

(2) Dividends received from an investment in associate will be presented as investment income in the consolidated financial statements.

	Statement 1	Statement 2
A	Correct	Correct
B	Correct	Incorrect
C	Incorrect	Correct
D	Incorrect	Incorrect

INTERPRETATION OF FINANCIAL STATEMENTS

The following data relate to questions 390 to 401. Barnstorm case-study.

Note: The following questions, based upon the financial statements of Barnstorm presented below are designed as a revision aid to test your knowledge of definitions and calculations of accounting ratios. You will not necessarily be required to state the ratio definition and calculate the ratio for two years in the real exam.

You should calculate all ratios to two decimal places.

The financial statements of Barnstorm for the year ended 31 July 20X4, with comparatives, are presented below.

Statement of profit or loss and other comprehensive income – year ended 31 July 20X4.

	20X4	20X3
	$000	$000
Revenue	1,391,820	1,159,850
Cost of sales	(1,050,825)	(753,450)
Gross profit	340,995	406,400
Operating expenses	(161,450)	(170,950)
Finance costs	(10,000)	(14,000)
Profit before tax	169,545	221,450
Tax	(50,800)	(66,300)
Profit for the year	118,745	155,150
Other comprehensive income:		
Revaluation surplus on land and buildings	10,000	
Total comprehensive income for the year	128,745	155,150

Statement of financial position at 31 July 20X4

	20X4	20X3
	$000	$000
Non-current assets		
Property, plant and equipment	559,590	341,400
Current assets		
Inventory	109,400	88,760
Receivables	419,455	206,550
Bank		95,400
	1,088,445	732,110

Equity and reserves		
$1 ordinary shares	140,000	100,000
Share premium	40,000	20,000
Revaluation reserve	10,000	
Retained earnings	406,165	287,420
	596,165	407,420
Non-current liabilities		
10% Bank loan 20X7	61,600	83,100
Current liabilities		
Payables	345,480	179,590
Bank overdraft	30,200	
Taxation	55,000	62,000
	1,088,445	732,110

390 State the definition and calculate the return on capital employed for the year ended 31 July 20X4, together with the comparative for the earlier year.

391 State the definition and calculate the gross profit margin for the year ended 31 July 20X4, together with the comparative for the earlier year.

392 State the definition and calculate the operating profit margin for the year ended 31 July 20X4, together with the comparative for the earlier year.

393 State the definition and calculate the asset turnover for the year ended 31 July 20X4, together with the comparative for the earlier year.

394 State the definition and calculate the current ratio for the year ended 31 July 20X4, together with the comparative for the earlier year.

395 State the definition and calculate quick 'acid test' ratio for the year ended 31 July 20X4, together with the comparative for the earlier year.

396 State the definition and calculate the inventory holding period for the year ended 31 July 20X4, together with the comparative for the earlier year.

397 State the definition and calculate the trade receivables collection period for the year ended 31 July 20X4, together with the comparative for the earlier year.

398 State the definition and calculate the trade payables payment period for the year ended 31 July 20X4, together with the comparative for the earlier year.

399 State the definition and calculate the debt-equity ratio for the year ended 31 July 20X4, together with the comparative for the earlier year.

400 State the definition and calculate the gearing ratio for the year ended 31 July 20X4, together with the comparative for the earlier year.

401 State the definition and calculate interest cover for the year ended 31 July 20X4, together with the comparative for the earlier year.

402 W Co had sales of $20,000 and cost of sales of $15,400.

What W Co's gross profit margin?

A   77%

B   129%

C   43%

D   23%

403 The following extract relates to X Co for the years ended 30 June 20X5 and 20X6:

	20X5	20X6
Revenue	20,000	26,000
Cost of sales	(15,400)	(21,050)
Gross profit	4,600	4,950
Less expenses	(2,460)	(2,770)
Operating profit	2,140	2,180

What was the operating profit margin for 20X5 and 20X6?

	20X5	20X6
A	10.7%	8.38%
B	8.38%	10.7%
C	23%	19%
D	12%	10%

404 The following extract relates to Y Co for 20X5 and 20X6:

	20X5	20X6
Statement of profit or loss extract	$	$
Revenue	20,000	26,000
Statement of financial position extract		
Receivables	4,400	6,740
Cash	120	960

What is the receivables collection period for 20X5 and 20X6?

	20X5	20X6
A	80 days	95 days
B	82 days	108 days
C	75 days	111 days
D	95 days	80 days

405 The following extract of the statement of profit or loss relates to Z Co for the year ended 30 September 20X6:

	20X6
Statement of profit or loss extract	
Gross profit	15,175
Expenses	(2,460)
Profit before interest and tax	12,715
Finance cost	(5,000)
Profit before tax	7,715
Tax	(1,515)
Profit after tax	6,200

What is interest cover for the year?

A   2.54 times

B   3.03 times

C   1.54 times

D   1.24 times

406 Given a selling price of $700 and gross profit mark-up of 40%, what is the cost of an item?

A $280

B $420

C $500

D $980

407 A Co had sales of $220,000 and purchases of $160,000, together with opening inventory and closing inventory of $24,000 and $20,000 respectively.

What was inventory holding period in days (based on the average level of inventory for the period)?

- A   44.5 days
- B   22.2 days
- C   53.4 days
- D   49.0 days

408 **What is the formula for calculating the inventory holding period in days?**

- A   Cost of goods sold divided by average inventories × 365
- B   Sales divided by average inventories at cost × 365
- C   Sales divided by average inventories at selling price × 365
- D   Average inventories at cost divided by cost of goods sold × 365

409 B Co had the following details extracted from its statement of financial position:

	$000
Inventory	3,800
Receivables	2,000
Bank overdraft	200
Payables	2,000

What was the current ratio based upon the available information?

- A   1.72:1
- B   2.90:1
- C   2.64:1
- D   3.00:1

410 **D Co's gearing ratio would rise if:**

- A   a decrease in long-term loans is less than a decrease in shareholder's funds
- B   a decrease in long-term loans is more than a decrease in shareholder's funds
- C   interest rates rose
- D   interest rates fell

411 R Co had the following details extracted from its statement of financial position:

	$000
Inventory	3,800
Receivables	2,000
Bank overdraft	200
Payables	2,000

Based upon the available information, what was the quick (acid test) ratio of R Co?

A   2.63 : 1

B   0.9 : 1

C   29.0 : 1

D   1 : 1

412 Extracts from the financial statements of Miller for the year ended 31 May 20X2 are shown below:

	$000
Revenue	475
Cost of sales	(342)
Gross profit	133
Expenses	(59)
Finance cost	(26)
Profit before tax	48

What was the interest cover ratio for the year ended 31 May 20X2?

A   2.85

B   1.85

C   5.12

D   0.35

413 The following extract relates to R Co 20X6 and 20X5:

	20X6	20X5
Statement of profit or loss extract	$	$
Cost of sales	55,000	48,000
Statement of financial position extract		
Trade payables	4,400	5,300
Overdraft	120	960

Calculate the payables payment period of R Co for 20X6 and 20X5.

20X6	days
20X5	days

414 The following extracts relate to T Co or 20X3 and 20X2:

	20X3	20X2
	$	$
Inventory	18,000	16,000
Trade receivables	17,500	21,050
Cash and equivalents	3,095	
	38,595	37,050
Current liabilities		
Trade payables	20,750	18,500
Bank overdraft		500
	20,750	19,000

Calculate the current ratio of T Co for 20X3 and 20X2.

20X3	
20X2	

415 An increase in the gearing ratio could be caused by the issue of ordinary shares for cash during the year.

Is the statement above true or false?

A   True

B   False

416 An increase in return on capital could be caused by an increase in long-term loans taken out by the business during the year.

Is the statement above true or false?

A   True

B   False

417 A reduction in the unit purchase cost of raw materials whilst the unit selling price remains unchanged will increase the gross profit margin.

Is the statement above true or false?

A   True

B   False

418 The following extracts relate to MN Co for 20X8 and 20X7:

	20X8	*20X7*
Issued share capital	50,000	50,000
Share premium	5,500	5,500
Retained earnings	34,500	24,500
	90,000	80,000
Non-current liabilities		
10% Bank loan	4,500	5,600
Current liabilities		
Bank overdraft	3,000	500

Calculate the debt/equity ratio of MN Co for 20X8 and 20X7.

20X8	
20X7	

419 Which one of the following is likely to increase the trade receivables collection period?

A Offering credit customers a significant discount for prompt payment within seven days of receipt of invoice

B Application of effective credit control procedures

C Poor application of credit control procedures by a business

D An increasing volume of credit sales during an accounting period

420 Which one of the following is likely to reduce the trade payables payment period?

A Offering credit customers a significant discount for prompt payment within seven days of receipt of invoice

B Paying trade suppliers within seven days of receipt of invoice to obtain a discount

C Buying proportionately more goods on a cash basis, rather than on a credit basis

D Buying an increasing volume of credit purchases during an accounting period

421 Which one of the following is likely to increase the inventory holding period?

A Building up inventory levels in preparation of a sales and marketing campaign later in the year

B Scrapping of old and obsolete items of inventory

C Only ordering goods from a reliable supplier upon receipt of a customer order

D Implementation of effective goods requisitioning and ordering policies

422 You have been advised that a business has an inventory turnover of 8.49.

What is the average number of days that inventory is retained in the business prior to its sale?

423 During the year, A Co made a bonus issue of shares to its shareholders.

What is the impact of this upon the gearing ratio?

A   The gearing ratio will increase

B   The gearing ratio will decrease

C   There will be no change to the gearing ratio

D   It is not possible to determine the impact on the gearing ratio as there is insufficient information available

424 **Which of the following statements could explain why return on capital for an entity increased from 20% in 20X7 to 25% in 20X8?**

(1)   The entity reduced long-term borrowings during 20X8.

(2)   The entity managed to increase in profit margin during 20X8.

(3)   The entity made an issue of shares for cash during 20X8 to finance capital expenditure.

A   None of the above

B   (2) and (3) only

C   (1) and (3) only

D   (1) and (2) only

425 During the year, B Co made a rights issue of shares to its shareholders.

What was the impact of this upon the gearing ratio?

A   It is not possible to determine the impact on the gearing ratio as there is insufficient information available

B   The gearing ratio increased

C   The gearing ratio decreased

D   The gearing ratio remained unchanged

426 In an attempt to increase sales revenue during the year, C Co offered extended credit terms to its major customers. Whilst many major customers took advantage of the extended credit period, C Co did not increase its volume of sales.

What impact did this have upon the current ratio?

A   There was no change to the current ratio

B   It is not possible to determine the impact on the current ratio as there is insufficient information available

C   The current ratio increased

D   The current ratio decreased

427 On 1 July 20X5, D Co raised $5 million from an issue of ordinary shares. D Co then immediately used this cash to repay a loan of $5 million, which was not due for repayment until 30 June 20X9.

What impact did this have upon the debt/equity ratio?

A   It is not possible to determine the impact on the debt/equity ratio as there is insufficient information available

B   The debt/equity ratio increased

C   The debt/equity ratio decreased

D   There will be no change to the debt/equity ratio

428 XYZ Co has the following working capital ratios:

	20X9	20X8
Current ratio	1.2:1	0.9:1
Receivables days	60 days	50 days
Payables days	45 days	35 days
Inventory turnover	36 days	45 days

Which of the following statements regarding XYZ Co is true?

A   XYZ Co is taking longer to pay suppliers in 20X9 than in 20X8

B   XYZ Co is suffering a worsening liquidity position in 20X9

C   XYZ Co is managing inventory less efficiently in 20X9 in comparison with 20X8.

D   XYZ Co is reiving cash from customers more quickly in 20X9 than in 20X8

429 **State whether each of the following statements is true or false.**

True/False

(1)   A statement of cash flows prepared using the direct method produces a different figure for investing activities in comparison with that produced if the indirect method is used.

(2)   A bonus issue of shares does not feature in a statement of cash flows.

(3)   The amortisation charge for the year on intangible assets will appear as an item under 'Cash flows from operating activities' in a statement of cash flows.

(4)   Loss on the sale of a non-current asset will appear as an item under 'Cash flows from investing activities' in a statement of cash flows.

430 **Which one of the following statements is true?**

A   Analysis of financial performance should include both financial and non-financial information available.

B   An entity will always have a poor quick or acid test ratio if is highly geared.

C   The use of financial ratios to evaluate performance is not appropriate for sole traders.

D   Calculation of financial ratios for one accounting period only provides sufficient information to assess financial performance.

Section 2

MULTI-TASK QUESTIONS

1   ICE

The trial balance of Ice, an entity, as at 31 December 20X1 is presented below.

	Dr $	Cr $
Revenue		600,000
Purchases	240,000	
Administrative expenses	185,000	
Distribution expenses	75,000	
Plant and machinery – cost	120,000	
Plant and machinery – accumulated depreciation at 1 January 20X1		15,000
Trade receivables	20,500	
Allowance for receivables – 1 January 20X1		2,000
Inventory – 1 January 20X1	24,000	
Share capital		5,000
Trade payables		29,000
Retained earnings – 1 January 20X1		43,500
6% Loan – repayable 31 December 20X4		100,000
Cash	130,000	
Total of balances	**794,500**	**794,500**

The following notes are relevant to the preparation of the financial statements for the year ended 31 December 20X1:

(i)   It has been determined that trade receivables of $1,000 are irrecoverable. No adjustment is required to the allowance for receivables.

(ii)   Depreciation on plant and machinery is charged at 20% per annum on a reducing balance basis. Depreciation is charged to cost of sales.

(iii) The loan was taken out on 1 April 20X1. No interest has been accrued.

(iv)   Closing inventory has been correctly valued at $30,000.

(v)   A customer bought goods on credit from Ice for $500 on 10 December 20X1. They returned these goods on 30 December 20X1. No entries have been posted for this return.

(vi)   Ice is being sued by an ex-employee for unfair dismissal. Legal advisers think it is probable that Ice will lose the case and that they will have to pay damages of $50,000 in 20X2. Legal costs are charged to administrative expenses.

(vii)   The current year tax bill has been estimated at $6,000.

Required:

Prepare the statement of profit or loss for Ice for the year ended 31 December 20X1 and a statement of financial position as at 31 December 20X1.

(Total: 15 marks)

2   WILLOW

You have been asked to help prepare the financial statements of Willow for the year ended 30 June 20X1. The entity's trial balance as at 30 June 20X1 is shown below.

	Debit	Credit
	$000	$000
Share capital		50,000
Share premium		25,000
Revaluation reserve at 1 July 20X0		10,000
Land & buildings – value/cost	120,000	
accumulated depreciation at 1 July 20X0		22,500
Plant and equipment – cost	32,000	
accumulated depreciation at 1 July 20X0		18,000
Trade and other receivables	20,280	
Trade and other payables		8,725
5% bank loan repayable 20X5		20,000
Cash and cash equivalents	2,213	
Retained earnings at 1 July 20X0		12,920
Sales		100,926
Purchases	67,231	
Distribution costs	8,326	
Administrative expenses	7,741	
Inventories at 1 July 20X0	7,280	
Dividends paid	3,000	

The following information is relevant to the preparation of the financial statements:

(i)   The inventories at the close of business on 30 June 20X1 cost $9,420,000.

(ii)   Depreciation is to be provided for the year to 30 June 20X1 as follows:

Buildings   4% per annum   Straight line basis

This should all be charged to administrative expenses

Plant and equipment   20% per annum   Reducing balance basis

This is to be apportioned as follows:

	%
Cost of sales	70
Distribution costs	20
Administrative expenses	10

Land, which is non-depreciable, is included in the trial balance at a value of $40,000,000. At 30 June 20X1, a surveyor valued it at $54,000,000. This revaluation is to be included in the financial statements for the year ended 30 June 20X1.

(iii) It has been decided to write off a debt of $540,000 which will be charged to administrative expenses.

(iv) Included within distribution costs is $2,120,000 relating to an advertising campaign that will commence on 1 January 20X1 and run to 31 December 20X1.

(v) Loan interest has not yet been accounted for.

(vi) The tax charge for the year has been calculated at $2,700,000.

Required:

Prepare the statement of profit or loss and other comprehensive income of Willow for the year ended 30 June 20X1 and the statement of financial position as at 30 June 20X1.

(Total: 15 marks)

3   CLERC

You are about to commence preparation of the financial statements of Clerc for the year ended 31 December 20X9. The entity's trial balance as at 31 December 20X9 is shown below.

	Debit $	Credit $
Share capital		100,000
Share premium		20,000
Revaluation reserve at 1 January 20X9		50,000
Trade and other payables		13,882
Land & buildings – value/cost	210,000	
accumulated depreciation at 1 January 20X9		30,000
Plant and machinery – cost	88,000	
accumulated depreciation at 1 January 20X9		16,010
Trade and other receivables	8,752	
Accruals		3,029
5% bank loan repayable 20Y3		40,000
Cash and cash equivalents	6,993	
Retained earnings at 1 January 20X9		23,893
Sales		178,833
Purchases	130,562	
Distribution costs	7,009	
Administrative expenses	7,100	
Inventories at 1 January 20X9	17,331	
Bank interest received		100

The following information is relevant

(i) The interest for the year on the bank loan has not yet been paid or accrued.

(ii) Land, which is non-depreciable, is included in the trial balance at a value of $110,000. At 31 December 20X9 it was revalued to $150,000 and this revaluation is to be included in the financial statements.

(iii) Depreciation is to be provided for the year to 31 December 20X9 as follows:

Buildings	10% per annum	Straight line basis
Plant and machinery	20% per annum	Reducing balance basis

As part of the buildings contains the office accommodation and part of the buildings contains the plant and machinery, the depreciation for the 'Buildings' should be allocated between cost of sales and administrative expenses as follows:

	%
Cost of sales	40
Administrative expenses	60

(iv) Included in trade receivables is a balance of $1,720 that is considered to be irrecoverable due to the customer going into administration and the Directors of Clerc have decided to write off this receivable.

(v) Inventories at the close of business on 31 December 20X9 were valued at cost of $19,871. Included in this amount was an inventory line at a cost of $4,000 that, due to change in legislation, is now illegal. Clerc could rectify the items at a cost of $2,500 and plans to do so. The items usually retail to customers at $6,000.

(vi) The tax charge for the year has been calculated at $7,162.

Required:

Prepare the statement of profit or loss and other comprehensive income of Clerc for the year ended 31 December 20X9 and the statement of financial position as at 31 December 20X9.

(Total: 15 marks)

4 CARBON

Carbon is a limited liability entity. A trial balance for the year ended 31 December 20X5 is presented below.

	Dr $	Cr $
Revenue		450,000
Purchases	180,000	
Administrative expenses	140,000	
Distribution expenses	56,000	
Plant and machinery – cost	150,000	
Plant and machinery – accumulated depreciation at 1 January 20X5		30,000
Trade receivables	36,000	
Allowance for receivables – 1 January 20X5		2,500
Inventory – 1 January 20X5	33,000	
Share capital		10,000
Trade payables		32,000
Retained earnings – 1 January 20X5		25,500
8% Loan – repayable 31 December 20X9		50,000
Cash	5,000	
	600,000	600,000

The following notes are relevant to the preparation of the financial statements for the year ended 31 December 20X5:

(i) The current year tax charge has been estimated at $5,000.

(ii) It has been determined that trade receivables of $1,500 are irrecoverable. In addition, it was decided that the allowance for receivables should be increased by $1,000.

(iii) Depreciation on plant and machinery is charged at 20% per annum on a reducing balance basis. Depreciation is charged to cost of sales.

(iv) The loan was taken out on 1 October 20X5. No interest has been accrued.

(v) Closing inventory has been correctly valued at $27,000.

(vi) A customer bought goods on credit from Carbon for $1,000 on 5 December 20X5. The customer returned these goods on 28 December 20X5. No entries have been posted for this return.

(vii) Carbon is being sued by a customer regarding the sale of goods that the customer believes to be defective. Legal advisers think that it is probable that Carbon will lose the case and that they will have to pay damages of $20,000 in 20X6. Legal expenses are charged to administrative expenses.

Required:

Prepare a statement of profit or loss of Carbon the year ended 31 December 20X5 and a statement of financial position as at 31 December 20X5.

(Total: 15 marks)

5   MARKUS

Markus has prepared a trial balance for his business at 30 April 20X3 which is presented below.

	Dr $	Cr $
Capital account – 1 May 20X2		30,000
Finance costs	300	
Bank		7,400
Administrative expenses	65,800	
Distribution expenses	31,200	
Plant and machinery – cost	72,000	
Plant and machinery – accumulated depreciation at 1 May 20X2		25,000
Trade receivables	20,000	
Allowance for receivables – 1 May 20X2		3,150
Revenue		230,000
Inventory – 1 May 20X2	18,750	
Drawings	18,000	
Trade payables		17,500
Purchases	90,000	
6% Loan – repayable 31 July 20X5		3,000
	———	———
	316,050	316,050
	———	———

The following notes are relevant to the preparation of the financial statements for the year ended 30 April 20X3:

(i)   Markus took goods which cost $5,000 for personal use during the year, but this has not been recorded.

(ii)   It has been determined that trade receivables of $600 are irrecoverable. In addition, it was decided that the allowance for receivables should be reduced by $500.

(iii)   Depreciation on plant and machinery is charged at 15% per annum on a reducing balance basis. Depreciation is charged to cost of sales.

(iv)   The loan was taken out on 1 August 20X2 and interest has not yet been paid or accrued.

(v)   Closing inventory had been valued at $17,500. It was subsequently discovered that some items of inventory which had cost $5,000 had a net realisable value of $3,750.

(vi)   At 30 April 20X3, a prepayment for insurance paid in advance of $400 had not yet been accounted for. Insurance is classified as an administrative expense.

(vii) At 30 April 20X3, an accrual for freight and delivery expenses amounting to $350 had not yet been accounted for. Freight and delivery expenses are classified as distribution expenses.

Required:

Prepare a statement of profit or loss of Markus the year ended 30 April 20X3 and a statement of financial position as at 30 April 20X3.

(Total: 15 marks)

6   FIREWORK

The following financial statements and supporting information relate to Firework, a limited liability entity:

Statement of profit or loss and other comprehensive income for the year ended 30 June 20X5

	$000
Revenue	113,250
Cost of sales	(77,500)
Gross profit	35,750
Distribution costs	(3,000)
Administration expenses	(1,000)
Interest payable	(750)
Profit before tax	31,000
Income tax expense	(6,000)
Profit for the year	25,000
Other comprehensive income:	
Revaluation of property, plant and equipment	2,000
Total comprehensive income for the year	27,000

Firework – Statement of financial position at 30 June 20X5

	20X5 $000	20X4 $000
ASSETS		
Non-current assets		
Property, plant and equipment	110,000	93,000
Current assets		
Inventories	36,000	30,000
Trade receivables	40,000	35,000
Cash and equivalents	Nil	10,000
Total assets	186,000	168,000

EQUITY AND LIABILITIES

Equity share capital	20,000	15,000
Share premium	8,000	3,000
Revaluation reserve	10,000	8,000
Retained earnings	96,000	85,000
Total equity	**134,000**	**111,000**
Non-current liabilities		
Bank loan	7,000	17,000
Current liabilities		
Trade payables	36,500	30,000
Income tax	6,500	10,000
Bank overdraft	2,000	Nil
Total equity and liabilities	**186,000**	**168,000**

Notes:

The following information is relevant to the financial statements of Firework:

(i)   During the year ended 30 June 20X5, Firework disposed of several items of plant and equipment for sale proceeds of $8,000,000. The loss on disposal of $2,000,000 is included within cost of sales. The depreciation charge for the year was $15,000,000.

(ii)   Firework estimated that the income tax liability arising on the profit for the year ended 30 June 20X5 was $6,500,000.

Required:

Based upon the available information, prepare a statement of cash flows using the indirect method for Firework for the year ended 30 June 20X5 in accordance with the requirements of IAS 7 Statement of Cash Flows.

(Total: 15 marks)

7 CRACKER

The following financial statements and supporting information relate to Cracker, a limited liability entity:

Statement of profit or loss and other comprehensive income for the year ended 31 March 20X1

	$000
Revenue	88,740
Cost of sales	(73,750)
Gross profit	14,990
Distribution costs	(1,200)
Administration expenses	(610)
	13,180
Profit on disposal of plant and equipment	300
Investment income	320
Interest payable	(2,150)
Profit before tax	11,650
Income tax expense	(2,900)
Profit for the year	8,750

There were no items of other comprehensive income during the year.

Cracker – Statement of financial position at 31 March 20X1

	20X1	20X0
ASSETS	$000	$000
Non-current assets		
Property, plant and equipment	73,000	70,500
Current assets		
Inventories	27,500	25,500
Trade receivables	37,500	33,000
Cash and equivalents	4,250	1,250
Total assets	142,250	130,250

EQUITY AND LIABILITIES

Equity share capital	11,000	10,000
Share premium	610	Nil
Retained earnings	74,790	66,040
Total equity	86,400	76,040
Non-current liabilities		
10% Debenture	23,500	20,000
Current liabilities		
Trade payables	29,450	31,900
Income tax	2,900	2,310
Total equity and liabilities	142,250	130,250

Notes:

The following information is relevant to the financial statements of Cracker:

(i) During the year ended 31 March 20X1, Cracker disposed of some items of plant and equipment. The carrying amount of these items at the date of disposal was $800,000. The depreciation charge for the year was $500,000.

(ii) Cracker estimated that the income tax liability arising on the profit for the year ended 31 March 20X1 was $2,900,000.

Required:

Based upon the available information, prepare a statement of cash flows using the indirect method for Cracker for the year ended 31 March 20X1 in accordance with the requirements of IAS 7 Statement of Cash Flows.

(Total: 15 marks)

8   SPARKLER

The following financial statements and supporting information relate to Sparkler, a limited liability entity:

Statement of profit or loss and other comprehensive income for the year ended 30 September 20X9

	$000
Revenue	94,800
Cost of sales	(71,100)
Gross profit	23,700
Distribution costs	(2,500)
Administration expenses	(1,000)
Profit on disposal of plant and equipment	500
Interest payable	(2,700)
Profit before tax	18,000
Income tax expense	(3,500)
Profit for the year	14,500
Other comprehensive income:	
Revaluation surplus on property, plant and equipment	3,000
Total comprehensive income for the year	17,500

Sparkler – Statement of financial position at 30 September 20X9

	20X9	20X8
	$000	$000
ASSETS		
Non-current assets		
Property, plant and equipment	95,000	85,000
Current assets		
Inventories	30,750	36,000
Trade receivables	39,250	45,000
Cash and equivalents	3,000	Nil
Total assets	168,000	166,000

EQUITY AND LIABILITIES		
Equity share capital	30,000	24,000
Share premium	10,000	8,000
Revaluation reserve	3,000	Nil
Retained earnings	60,875	66,500
Total equity	103,875	98,500
Non-current liabilities		
10% Debenture	25,000	20,000
Current liabilities		
Bank overdraft	Nil	4,500
Trade payables	35,000	38,500
Income tax	3,500	4,000
Accrued interest	625	500
Total equity and liabilities	168,000	166,000

The following information is relevant to the financial statements of Sparkler during the year ended 30 September 20X9

(a) Sparkler disposed of some items of plant and equipment for sale proceeds of $2,000,000. The carrying amount of the items disposed of was $1,500,000.

(b) Sparkler purchased property plant and equipment at a cost of $21,000,000. In addition, land and buildings were revalued during the year.

(c) Sparkler estimated that the income tax liability arising on the profit for the year was $3,500,000.

Required:

Based upon the available information, prepare a statement of cash flows using the indirect method for Sparkler for the year ended 30 September 20X9 in accordance with the requirements of IAS 7 Statement of Cash Flows.

(Total: 15 marks)

9 OUTFLOW

The following financial statements and supporting information relate to Outflow, a limited liability entity:

Statement of profit or loss and other comprehensive income for the year ended 30 April 20X2

	$000
Revenue	34,760
Cost of sales	(33,560)
	———
Gross profit	1,200
Distribution and administration expenses	(4,500)
Interest payable	(1,000)
	———
Loss before tax	(4,300)
Income tax	500
	———
Loss for the year	(3,800)
Other comprehensive income:	
Revaluation surplus on property, plant and equipment	2,000
	———
Total comprehensive income for the year	(1,800)
	———

Outflow – Statement of financial position at 30 April 20X2

	20X2	20X1
	$000	$000
ASSETS		
Non-current assets		
Property, plant and equipment – cost or val'n	260,000	245,000
Property, plant and equipment – accumulated dep'n	(150,000)	(145,000)
	———	———
	110,000	100,000
Current assets		
Inventories	30,000	33,000
Trade receivables	48,750	52,000
Income tax recoverable	500	Nil
	———	———
Total assets	189,250	185,000
	———	———

EQUITY AND LIABILITIES	$000	$000
Equity share capital @ $1 each	44,000	40,000
Share premium	5,000	4,000
Revaluation reserve	22,000	20,000
Retained earnings	72,450	77,250
Total equity	143,450	141,250
Non-current liabilities		
Long-term bank loan	15,500	8,000
Current liabilities		
Bank overdraft	4,000	3,250
Trade payables	26,300	27,500
Income tax	Nil	5,000
Total equity and liabilities	189,250	185,000

The following information is relevant to the financial statements of Outflow during the year ended 30 April 20X2:

(a) Outflow scrapped numerous items of plant and equipment during the year. The items scrapped were originally purchased for $7,000,000 and they had a carrying amount of $1,000,000 at the date of disposal. The gain or loss on scrapping is included within cost of sales.

(b) Outflow made a depreciation charge for the year of $11,000,000 and several buildings had been revalued during the year.

(c) Outflow estimated that it would receive a tax refund of $500,000 as a result of making a loss before tax for the year ended 30 April 20X2.

Required:

Based upon the available information, prepare a statement of cash flows using the indirect method for Outflow for the year ended 30 April 20X2 in accordance with the requirements of IAS 7 Statement of Cash Flows.

(Total: 15 marks)

10   PATTY AND SELMA

The statements of profit or loss for two entities, Patty and Selma, for the year ended 31 December 20X1 are presented below:

	Patty	Selma
	$000	$000
Revenue	987	567
Cost of sales	(564)	(335)
Gross profit	423	232
Administrative expenses	(223)	(122)
Operating profit	200	110
Finance costs	(50)	(30)
Profit before tax	150	80
Taxation	(40)	(25)
Profit for the year	110	55

The following notes are relevant to the preparation of the consolidated financial statements:

Patty bought 70% of the ordinary shares in Selma several years ago.

(i)   During the year ended 31 December 20X1, Selma sold goods to Patty for $120,000 making a cost mark up of 20%. One quarter of these goods remained in the inventory of Patty at the year end.

Required:

(a)   **Using the individual entity financial statements, calculate the following ratios for Patty and Selma for the year ended 31 December 20X1:**

(i)   **Gross profit margin**

(ii)   **Operating profit margin**

(iii)   **Interest cover.**   **(6 marks)**

(b)   **Prepare a consolidated statement of profit or loss and other comprehensive income for the year ended 31 December 20X1.**   **(9 marks)**

(Total: 15 marks)

11   CUBE AND PRISM

The statements of financial position for Cube and Prism as at 31 December 20X1 are presented below:

Assets	Cube	Prism
Non-current assets	$	$
Property, plant and equipment	270,000	179,000
Investments	300,000	–
Current assets		
Inventories	95,000	50,000
Trade and other receivables	110,000	99,000
Cash and cash equivalents	8,000	51,000
Total assets	783,000	379,000
Equity and liabilities		
Equity		
Share capital	80,000	40,000
Revaluation surplus	20,000	10,000
Retained earnings	435,000	209,000
Liabilities		
Long-term loans	200,000	70,000
Trade and other payables	48,000	50,000
Total equity and liabilities	783,000	379,000

The following notes are relevant to the preparation of the consolidated financial statements:

(i)   Cube acquired 75% of the ordinary shares of Prism for $300,000 several years ago. At the acquisition date, the retained earnings of Prism were $120,000 and revaluation surplus was $10,000. The fair value of the non-controlling interest at the date of acquisition was $55,000.

(ii)   The fair values of the net assets of Prism at the acquisition date approximated their carrying amounts, with the exception of some land. This land was held in the financial statements of Prism at its cost of $100,000 but was estimated to have a fair value of $170,000. This land is still held at 31 December 20X1.

(iii) During the year, Cube sold goods to Prism for $30,000 making a gross profit margin on the sale of 30%. One third of these goods are still included in the inventories of Prism.

Required:

(a) Using the individual financial statements, calculate the following ratios for Cube and Prism for the year ended 31 December 20X1:

    (i)   The quick ratio (x:1)

    (ii)   Gearing (in terms of the percentage of capital employed represented by borrowings)

    (iii) All ratios should be calculated to one decimal place.   **(4 marks)**

(b) Prepare the consolidated statement of financial position for the Cube group as at 31 December 20X1.   **(11 marks)**

                                           (Total: 15 marks)

12 BRYSON AND STOPPARD

Bryson acquired 75% of the issued share capital of Stoppard on 1 January 20X1 for $8,720,000. At that date Stoppard had issued share capital of $4,800,000. For the year ended 31 March 20X1, Stoppard made a profit after tax of $640,000.

Extracts of the statements of financial position for the two entities at 31 March 20X1 are as follows:

	Bryson $000	Stoppard $000
Assets		
Investment in Stoppard	8,720	
Non-current assets	11,280	3,670
Current assets	5,760	5,010
Total assets	25,760	8,680
Equity and liabilities	$000	$000
Equity		
Share capital	9,200	4,800
Retained earnings	12,480	1,290
Total equity	21,680	6,090
Non-current liabilities	1,440	1,180
Current liabilities	2,640	1,410
Total equity and liabilities	25,760	8,680

The following information is relevant to the preparation of the consolidated financial statements:

(i)   At acquisition, the fair value of land owned by Stoppard exceeded its cost by $1,000,000. This land was still owned at 31 March 20X1.

(ii)   During the year Bryson sold goods to Stoppard for $500,000 making a profit of $50,000. Eighty per cent of the goods remained in Stoppard's inventory at the year end. At 31 March 20X1 Bryson was still owed half of the total amount invoiced to Stoppard for these goods.

(iii)   At 1 January 20X1, the fair value of the non-controlling interest at the date of acquisition was $2,200,000.

Required:

(a)   **Calculate the current ratio for Bryson and Stoppard as at 31 March 20X1 based upon the individual financial statements of each entity.**   **(2 marks)**

(b)   **Prepare the consolidated statement of financial position for Bryson plc and its subsidiary undertaking as at 31 March 20X1.**   **(13 marks)**

(Total 15 marks)

13   PEN AND STAPLE

The statements of profit or loss for two entities, Pen and Staple, for the year ended 31 December 20X4 are presented below:

	Pen	Staple
	$000	$000
Revenue	1,500	700
Cost of sales	(775)	(370)
Gross profit	725	330
Administrative expenses	(317)	(135)
Operating profit	408	195
Finance costs	(60)	(35)
Profit before tax	348	160
Taxation	(96)	(45)
Profit for the year	252	115

The following notes are relevant to the preparation of the consolidated financial statements:

(i)   Pen bought 70% of the ordinary shares in Staple on 1 January 20X1.

(ii)   During the year ended 31 December 20X4, Staple sold goods to Pen for $150,000 making a mark-up on cost of 20%. One fifth of these goods remained in the inventory of Pen at the year end.

Required:

(a) Using the individual entity financial statements, calculate the following ratios for Pen and Staple for the year ended 31 December 20X4:

(i) Gross profit margin

(ii) Operating profit margin

(iii) Interest cover. **(6 marks)**

(b) Prepare a consolidated statement of profit or loss for the Pen group for the year ended 31 December 20X4. **(9 marks)**

(Total: 15 marks)

14 PEBBLE AND STONE

The statements of financial position for Pebble and Stone as at 31 December 20X6 are presented below:

Assets	Pebble	Stone
Non-current assets	$	$
Property, plant and equipment	300,000	225,000
Investments	400,000	–
Current assets		
Inventories	80,000	75,000
Trade and other receivables	60,000	140,000
Cash and cash equivalents	10,000	25,000
Total assets	850,000	465,000
Equity and liabilities		
Equity		
Share capital	80,000	60,000
Share premium	20,000	10,000
Retained earnings	295,000	250,000
Non-current liabilities		
Loans	300,000	85,000
Current liabilities		
Trade and other payables	155,000	60,000
Total equity and liabilities	850,000	465,000

The following notes are relevant to the preparation of the consolidated financial statements:

(i) Pebble acquired 80% of the ordinary shares of Stone for $400,000 on 1 January 20X2. At the acquisition date, the retained earnings of Stone were $150,000. The fair value of the non-controlling interest in Stone at the date of acquisition was $80,000.

(ii) At the date of acquisition, the fair values of the net assets of Stone approximated their carrying amounts, with the exception of a plot of land owned by Stone. This land was held in the financial statements of Stone at its cost of $150,000 but was estimated to have a fair value of $180,000. This land was still owned by Stone at 31 December 20X6.

(iii) During the year, Pebble sold goods to Stone for $50,000 making a gross profit margin on the sale of 25%. Two fifths of these goods are still included in the inventories of Stone at 31 December 20X6.

Required:

(a) **Prepare the consolidated statement of financial position for the Pebble group as at 31 December 20X6.** **(11 marks)**

(b) **Pebble is considering making an investment in another entity, Archive, which would be accounted for as an associate. Which TWO of the following factors would be relevant when accounting for an associate?**

- **Control of Archive**
- **Significant influence in Archive**
- **Owning the majority of the ordinary shares of Archive**
- **Owning between 20% and 50% of the ordinary shares of Archive**
- **Accounting for goodwill**
- **Accounting of non-controlling interests.** **(4 marks)**

(Total: 15 marks)

15 HELSINKI AND STOCKHOLM

The following statements of profit or loss relate to Helsinki and its subsidiary Stockholm for the year ended 31 December 20X6:

	Helsinki $000	Stockholm $000
Revenue	200,000	100,000
Cost of sales	(110,000)	(50,000)
Gross profit	90,000	50,000
Distribution costs	(20,000)	(10,000)
Administrative expenses	(40,000)	(20,000)
Operating profit	30,000	20,000
Investment income from Stockholm	7,500	
Profit before tax	37,500	20,000
Taxation	(10,500)	(6,000)
Profit for the year	27,000	14,000

The following notes are relevant to the preparation of the consolidated financial statements:

(i) Helsinki acquired three million of the equity shares of Stockholm on 30 June 20X6 when Stockholm had a total of four million equity shares in issue. Helsinki paid a total of $25 million to acquire the shares.

(ii) At 30 June 20X6, the retained earnings of Stockholm were $20 million and the carrying amounts of the net assets of Stockholm approximated to their fair values.

(iii) It is group accounting policy to account for non-controlling interest at its fair value. At the date of acquisition, the fair value of the non-controlling interest in Stockholm was $7 million.

(iv) During the post-acquisition period, Stockholm sold goods to Helsinki. The goods originally cost $10 million and they were sold to Helsinki at a mark-up of 25%. At 31 December 20X6, Helsinki still had 40% of these goods within its inventory.

Required:

(a) **Calculate goodwill arising on acquisition of Stockholm by Helsinki.** **(4 marks)**

(b) **Prepare the consolidated statement of profit or loss for the Helsinki group for the year ended 31 December 20X6.** **(11 marks)**

(Total: 15 marks)

16 PEDANTIC

On 1 October 20X7, Pedantic acquired 60% of the equity share capital of Sophistic in a share exchange of two shares in Pedantic for three shares in Sophistic. The issue of shares has not yet been recorded by Pedantic. At the date of acquisition shares in Pedantic had a market value of $6 each. Below are the summarised draft financial statements of both entities.

Statement of profit or loss for the year ended 30 September 20X8

	Pedantic	Sophistic
	$000	$000
Revenue	85,000	42,000
Cost of sales	(63,000)	(32,000)
Gross profit	22,000	10,000
Distribution costs	(4,000)	(3,500)
Administrative expenses	(8,000)	(1,000)
Finance costs	(600)	(400)
Profit before tax	9,400	5,100
Income tax expense	(2,162)	(1,000)
Profit for the year	7,238	4,100

Statements of financial position as at 30 September 20X8

	Pedantic $000	Sophistic $000
Assets		
Non-current assets		
Property, plant and equipment	40,600	12,600
Current assets	16,000	6,600
Total assets	56,600	19,200
Equity and liabilities		
Equity shares of $1 each	10,000	4,000
Retained earnings	35,400	6,500
	45,400	10,500
Non-current liabilities:		
10% loan notes	3,000	4,000
Current liabilities	8,200	4,700
Total equity and liabilities	56,600	19,200

The following information is relevant:

(i)   At the date of acquisition, the fair values of Sophistic's net assets were equal to their carrying amounts.

(ii)   Sales from Sophistic to Pedantic in the post-acquisition period were $6 million. Sophistic made a mark up on cost of 20% on these sales. One quarter of these goods remained in the inventory of Pedantic at the year-end.

(iii)   Other than where indicated, statement of profit or loss items are deemed to accrue evenly on a time basis.

(iv)   At 30 September 20X8, Sophistic had a receivable due from Pedantic of $1 million. This agreed with the amount payable to Sophistic in Pedantic's financial statements.

(v)   Pedantic has a policy of accounting for any non-controlling interest at fair value. The fair value of the non-controlling interest at the acquisition date was $5.9 million. Consolidated goodwill was not impaired at 30 September 20X8.

Required:

(a)   **Prepare the consolidated statement of profit or loss for Pedantic for the year ended 30 September 20X8.**   **(6 marks)**

(b)   **Prepare the consolidated statement of financial position for Pedantic as at 30 September 20X8.**   **(9 marks)**

(Total: 15 marks)

Section 3

ANSWERS TO MULTIPLE CHOICE TEST QUESTIONS

THE CONTEXT AND PURPOSE OF FINANCIAL REPORTING

1 D

The directors of a company run the company; however, they are not personally liable for its losses. A sole trader business is owned and operated by the proprietor (sole trader).

Partners are jointly and severally liable for any losses of the business.

A company is owned by the shareholders (members) and run by the directors/management team.

2 C

3 D

4 A

Management require very detailed information in order to make informed decisions with regard to operations (e.g. whether to shut down a particular product line or source new suppliers).

Other parties need far less detail:

- Investors are interested in profitability and the security of their investment.
- The government is interested in profits (for tax purposes) and sales performance (in order to assess how the economy is performing).
- Lenders are interested in whether a business is solvent and able to repay their debt.

5 A

- Accounting involves recording transactions as they occur and then summarising them in the form of the financial statements.
- Financial accounting describes the production of financial statements for external users.

6 C

7   C

Both financial and management accounts should be equally accurate and reliable.

8   A

9   C

10   A

Accounting standards provide guidance on common transactions. They cannot provide guidance on all types of transactions.

11   D

12   B

13   B

Tutorial note:

A sole trader may have employees. A sole trader is fully liable for the debts of the business. A sole trader may have more than one place of business, perhaps with the support of employees or managers acting on their behalf.

14   A

A limited liability company is a separate legal entity and can own assets and incur liabilities in its own name.

15   B

16   C

17   B

18   C and D

Issued share capital and revaluation surplus apply only to limited company financial statements.

19   B and C

Dividends paid and share premium account applies only to limited company financial statements.

20   C

21   B

The Framework is not an accounting standard itself, although it is used as a reference document when new standards are developed.

22   D

All of the remaining answers include only part of the full definition of an asset.

23   A

Equity or capital of the business is represented by the next assets of the business.

THE QUALITATIVE CHARACTERISTICS OF FINANCIAL INFORMATION

24   C

25   D

- If applicable, the going concern concept presumes, but does not guarantee, that a business will continue in operational existence for the foreseeable future.
- Commercial substance should always be reflected in financial statements, even where this differs from legal form.
- A revaluation surplus is not realised. However, it is credited in other comprehensive income in the statement of profit or loss and other comprehensive income and then included in the statement of changes in equity.

26   B and D

Tutorial note:

The remaining answers are fundamental qualitative characteristics of useful financial information.

27   D

28   D

If a business is a going concern, it is reasonable to assume that non-current assets will be used over their expected useful economic life. It is therefore appropriate to value a non-current asset at cost less accumulated depreciation, which represents the consumption of cost or value so far.

29   B

30   D

THE USE OF DOUBLE-ENTRY AND ACCOUNTING SYSTEMS

DOUBLE ENTRY BOOKKEEPING

31 B

- The computer does not qualify as inventory drawings as it is for the use of Oscar's daughter in her role as administrator to the business.

- The computer is being transferred from inventory to non-current assets by debiting the non-current assets account. It is no longer part of cost of sales and is removed from cost of sales by a credit.

32 B

Tutorial note:

Drawings, carriage outwards (an expense), prepayments, carriage outwards (expense) and opening inventory are all debit balances. Accruals, rental income and purchase returns are all credit balances.

33 C

34 A

35 D

	$	$
Sales		256,800
Cost of sales		
Opening inventory	13,400	
Purchases	145,000	
Carriage in	2,300	
Closing inventory	(14,200)	(146,500)
Gross profit		110,300
Discount received		3,900
Expenses		(76,000)
Carriage out		(1,950)
Net profit		36,250

36 $3,150

Bank

	$		$
Balance b/f	1,780	Drawings (4 × $200)	800
Receipt after trade discount	570		
Receipt from customer	400		
Bankings from canteen receipts	1,200	Balance c/f	**3,150**
	3,950		3,950

Trade discounts are deducted at source by the seller and only the reduced amount will be payable by the customer. Therefore, the net amount of $570 must have been received during the month.

37 $2,675

Bank

	$		$
Returns of goods purchased for cash	50	Overdraft at start of month	1,340
Rental income	1,300	Payments to credit suppliers	990
Receipts from customers	4,400	Reimbursement of petty cash float	45
		Payment of electricity bill	700
		Balance c/f	**2,675**
	5,750		5,750

38   C

39   A

40   C

41   D

An invoice is raised by a business and issued to a customer. It contains more than the amount due to be paid for goods and services supplied. It will also include the quantity and description of goods, the date of supply and the nett amount, sales tax applied and gross amount due.

42

A	Business assets will always equal business liabilities	False
B	Business assets will always exceed business liabilities	False
C	Business assets include proprietor's capital	False
D	Business liabilities include proprietor's capital	False

Tutorial note:

Statements A and B ignore proprietor's capital and therefore cannot be true. Statements C and D are false as proprietor's capital is neither a business asset nor a business liability.

43

A	The journal records all bank and cash transactions	False
B	The journal records all accounting transactions	False
C	The journal is a book of prime entry	True
D	The journal records all credit sales transactions	False

Tutorial note:

The journal records all transactions not already recorded in a book of prime entry. Bank and cash transactions are recorded in the cash book and petty cash book respectively. Credit sales transactions are recorded in the sales day book.

44

	Ledger Account:	$
Debit	Depreciation expense – motor vehicles	10,000
Credit	Accumulated depreciation – motor vehicles	10,000

45

	Ledger Account:	$
Debit	Irrecoverable debts expense	4,300
Credit	Trade receivables	4,300

46

	Ledger Account:	$
Debit	Sales revenue	2,500
Credit	Disposal of non-current asset	2,500

47

	Ledger Account:	$
Debit	Trade payables ledger control account	1,250
Credit	Trade receivables ledger control account	1,250

48

	Ledger Account:	$
Debit	Depreciation expense account	3,500
Credit	Accumulated depreciation provision account – buildings	3,500

49

	Ledger Account:	$
Debit	Trade payables ledger control account	250
Credit	Discount received – income	250

50

	Ledger Account:	$
Debit	Purchases	6,400
Credit	Trade payables ledger control account	6,400

51   **$500**

	$
Revenue	22,000
Purchases	(19,200)
(note: the business does not hold inventory)	
Rent	(5,400)
Bank interest	(825)
Heat and light	(4,475)
	_____
Loss for the year	(7,900)
	_____

Therefore closing capital for the accounting period ended 30 April 20X3 = $12,500 – $7,900 – $4,100 = $500.

LEDGER ACCOUNTS, BOOKS OF PRIME ENTRY AND JOURNALS

52 C

Day books include:

Sales day book	Purchases day book	Sales returns day book
Purchases returns day book	Cash book	Petty cash book
The journal		

53 B

$25 + $(7.25 + 12.75 + 15) = $60

> **Tutorial note:**
>
> *The petty cash float can always be calculated by adding together the amount in petty cash at the end of the month plus the vouchers evidencing expenditure for the month.*

54 B

55 $3,004

Receivables ledger control account

	$		$
Balance b/f	69,472		
Sales	697,104	Cash received	686,912
		Irrecoverable debts	1,697
		Sales returns (β)	**3,004**
		Balance c/f	74,963
	766,576		766,576

56 $385

	$
Opening float	150
Receipts	
Photocopier use	25
Bank	500
Payments	
Cheque cashed	(90)
Payments (β)	**385**
Closing float	200

57 B

Tutorial note:

A debit balance on a purchase ledger account means that the business is owed money by its supplier. This could be explained by the business mistakenly paying an invoice twice. (Alternatively, a business might pay the full invoice amount and then receive a credit note from the supplier following the return of faulty goods.)

58 $38,100

Payables ledger control account

	$		$
Bank	68,900	Balance b/f	34,500
Discounts received	1,200	Purchases (credit)	78,400
Purchase returns	4,700		
Balance c/f	38,100		
	———		———
	112,900		112,900
	———		———
		Balance b/f	38,100

59 $19,000

Receivables ledger control account

	$		$
Sales	250,000	Bank	225,000
Bank: cheque returned	3,500	Sales returns	2,500
		Irrecoverable debts	3,000
		Contra: trade payables	4,000
		Balance c/f	**19,000**
	———		———
	253,500		253,500
	———		———
Balance b/f	19,000		

60 C

Tutorial note:

The non-current asset register is not a book of prime entry. As the part-exchange value received is not a cash receipt, it will be recorded in the journal.

61   D

Mike has received cash (a debit entry) and the credit entry should be made to the trade payables control account to cancel out the debit entry recorded when the second payment was made in error.

62

	Ledger Account:	$
Debit	Trade receivables ledger control account	12,000
Credit	Sales	10,000
Credit	Sales tax	2,000

63

	Ledger Account:	$
Debit	Purchases (100/115 × $1,541)	1,340
Debit	Sales tax (15/115 × $1,541)	201
Credit	Payables ledger control account	1,541

Tutorial note:

The gross invoice value is credited to the payables ledger control account as that is the total liability due to the supplier. The debit entries comprise the net cost is accounted for as a purchase cost and the related sales tax element, which is recoverable.

64   A

- B describes a purchase order.
- C describes a supplier statement.
- D describes a remittance advice.

65   B

- The sales and purchases day books record credit sales and credit purchases respectively.

66 $70.00

	$
Balance of petty cash in hand	66.00
Add: Sundry purchases	22.00
Loan to sales manager	10.00
Purchase of staff drinks	19.00
Less: Sundry sales receipts	(47.00)
Imprest balance	70.00

RECORDING TRANSACTIONS AND EVENTS

SALES AND PURCHASES AND SALES TAX

67 $655.50

	$
Price	600.00
Less: trade discount (5% × $600)	(30.00)
	570.00
Add: sales tax at 15% (15% × $570)	85.50
	655.50

Tutorial note:

Sales tax is always charged on the selling price net of trade (bulk purchase) discount given.

68 $75,788

<table>
<thead>
<tr><th colspan="2" align="center">Sales tax</th><th></th><th></th></tr>
<tr><th></th><th>$</th><th></th><th>$</th></tr>
</thead>
<tbody>
<tr><td></td><td></td><td>Balance b/f</td><td>23,778</td></tr>
<tr><td>Tax on purchases</td><td></td><td>Tax on sales</td><td></td></tr>
<tr><td>$\dfrac{17.5\%}{117.5\%} \times \$590,790$</td><td>87,990</td><td>17.5% × $800,000</td><td>140,000</td></tr>
<tr><td>**Balance c/f**</td><td>**75,788**</td><td></td><td></td></tr>
<tr><td></td><td>163,778</td><td></td><td>163,778</td></tr>
<tr><td></td><td></td><td>Balance b/f</td><td>75,788</td></tr>
</tbody>
</table>

69 **$962.50**

Sales tax

	$		$
Tax on purchases (input tax)		Tax on sales (output tax)	4,112.50
($18,000 × 17.5%)	3,150.00	($27,612.5 × 17.5/117.5)	
Balance c/f	962.50		
	————		————
	4,112.50		4,112.50
	————		————
		Balance b/f	962.50

70 **C**

	$
Sales net of sales tax	90,000
Purchases net of sales tax	(72,000)
	————
	18,000
	————
Tax payable @ 10%	$1,800

As sales exceed purchases, the excess sales tax is payable to the tax authorities.

71 **$5,300**

Sales tax

	$		$
Tax on purchases	6,000	Balance b/f	3,400
Bank	2,600	Tax on sales	10,500
Balance c/f	5,300		
	————		————
	13,900		13,900
	————		————
		Balance b/f	5,300

Tax on sales (outputs) = 17.5% × $60,000 = $10,500

Tax on purchases (inputs) = (17.5/117.5) × $40,286 = $6,000

72 **B**

Sales revenue is recorded exclusive of sales tax in the statement of profit or loss.

73 **B**

The receivables account should be debited with the full amount payable, including the tax. The entry in the sales account should be for the sales value excluding sales tax. Sales tax payable to the tax authorities should be credited to the sales tax account (liability = credit balance).

74   A

The receivables account should be credited with the full amount of the sales return, including the tax. The Sales returns account should be debited with the value of the returns excluding the sales tax. The sales tax account should be debited with the amount of tax on the returns (since the tax is no longer payable).

75   C

The supplier is owed the full amount of the invoice, including the sales tax, so the credit entry in the supplier account must be $9,200. The non-current asset account is recorded at cost excluding the sales tax. The input tax is recoverable, so debit the sales tax account with $1,200.

76   A

- If input tax (tax on purchases) exceeds output tax (tax on sales), the difference is recoverable from the tax authorities.
- Sales and purchases are reported net of sales tax.
- Sales tax cannot be recovered on certain expenses (such as client entertaining) and purchases (such as cars).

77 $578,200

Trade payables

	$		$
Cash paid	542,300	Balance b/f	142,600
Discounts received	13,200		
Goods returned	27,500		
Balance c/f	137,800	Purchases (β)	578,200
	720,800		720,800

78 $84,000

Trade receivables

	$		$
Balance b/f	10,000	Receipts from sales	85,000
Sales (β)	**84,000**		
		Balance c/f	9,000
	94,000		94,000

79 C

Cash

	$		$
Balance b/f	300	Bankings	50,000
Proceeds of sale of car	5,000	Wages	12,000
Sales (β)	**81,100**	Drawings	24,000
		Balance c/f	400
	86,400		86,400

80 A

The balance on the sales tax account is calculated as:

Credit sales ($121,000/100 × 20) =	$24,200
Credit purchases ($157,110/120 × 20) =	($26,185)
	($1,985)

The sales tax on the credit purchases (input tax) exceeds the sales tax on sales (output tax), the balance on the account represents an amount due to Alan, therefore is an asset, a debit.

81 A

Carriage inwards is an expense incurred in bringing goods purchased into the business, and carriage outwards is an expense incurred in delivering goods to customers.

82 C

The receivables account should be credited with the full amount of the sales return, including the sales tax. The sales returns (returns inwards) should be debited with the value of the returns excluding the sales tax. The sales tax account should be debited with the amount of tax on the returns (as the output tax will no longer be payable).

83 $920.00

	$
Price	800.00
Less: trade discount (8% × $800)	(64.00)
	736.00
Add: sales tax (25% × $736)	184.00
	920.00

84   C

Trade discount is always deducted when calculating the amount invoiced by the seller. In addition, as Smith is not expected to take account of the early settlement discount terms, the amount of revenue receivable is calculated after deduction of trade discount only at $950 ($1000 × 95%). When Smith subsequently pays early to be eligible for the discount, the accounting entries should reflect that fact and record settlement of the amount outstanding and also reduced revenue.

Debit Cash $912 ($950 × 96%), Debit Revenue $38 ($950 × 4%), and Credit Trade receivables $950.

85   B

Trade discount is always deducted when calculating the amount invoiced by the seller. In addition, as Jones is expected to take account of the early settlement discount terms, the amount of revenue receivable is calculated after deduction of both trade discount and early settlement discount, a total of $2,280 ($2,500 × 95% × 96%). When Jones subsequently pays early to be eligible for the discount, the accounting entries should reflect the receipt of cash and clearance of the trade receivable for the amount expected as follows:

Debit Cash $2,280 and Credit Trade receivables $2,280.

86   D

Trade discount is always deducted when calculating the amount invoiced by the seller. In addition, as Black is expected to take account of the early settlement discount terms, the amount of revenue receivable is calculated after deduction of both trade discount and early settlement discount, a total of $4,104 ($4,500 × 95% × 96%). When Black subsequently pays outside the settlement discount period, the full amount of the receivable $4,275 ($4,500 × 95%) is due. The additional cash received in excess of the receivable amount of $171 is therefore accounted for as a cash sale as follows:

Debit Cash $4,275, Credit Revenue $171 and Credit Trade receivables $4,104.

87   A

Trade discount is always deducted when calculating the amount invoiced by the seller. In addition, as White is not expected to take account of the early settlement discount terms, the amount of revenue receivable is calculated after deduction of trade discount only, a total of $3,515 ($3,700 × 95%). When White subsequently pays outside the settlement discount period as expected, the full amount of the receivable is due.

Debit Cash $3,515, and Credit Trade receivables $3,515.

88   B

Trade discount is always deducted and, in addition, as Green is expected to take account of the early settlement discount terms, the amount of revenue receivable is calculated after deduction of trade discount and early settlement discount, a total of $1,276.80 ($1,400 × 96% × 95%). When Green subsequently pays outside the settlement discount period, the full amount of $1,344 ($1,400 × 96%) is due and the additional amount received of $67.20 ($1,344.00 − $1,276.80) is accounted for as a cash sale.

Debit Cash $1,344, and Credit Trade receivables $1,276.80 and Credit Revenue $67.20.

INVENTORY

89 $500

- The inventory should be valued at the lower of cost and NRV.
- Cost is $500.
- NRV is $1,200 – $250 = $950.
- The correct valuation is therefore $500.

90 A

	$
Opening inventory + units purchased	440
Units sold	(290)
Closing inventory (units)	150

FIFO Closing inventory: 150 units @ $2.78 $417

AVCO Weighted average cost	$
100 units @ $2.52	252
140 units @ $2.56	358
200 units @ $2.78	556
440	1,166

Average cost per unit	1,166/440 = $2.65
	$
	440.00
Closing inventory: 150 units @ $2.65	$397.50
FIFO higher by (417.00 – 397.50)	$19.50

Tutorial note:

The periodic weighted requires the total cost of the inventory to be divided by the total units in the period to determine the weighted average cost for the period. This weighted average figure will then be used to value the inventory.

The continuous weighted method requires the weighted average to be calculated every time there is a purchase.

91   B

- If prices have fallen during the year, AVCO will give a higher value of closing inventory than FIFO, which values goods for resale at the latest prices.
- Where the value of closing inventory is higher, profits are higher.

92 $56,640

- The number of units held at the year-end is 1,180 (1,200 – 20).
- The sale on 31 December provides evidence of a net realisable value $2 below cost. Therefore each unit should be valued at its net realisable value:
- 1,180 units × $48 = $56,640.

93   C

Tutorial note:

Inventory should be valued at the lower of cost and net realisable value. Replacement cost is irrelevant.

94   C

- When inventory is included in purchases at cost and closing inventory at cost, the effect on profit is nil (the same amount is both a debit and a credit in the statement of profit or loss).
- In this case, only the credit is recorded (closing inventory). Therefore profit is overstated by the cost of the fabric.
- The inventory valuation is not misstated, as it includes the fabric received on 29 June.

95   A

Tutorial note:

Inventory drawings are credited to purchases in order to remove them from cost of sales, as these goods have not been sold.

96   B

At the year-end:

1   Opening inventory must be removed from the statement of financial position inventory account (a credit) and expensed to the statement of profit or loss as part of cost of sales (a debit).

2   Closing inventory must be debited on to the statement of financial position as an asset and removed from the cost of sales (a credit).

---

97 $39,900

	$
Value at 7 July 20X6	38,950
Sales since year end (100/125 × $6,500)	5,200
Purchase since year end	(4,250)
Value at 30 June 20X6	39,900

98 $155

	Items	Unit value	
		$	$
Opening inventory	6	15	90
January: purchases	10	19.80	198
	16	18	288
February: sales	(10)	18	(180)
	6	18	108
March: purchases	20	24.50	490
	26	23	598
March: sales	(5)	23	(115)
	21	23	483

	$
Sales (15 × $30)	450
Cost of sales ($180 + $115)	(295)
Gross profit	155

99 $1,110

Date		Units	Unit value	Inventory value
			$	$
1 October	Opening inventory	60		720
8 October	Purchase 40 units at $15	40		600
14 October	Purchase 50 units at $18	50		900
		150	14.80	2,220
21 October	Sold 75 units: cost	(75)	14.80	(1,110)
31 October	Closing inventory	75	14.80	1,110

100 A

The net realisable value of inventory items is the selling price less the 4% commission payable.

	NRV	Lower of cost or NRV
	$	$
Henry VII	2,784	2,280
Dissuasion	3,840	3,840
John Bunion	1,248	1,248
		7,368

101 D

The closing inventory of 12 items (15 – 5 + 10 – 8) comprise

	$
10 items at $3.50 each	35.00
2 items at $3 each	6.00
Cost on a FIFO basis is	41.00

102 B

Tutorial note:

If the inventory was not included in the original valuation of closing inventory, closing inventory will be increased by $1,000 (the lower of cost and net realisable value). Since closing inventory is $1,000 higher, cost of sales is $1,000 lower and profit $1,000 higher.

103 $4,700

	Net realisable value	Lower of cost or NRV	Units	Value
	$	$		$
Basic	8	6	200	1,200
Super	8	8	250	2,000
Luxury	10	10	150	1,500
Total value				4,700

104 A

When prices are rising, FIFO will give a higher valuation for closing inventory, because the closing inventory will consist of the most recently-purchased items. Higher closing inventory means lower cost of sales and higher profit.

105 C

In contrast, if continuous weighted average cost per unit is calculated, a new cost per unit is calculated each time a purchase is made.

106 A

In contrast, if periodic weighted average cost per unit is calculated, this would be done at the end of the accounting period.

107 $85.00

	Units	Unit cost $	Total cost $
2 Feb	10	5.00	50.00
5 Feb	(6)	5.00	(30.00)
	——		——
	4		20.00
7 Feb	10	6.50	65.00
	——		——
	14	6.07	85.00
	——		——

108 $80.50

Total cost of purchases/total units) = ((10 × $5.00) + (10 × $6.50))/20 units = $5.75 per unit. Closing inventory valuation is therefore 14 units × $5.75 = $80.50.

109 $73.50

Total cost of purchases/total units) = ((4 × $4.00) + (10 × $5.00) + (10 × $6.00))/24 units = $5.25 per unit. Cost of sales is therefore 14 units × $5.25 = $73.50.

110 $71.70

	Units	Unit cost $	Total cost $
1 Apr	4	4.00	16.00
12 Apr	10	5.00	50.00
	——		
	14	66.00/14 = 4.71	66.00
15 Apr	(6)	4.71	(28.26)
	——		——
	8		37.74
17 Apr	10	6.00	60.00
	——		——
	18	97.74/18 = 5.43	97.74
25 Apr	(8)	5.43	(43.44)
	——		——
	10		54.30
	——		——

Cost of sales = $28.26 + $43.44 = $71.70.

TANGIBLE AND INTANGIBLE NON-CURRENT ASSETS

111 C

Asset register	$	Ledger accounts	$
Carrying amount per question	85,600	Carrying amount per question	130,000
Addition of land	30,000	Disposal at carrying amount	(14,400)
	115,600		115,600

112 A

			$
1.1.X4	Cost		235,000
	Depreciation at 30%		(70,500)
y/e 31.12.X4	Carrying amount		164,500
	Depreciation at 30%		(49,350)
y/e 31.12.X5	Carrying amount		115,150
	Depreciation at 20%		(34,545)
y/e 31.12.X6	Carrying amount		80,605
	Accumulated depreciation (70,500 + 49,350 + 34,545)		154,395

Therefore

(1)	Uplift cost account to valuation	Dr Cost $65,000
(2)	Remove depreciation to date	Dr Accumulated depreciation $154,395
(3)	Send the balance to the revaluation surplus	Cr Revaluation surplus $219,395

113 D

A non-current asset register is a detailed schedule of non-current assets, and is not another name for non-current asset ledger accounts in the general ledger.

114 C

115 $192,600

			$
Depreciation on additions:	20% × $48,000 × 6/12	=	4,800
Depreciation on disposals:	20% × $84,000 × 9/12	=	12,600
Depreciation on other assets:	20% × (960,000 – 84,000)	=	175,200
			192,600

116 $50,600

	$
Cost of plant	48,000
Delivery	400
Modifications	2,200
	50,600

Tutorial note:

The warranty cost cannot be capitalised. This is a revenue expense which must be debited to the statement of profit or loss.

117 B

		$
Year 1	Cost	2,400.00
	Depreciation at 20%	(480.00)
Year 2	Carrying amount	1,920.00
	Depreciation at 20%	(384.00)
Year 3	Carrying amount	1,536.00
	Depreciation at 20%	(307.20)
Year 4	Carrying amount	1,228.80
	Sale proceeds	1,200.00
	Loss on disposal	(28.80)

118 B

	$	$
Original balance		125,000
Carrying amount of assets sold:		
Proceeds	9,000	
Less: Profit	(2,000)	
		(7,000)
Adjusted balance		118,000

119 **$86,000**

	$
Purchase cost of machine	80,000
Installation	5,000
Pre-production safety testing	1,000
	86,000

A non-current asset should be measured initially at its cost. 'Cost' means the amounts incurred to acquire the asset and bring it into working condition for its intended use. These include the purchase cost, initial delivery and handling costs, installation costs and professional fees. Costs of testing whether the asset is working properly may be included, but staff training costs cannot be capitalised.

120 **A**

	$
Cost	5,000
Year 1 (20% × 5,000)	(1,000)
Year 2 (20% × 4,000)	(800)
Year 3 (20% × 3,200)	(640)
Carrying amount at time of disposal	2,560
Sale proceeds	2,200
Loss on disposal	360

121 **$4.72 million**

	$m
Non-current assets at cost	10.40
Accumulated depreciation	(0.12)
Carrying amount	10.28
Revaluation amount	15.00
Transfer to revaluation surplus	4.72

122 **D**

Painting and replacing windows are maintenance and repairs, and so are classified as 'revenue expenditure' and must be expensed through the statement of profit or loss. The purchase of a car for resale means that the car is an item of inventory for the business, not a non-current asset. Legal fees incurred in purchasing a building are included in the cost of the building, and so are part of the non-current asset cost, i.e. capital expenditure.

123 D

<table>
<tr><td colspan="4" align="center">**Disposals account**</td></tr>
<tr><td></td><td>$</td><td></td><td>$</td></tr>
<tr><td>Cost</td><td>12,000</td><td>Accumulated depreciation
(3 yrs × 20% × $12,000)</td><td>7,200</td></tr>
<tr><td>Profit (β)</td><td>200</td><td>Proceeds (part exchange allowance)</td><td>5,000</td></tr>
<tr><td></td><td>12,200</td><td></td><td>12,200</td></tr>
</table>

124 $510,000

	Cost	Accum dep'n	Carrying amount
	$000	$000	$000
Opening balance	860	397	
Disposal	(80)	(43)	
	780	354	
Purchase	180		
Depreciation (10%)		96	
	960	450	510

125 C

126 $12,450

1 Jan – 30 June: 3% of $380,000 × 6/12 = $5,700

1 July – 31 December: 3% of $450,000 × 6/12 = $6,750

Charge for the year: $5,700 + $6,750 = $12,450

127 D

Do not include the vehicle tax in the cost of the car. Road tax is a revenue expense item.

		Acc dep'n	Proceeds	Profit
	$	$	$	$
Cost of asset	10,000			
Depreciation 20X1 (25% × $10,000)	(2,500)	2,500		
Depreciation 20X2 (25% × ($10,000 – $2,500))	(1,875)	4,375		
Depreciation 20X3 (25% × ($10,000 – $4,375))	(1,406)	5,781		
Depreciation 20X4 (25% × ($10,000 – $5,781))	(1,055)	6,836		
Carrying amount at time of disposal	3,164		5,000	1,836

128 D

The reducing balance method charges more depreciation in earlier years than in later years. It is therefore appropriate to use for assets such as motor vehicles that lose a large part of their value in the earlier years of their life.

129 $5,000 loss

Annual depreciation = $(40,000 – 10,000)/6 years = $5,000.

The machine was used for four years before disposal, giving accumulated depreciation of 4 × $5,000 = $20,000.

When the machine was sold, its carrying amount was $40,000 – $20,000 = $20,000. It was sold for $15,000, giving a loss on disposal of $5,000 as follows:

	$
Disposal proceeds	15,000
Carrying amount at disposal date	20,000
	———
Loss on disposal	5,000
	———

130 $3,610

Initial depreciation charge p.a. $\dfrac{\$20,000- \$500}{10\,years} = \$1,950$

Carrying amount at date of change $20,000 – $1,950 = $18,050

New depreciation charge (for y/e 30 June X9 onwards) $\dfrac{\$18,050}{5\,yrs} = \$3,610$

Note that the revision of estimations takes place in the year ended 30 June 20X9 before the depreciation for that year is charged.

131 A

Tutorial note:

When accounting for intangible assets using the revaluation model, movements in the carrying amount are accounted for in other comprehensive income and other components of equity.

132 B

Answer (A) is not precise enough – there must be an annual impairment review to ensure that the asset is not overstated in the financial statements.

133

	Capitalised ? Yes/No
Employment costs of staff conducting research activities	No
Cost of constructing a working model of a new product	Yes
Materials and consumables costs associated with conducting scientific experiments	No
Licence purchased to permit production and sale of a product for ten years	Yes

134 B

When accounting for intangible assets using the cost model, annual impairment charges are accounted for in the statement of profit or loss.

135

	Research expense	Intangible asset
Market research costs	Yes	
Patented product design costs		Yes
Product advertising	Yes	
Employee training costs	Yes	

136 A

Tutorial note:

An intangible asset may be internally generated (development costs per IAS 38) and may also be purchased – therefore answers B and D are incorrect. Answer C is incorrect as assets can normally be sold.

137   A

The revaluation surplus balance as at 31 October 20X2 is being asked for. When revaluing an asset, it is the carrying amount of the asset which is revalued, rather than the cost, and as the question states there is no annual transfer of the excess depreciation, the balance on the revaluation surplus can be found as: $150,000 – $81,600 = $68,400.

As the revaluation takes place on 1 November 20X1, a whole year's depreciation is calculated on the revalued amount. The new charge will take the revalued amount of $150,000 and depreciate the asset over its remaining useful economic life.

By looking at the accumulated depreciation brought forward you can tell how old the original asset is:

Original depreciation charge: $102,000/50 years = $2,040 per annum and as $20,400 is accumulated depreciation brought forward, then the asset must have already been held for 10 years. Therefore, the remaining useful economic life is 50 years – 10 years = 40 years.

The new depreciation charge should be calculated as: $150,000/40 years = $3,750.

138   A, C and D

139 $625 profit

The capitalised cost of the truck is $20,000 – the insurance cost is not capitalised but accounted for as an expense in profit or loss. The net cost of the truck is: $17,000 ($20,000 – $3,000) and the annual depreciation charge will be $2,125 ($17,000/8 years).

At the disposal date, the business had owned the truck for exactly five years – therefore accumulated depreciation to disposal date is $10,625, giving a net carrying amount of $9,375 ($20,000 – $10,625). As the trade-in allowance is $10,000, this will result in a profit on disposal of $625.

140   Option 1 – Optional and Option 2 – Statement of changes in equity

When an entity has revalued a non-current asset, it is **optional** to account for excess depreciation arising on the revaluation. When excess depreciation is accounted for, the accounting adjustment is reflected in **the statement of changes in equity**.

Tutorial note:

Note that when an entity does decide to account for excess depreciation, it must apply that accounting policy every year and cannot apply the policy in some years and not in others.

141 $900 loss

The cost of the asset is $15,000 – the cost of the maintenance agreement is not capitalised but accounted for as a payment in advance and charged to profit or loss as an expense over three years. The net cost of the asset is: $13,000 ($15,000 – $2,000) and will be depreciated at 20% per annum.

At the disposal date, the business had owned the asset for 3.5 years – therefore accumulated depreciation to disposal date is $9,100, giving a net carrying amount of $5,900 ($15,000 – $9,100). As the trade-in allowance was $5,000, this will result in a loss on disposal of $900.

142 C

The costs of a development project are capitalised only if:

- The project is separately identifiable.
- Expenditure can be reliably measured.
- It is commercially viable.
- It is technically feasible.
- It is projected to be profitable.
- Resources are available to complete it.
- Project 2 falls short of these criteria: it does not appear that the appetite suppressant properties of the substance have yet been confirmed and therefore it is not yet commercially viable.
- Project 3 may not be completed and therefore does not meet all six criteria.
- The costs of projects 2 and 3 should be expensed to the statement of profit or loss and other comprehensive income.

143 $147,292

	$
Project A	34,000
Project B	78,870
Project C ($290,000 + $19,800) × 4/36	34,422
	————
	147,292
	————

- Project A is a research project and all costs should be written off to the statement of profit or loss and other comprehensive income as incurred.
- Project B is a development project. Costs can only be capitalised once the capitalisation criteria are met. Those costs incurred before this was the case cannot be reinstated as an asset.
- Project C is a development project which has resulted in capitalised expenditure. This asset must be amortised over the 36 months of sales of the product. Amortisation for the current year should be 4 months (1 September to 31 December 20X5).

ACCRUALS AND PREPAYMENTS

144 $453,600

Rental income (property 1 and 2)

	$		$
Balance b/f	5,400	Balance b/f	12,300
Statement of profit or loss rental income (β)	453,600	Cash received (280,000 +160,000)	440,000
Balance c/f	6,700	Balance c/f	13,400
	465,700		465,700
Balance b/f	13,400	Balance b/f	6,700

145 $858,600

Rental income

	$		$
Balance b/f	42,300	Balance b/f	102,600
Statement of profit or loss (β)	858,600	Cash received	838,600
Balance c/f	88,700	Balance c/f	48,400
	989,600		989,600

146   A

		$
Statement of profit or loss	9/12 × $10,800	8,100
	3/12 × $12,000	3,000
		11,100
Statement of financial position prepayment	9/12 × $12,000	9,000

147 D

Statement of profit or loss (5/12 × $24,000) + (7/12 × $30,000) = $27,500

Statement of financial position $7,500 paid on 1 January therefore amount prepaid by tenant is:

2/3 × $7,500 = $5,000. For Vine this is prepaid/deferred income, i.e. income received in advance – a liability.

148 $385

Motor expenses

	$		$
Balance b/f (insurance)	80	Balance b/f (fuel)	95
Cash paid – petrol	95		
– other bills	245	Statement of profit or loss (β)	385
Balance c/f (petrol)	120	Balance c/f (insurance)	60
	540		540

The insurance prepayment covers 4 months as at the start of September. Therefore there must be a prepayment of 3 months at the end of September.

149 A

Charge to P&L = $1,800 × 7/12 = $1,050. Prepayment $1,800 × 5/12 = $750

150 Accrual $560 and P&L Expense $3,320

The accrual for May and June 20X3 is assumed to be 2/3 × $840 = $560.

Electricity expenses

	$		$
Bank	600	Opening balance b/f	300
Bank (720+900+840)	2,460		
Closing balance c/f	560	Statement of profit or loss	3,320
	3,620		3,620

151 $12,600

The premium for the year 1 July 20X2 to 30 June 20X3 was $13,200 × 1/1.1 = $12,000

Statement of profit or loss charge:

6 months at $12,000 plus 6 months at $13,200 = $6,000 + $6,600 = $12,600

152 B

The charge In the statement ot profit or loss will be the amount of interest incurred from 1 January (when the loan was taken out) to 30 September (the year end) i.e. 9/12 × 12% × $100,000 = $9,000. This represents three interest payments.

However, as only two interest payments were made (1 April and 1 July) the third payment due to be made on 1 October, which relates to the three months to 30 September, will be accrued: 3/12 × 12% × $100,000 = $3,000.

153 C

	$
Prepayment brought forward at the start of the year	10,000
Payment during the year	36,000
	———
	46,000
Less: Prepayment carried forward at the year end (7 months, therefore $36,000 × 7/12)	(21,000)
	———
Charge for insurance in the statement of profit or loss	25,000
	———

154 B

Accrued income is income not yet received for a service already provided (income received in arrears). The correct double entry to record accrued income is:

Dr Accrued income (statement of financial position), Cr Income (statement of profit or loss) which will increase profit.

155 B and C

The meter rental charge covers the period 1 Oct – 31 Dec and has been paid before the year end. Therefore, there is a prepayment of two months rental as follows: ($60 × 2/3) = $40.

The usage charge is paid in arrears and has been paid up to 30 Sept – therefore an accrual of one month is required as follows: ($135 × 1/3) = $45.

IRRECOVERABLE DEBTS AND ALLOWANCES FOR RECEIVABLES

156 D

Receivables ledger control account

	$		$
Balance b/f	34,500	Cash received	247,790
Credit sales (β)	278,090	Contra	1,200
		Irrecoverable debts	18,600
		Balance c/f	45,000
	312,590		312,590
Balance b/f	45,000		

Total sale = Credit sales + Cash sales

= $278,090 + $24,000 = $302,090

Note:

- Discounts received are relevant to the payables ledger control account.

- The double entry for the increase in allowance for receivables is:

Dr Irrecoverable debts expense   12,500

Cr Allowance for receivables   12,500

157 B

Receivables ledger control account

	$		$
Balance b/f	84,700	Contra with payables ledger control account	5,000
Credit sales	644,000	Irrecoverable debts	4,300
		Cash received from credit customers	625,780
		Balance c/f	93,620
	728,700		728,700

The double entry for a contra is Dr payables ledger control account (payables) and Cr receivables ledger control account (receivables).

Discounts received are relevant to payables not receivables. Cash sales should not feature in the receivables ledger control account.

The correct double entry for the increase in the allowance for receivables is Dr irrecoverable debts expense and Cr allowance for receivables.

158 A

		Allowance	Expense
	$	$	$
Receivables balance (draft)	58,200		
Irrecoverable debts	(8,900)		8,900
	49,300		
Specific allowance: Carroll	(1,350)	1,350	
Juffs	(750)	750	
Mary	(1,416)	1,416	
Allowance c/f		3,516	
Allowance b/f		5,650	
Decrease in allowance		2,134	(2,134)

Total expense = $8,900 – $2,134 = $6,766

159 B

Receivables ledger control account			
	$		$
Balance b/f (W)	13,150	Cash	115,500
Sales	125,000	Irrecoverable debts	7,100
		Balance c/f	15,550
	138,150		138,150

	b/f	c/f
	$	$
Gross receivables	13,150	15,550
Allowance	(1,150)	(2,100)
Net receivables	12,000	13,450

160 B

The write off of debts will reduce the gross receivables balance by $72,000 to $766,000.

The allowance is to be adjusted to $60,000 (hence an adjustment of $12,000).

The net balance is therefore $766,000 less $60,000, i.e. $706,000.

161 A

Year-end receivables	5% × $7,000,000	=	$350,000
Year-end allowance for receivables	4% × $350,000	=	$14,000
Allowance at start of year	100/120 × $14,000	=	$11,667
Increase in allowance		**=**	**$2,333**

Irrecoverable debts expense

	$		$
Write off of irrecoverable debts	3,200	Recovery of irrecoverable debts	450
Increase in allowance	2,333	Statement of profit or loss (β)	5,083
	———		———
	5,533		5,533
	———		———

162 B

Trade receivables

	$		$
Balance b/f	10,000	Receipts	90,000
Sales	100,000	Contra with payables	800
Irrecoverable debts recovered	1,000	Balance c/f	20,200
	———		———
	111,000		111,000
	———		———

163 C

When a debt is written off as irrecoverable, the transaction is recorded as:

Dr Irrecoverable debts account (expense) and Cr Receivables ledger control account.

Any subsequent change to the allowance for receivables should be dealt with as a separate matter.

164 A

Receivables

	$		$
Balance b/f	37,500	Contra with payables	15,750
Sales (credit)	357,500	Irrecoverable debts written off	10,500
		Bank (β)	329,750
		Balance c/f	39,000
	———		———
	395,000		395,000
	———		———

Cash sales do not affect receivables. Discounts received affect payables, not receivables.

The allowance for receivables does not affect the amount of receivables, but specific irrecoverable debts written off do affect receivables.

165 A

Receivables (5% of $2 million) = $100,000.

Required specific allowance for receivables = $4,000.

Current allowance for receivables = $4,000 × ¾ = $3,000.

Increase in allowance = $1,000. An increase in the allowance for receivables reduces profits.

166 A

	$
Irrecoverable debts written off (800 + 550)	1,350
Irrecoverable debt recovered	(350)
Reduction in allowance for receivables	(200)
Charge to statement of profit or loss	800

167 B

The allowance for receivables will reduce the carrying amount of receivables. An increase in an allowance for receivables will therefore reduce net current assets.

168 A

	$	$
Receivables balance	230,000	
Write off irrecoverable debts	(11,429)	11,429
Specific allowances – Emily		450
– Lulu		980
	218,571	
Total allowance at end of year		12,859
Allowance b/f		(11,700)
Increase in allowance = Dr to statement of profit or loss		1,159

169 D

> **Tutorial note:**
>
> *In comparison with making cash sales, the provision of credit will not improve the cash flow position of the business, rather it may result in a deterioration of cash flow. This is particularly true as some customers will be late in paying and others will not pay at all.*

170 C

> **Tutorial note:**
>
> *An aged receivables analysis is a list of how much each credit customer owes and how old their debt is. It enables the credit control function to identify which customers to chase, and also helps in the calculation of the allowance for receivables at the year-end. Separate information should be maintained of credit approval of customers, together with agreed limits.*

171 $6,966

Adjust the receivables control account for the specific allowance

	$	$
Balance on the receivables control account:	425,700	
Less: irrecoverable debts	(8,466)	8,466
	417,234	
Specific allowance required	(2,400)	2,400
Irrecoverable debt recovered		(2,000)
		8,866

The question states that the allowance for receivables at 1 April 20X3 was $1,900. The receivables expense for the year ended 31 March 20X4 is therefore $8,866 − $1,900 = $6,966.

PROVISIONS AND CONTINGENCIES

172 A

> **Tutorial note:**
>
> *Based upon the stated and publicised policy it would appear probable that customers who return goods in accordance with the policy will expect to receive a refund – this requires a provision. The outcome of the legal claim has been assessed as only possible (rather than probable) that there will be an outflow of economic benefits. This does not require a provision, only a disclosure note of the contingent liability.*

173 A

174 A

Warranties meet the criteria required to create a provision; a provision should be made for the best estimate of the obligation. The likelihood of a liability arising for Quidditch as a result of the guarantee is assessed as possible. A provision cannot be recognised in the financial statements unless the likelihood is probable.

175 C

A is incorrect – a contingent asset is only recognised and accounted for if it is virtually certain to arise.

B is incorrect as only contingent assets which are regarded as probable are disclosed in the financial statements.

D is incorrect as a contingent liability which is regarded as probable must be recognised and accounted for in the financial statements.

176 D

A is incorrect – a contingent asset is only recognised and accounted for if it is virtually certain to arise.

B is incorrect as contingent assets can be recognised if they are virtually certain.

C is incorrect as a contingent liability which is regarded as remote can be ignored when preparing the financial statements.

For the same reason, D is correct as contingent liabilities which are regarded as remote can be ignored when preparing the financial statements.

177 B

(1) is incorrect – a provision may be classified as a non-current liability when the probable outflow of economic benefits is expected to occur more than twelve months from the reporting date.

(2) is correct as normally a liability can be precisely quantified whereas quantification of a provision requires estimation and judgement.

(3) is correct – there is a future probable outflow of economic benefits, but the exact amount and/or date of the outflow is still to be confirmed.

178 C

Tutorial note:

IAS 37 requires that a provision should be recognised when it is probable that there will be a future outflow of economic benefits as a result of a past event.

Based upon the licence terms, damage has already been caused which will cost $5 million to rectify in 20X7 or later. This should be recognised and classified as a non-current liability. If damage has not yet been caused, there is not yet an obligation to rectify it. Therefore at 31 August 20X4 no provision can be made for expected future damage.

179 D

IAS 37 requires that a provision should be recognised when it is probable that there will be a future outflow of economic benefits as a result of a past event. Therefore, a provision to settle customer claims should be recognised. As it is only probable that the counter-claim against Bottler will succeed, it cannot be recognised in the statement of financial position – it is disclosed in a note to the financial statements.

180 C

An increase in the provision from $10,000 to $13,000 requires that a charge is made in profit or loss and that the provision balance within current liabilities is increased by the same amount.

181 B

Tutorial note:

IAS 37 requires that a provision should be recognised when it is probable that there will be a future outflow of economic benefits as a result of a past event. Contingent liabilities that are regarded as possible, rather than probable, should be the subject of a disclosure note in the financial statements.

CAPITAL STRUCTURE AND FINANCE COSTS

182 D

Statement 1 referring to capitalisation of reserves applies to a bonus issue and is therefore incorrect. A rights issue does not 'capitalise entity reserves', as a rights issue but raises cash resources at an issue price less that market value.

A rights issue is being offered to existing shareholders and does bring in cash but at a discounted price compared to the market value of a share. Statement 2 refers to a discounted price compared to nominal value – this is incorrect.

183 A

On issue of redeemable preference shares, the two items effected would be cash, as cash is coming in from the issue of shares and secondly, long-term debt. This is because, although legally they are shares, in substance redeemable preference shares are more like debt (as they have fixed return and are repayable/redeemable at a future date).

184 D

Opening retained earnings + profit – prior year final dividend = closing retained earnings

Opening retained earnings = $79,285 – $12,200 – $320,568

Opening retained earnings = $253,483

185 **$15,000**

	$
Net profit for the year	36,000
Dividend	(21,000)
Added to retained earnings	15,000

You should recognise that it is the profit for the period less any dividend paid that is added to the retained earnings balance. Accounting for the revaluation does not affect retained earnings for the year – this is accounted for through other comprehensive income and revaluation surplus within other components of equity.

186 **B**

187 **A and D**

188 **C**

Tutorial note:

A rights issue is an issue of shares for cash. It is usually made at less than full market price to encourage current shareholders to take up the share issue.

189 **C**

A bonus issue of shares is a free issue of shares to current shareholders on a pro-rata basis in relation to their current shareholding.

190 **B**

Dividends received are accounted for in the statement of profit or loss as income. Dividends paid are accounted for in the statement of changes in equity.

191 **C**

Tutorial note:

Dividends are paid from retained earnings. They must be accounted for as an expense in the statement of profit or loss.

192

Debit or credit	Ledger account	$
Debit	Bank (20,000 × $1.75)	35,000
Credit	Share capital ($20,000 × $1)	20,000
Share premium	Share premium ($20,000 × $0.75)	15,000

193 B

The accounting entries would be:

Dr Share premium $31,250

Cr Share capital (250,000/4) = 62,500 × $0.50 = $31,250

194 D

Redeemable preference shares have the characteristics of a liability as they will be redeemed at some future date which will require an outflow of economic benefits. They should be classified as a liability, rather than equity.

195 B

PREPARING A TRIAL BALANCE

FROM TRIAL BALANCE TO FINANCIAL STATEMENTS

196 C

	$	$
Plant and machinery	89,000	
Property	120,000	
Inventory	4,600	
Payables		6,300
Receivables	5,900	
Bank overdraft		790
Loan		50,000
Capital		100,000
Drawings	23,000	
Sales		330,000
Purchases	168,200	
Sales returns	7,000	
Sundry expenses	73,890	
Discounts received (β)		4,500
	491,590	491,590

197 D

When a trial balance agrees, this does not confirm that no errors have been made in the accounting records. Only those errors resulting from accounting entries without an equal debits and credits will be highlighted by the trial balance. An entity will prepare the statement of profit or loss and other comprehensive income, the statement of financial position, the statement of cash flows and the statement of changes in equity. The trial balance is not one of the financial statements prepared by an entity for its shareholders.

198 C

All three are limitations of a trial balance:

- figures in the trial balance are not necessarily the final figures to be reported in the financial statements; they are subject to year-end adjustments
- errors of commission (where an entry has been posted to the wrong account) are not identified by the trial balance since an equal debit and credit entry are still posted
- although a trial balance can identify if double entry has broken down, it does not indicate in which accounts wrong entries were made.

199 A

	$	$
Sales		120,000
Opening inventory	2,600	
Purchases	78,900	
Closing inventory	(1,900)	(79,600)
	———	———
Gross profit		40,400
Rental expense (3,400 – 200)	3,200	
Sundry expenses	13,900	
Bank interest	(270)	
Decrease in allowance	(120)	(16,710)
	———	———
Net profit		23,690
		———

200 C

	Dr $	Cr $
Premises/Acc Dep'n	500,000	120,000
Inventory	23,000	
Share capital		200,000
Retained earnings		105,000
Receivables	43,500	
Carriage in	1,500	
Allowance for receivables		3,400
Bank overdraft		1,010
Payables		35,900
Sales		500,080
Purchases	359,700	
Sales returns	10,300	
Sundry expenses	14,000	
Suspense	13,390	
	———	———
	965,390	965,390

201 B

	Increase $	Decrease $	$
Closing inventory	45,700		
Depreciation (20% × $470,800)		94,160	
Irrecoverable debt		230	
Deferred income		6,700	
	———	———	
	45,700	101,090	
Decrease in net assets	———	———	55,390

202 C

	Charge for the year				Closing
	$				$
Rent	24,000	Rent accrual			**2,000**
		(12 × $2,000)	Due	24,000	
		Paid		22,000	
		Accrual		2,000	
Insurance	28,000	Insurance prepayment			**2,000**
		Paid		30,000	
		Due		28,000	
		Prepayment		2,000	

The rental charge in the statement of profit or loss will be $24,000 ($2,000 × 12 months). Only $22,000 has been paid, therefore an accrual of $2,000 will appear in the statement of financial position. The insurance charge will be according to the notes given after the trial balance totalling $28,000. The amount paid is $30,000, thus a prepayment of $2,000 will appear in the statement of financial position.

Note: In the trial balance the amount paid will be shown.

203 A

		$
Irrecoverable debts	1,600 + 3,000	4,600
Decrease in allowance for receivables (W1)		(440)
Total irrecoverable debt expense		4,160

Receivables	(29,600 – 3,000)	26,600
Less: Closing allowance for receivables		(2,660)
Net closing receivables		23,940

(W1)

Closing allowance for receivables	2,660
Opening allowance for receivables	3,100
Decrease in allowance for receivables	440

204 B

Depreciation charge	= Closing cost × percentage depreciation rate
	= **$5,000** (10% × $50,000)
Closing accumulated depreciation	= Accumulated depreciation b/f + charge for the year
	= $15,000 + $5,000
	= $20,000
Carrying amount	= Closing cost less closing accumulated depreciation
Carrying amount	=$50,000 – $20,000
	= **$30,000**

205 D

Depreciation charge	= (Closing cost – accumulated depreciation b/f) × percentage depreciation rate
	= ($50,000 – $21,875) × 25%
	= $7,031
Closing accumulated depreciation	= Accumulated depreciation b/f + charge for the year
	= $21,875 + $7,031
	= $28,906
Carrying amount	= Closing cost less closing accumulated depreciation
Carrying amount	= $50,000 – $28,906
Carrying amount	= $21,094

206 C and D

CONTROL ACCOUNT RECONCILIATIONS

207 C

208 B

	PLCA $		Payables ledger $
Draft balance	768,420	Draft balance	781,200
Reverse incorrect debit entry	28,400		
Discounts received – correct entry	(15,620)		
Revised balance	781,200		781,200

Items A and D would explain the discrepancy if the balance on the control account was $12,780 greater than the balance on the payables ledger.

Item C would explain the balance on the payables ledger being $25,560 greater than the balance on the control account.

209 A

Payables ledger control account

	$		$
Contras against debit balances in receivables ledger	48,000	Balance b/f	318,600
Cash paid to suppliers	1,367,000	Purchases	1,268,600
Purchase returns	41,200		
Discounts received	8,200		
Balance c/f	122,800		
	1,587,200		1,587,200

210 D

	Payables ledger	Supplier statement
	$	$
Per question	230	3,980
Cheque (1)		(270)
Goods returned (2)		(180)
Contra (3)		(3,200)
Revised balance	230	330

Difference $100 (330 – 230)

211 A

The control account has been debited by $10 more than it should have been. The account should be credited. This error would have had no effect on the receivables ledger and so part of the difference has been explained.

212 B

	Lord's records
	$
Per question	14,500
Unrecorded discount	(150)
Revised balance = supplier statement	14,350

Lord believes that he owes $150 more than the supplier has stated. Items A, C and D would result in q different outcome.

213 D

Items A and B will result in an error in the control account. Item C will result in an error in the total of individual customer account balances. Item D will not affect either of the totals, although there are errors in the individual accounts of the two customers affected, with one account balance too high and the other too low by the same amount.

214 D

	SLCA
	$
Draft balance per question	37,642
Correction of misposted contra	(1,802)
Revised balance = receivables ledger balance	35,840

The balance on the control account exceeds the total of the individual account balances by $1,802. Items A, B and C would all have the effect of making the total of the individual account balances higher by $1,802. Item D, however, by recording a credit item as a debit item in the control account, has made the control account debit balance too high by $901 × 2 = $1,802.

215 B

	$		$
Balance per ledger account	260	Balance per supplier's statement	1,350
Cash discount disallowed	80	Less: Goods returned	(270)
		Less: Cash in transit	(830)
Adjusted ledger account balance	340	Revised balance	250

Unreconciled difference = ($340 – $250) = $90

216 D

The purchase day book has been undercast by $500 (i.e. the total is $500 lower than it should be). As a result of this, the purchases account has been debited and the payables ledger control account (total payables) credited with $500 too little.

The sales day book has been overcast by $700. As a result, the sales account has been credited and the receivables ledger control account (total receivables) has been debited with $700 too much.

As a result of these errors, the control account balances need to be adjusted, and profit reduced by ($500 + $700) $1,200, by reducing sales and increasing purchases.

Neither error affects the entries in the accounts of individual customers and suppliers.

217 A

As a result of the error, total payables are understated by $259,440 − $254,940 = $4,500. To correct the error, increase the balance in the payables ledger control account by crediting the control account.

The error has affected the control account only, and not the entries in the individual supplier account for Figgins in the purchase ledger, so the total of suppliers' balances is unaffected.

218 B

Error (1) Total sales and total receivables have been recorded $370 too much. Credit the receivables ledger control account by $370.

Error (2) Total receivables has been recorded ($940 − $490) $450 too little. Credit the receivables ledger control account by $450.

As a result of these two errors, total receivables have been under-credited by $820 ($450 + $370).

The errors have not affected the accounts of individual customers.

219 $367,300

	$
Trade payables b'fwd 1 May 20X4	130,000
Purchases for the year – bal fig	**367,300**
Cash paid	(340,000)
Contra with trade receivables ledger	(3,800)
Discount received	(3,500)
	————
Trade payables c'fwd 30 April 20X5	150,000
	————

BANK RECONCILIATIONS

220 D

Cash book	$	
Cash book balance per question	(1,350)	Credit therefore overdrawn
Standing order not yet recorded	(300)	
	_____	
Revised cash book balance	(1,650)	
	_____	

	$
Balance per bank statement (β)	(1,707)
Unpresented cheques	(56)
Uncleared lodgements	128
Bank error	(15)
	_____
Revised balance = cash book balance	(1,650)
	_____

On the bank statement the overdrawn balance is shown as a debit (i.e. from the bank's perspective they are owed money).

221 B

Note that the draft ledger account balance shows an overdraft, however the bank statement shows a positive balance:

	Bank statement	Ledger account
	$	$
Balance per question	250	(190)
Unpresented cheques	(150)	
Misposting of cash receipt		260
Bank interest		30
	_____	_____
	100	100
	_____	_____

222 C

Item 1 – unpresented cheques are those issued by a business but not yet banked by the recipient. They should be deducted from the balance shown on the bank statement in order to reflect the true bank balance.

Item 2 – a dishonoured cheque is recorded by crediting the cash book. The cheque would previously have been debited to cash when received. The credit is the reversal of that entry.

Item 3 – a bank error should be corrected by amendment to the balance per the bank statement.

Item 4 – from the bank's perspective an overdraft means that they are owed money by the customer. Hence it is shown as a debit (an asset to the bank) in the bank statement.

223 B

	$
Balance per bank statement (overdrawn)	(38,640)
Add: Lodgement not credited	19,270
	(19,370)
Less: Unpresented cheques	(14,260)
Balance per cash book	(33,630)

224 B

	$
Balance per bank statement	(200)
Unpresented cheques	(1,250)
Error	97
Uncleared lodgements	890
Revised balance = revised cash book balance	(463)

225 B

	$		$
Cash book balance	(8,970)	Bank statement balance (β)	(11,200)
Bank charges	(550)	Unpresented cheques	(3,275)
		Uncleared lodgements	5,380
		Bank error	(425)
Revised cash book balance	(9,520)	Revised cash book balance	(9,520)

226 B

Cash

	$		$
Original balance (β)	11,960	Dishonoured cheque	300
Error: receipt recorded as payment (2 × $195)	390	Bank charges	50
		Balance c/f (= revised bank balance)	12,000
	12,350		12,350

	$
Bank statement balance	13,400
Unpresented cheques	(1,400)
Revised balance	12,000

227 D

	$
Balance per bank statement	(715)
Less: Unpresented cheques	(824)
	(1,539)
Add: Outstanding lodgements	337
	(1,202)
Less: Bank error	(25)
Statement of financial position/cash book overdraft	(1,227)

228 D

Cash

	$		$
Reversal of standing order (entered twice)	125	Draft balance	5,675
Revised balance	6,450	Dishonoured cheque	900
	6,575		6,575

The dishonoured cheque for $450 should have been credited to the bank balance. Instead it was debited. The bank balance is therefore too high by $900.

229 B

Cash book

	$		$
Cash sales	1,450	Balance b/f	485
Cash receipts	2,400	Payments to suppliers	
		(95% × $1,800)	1,710
		Dishonoured cheques	250
		Balance c/f	1,405
	———		———
	3,850		3,850
	———		———

230 B

	$
Balance per bank statement	(800)
Unpresented cheque	(80)
	———
Revised bank balance	(880)
	———

The dishonoured cheque requires adjustment in the cash book. After this adjustment, the cash book balance will equal the revised bank balance.

231 B

Cash

	$		$
Draft balance	2,490		
		Bank charges	50
		Dishonoured cheque	140
		Revised balance	2,300
	———		———
	2,490		2,490
	———		———

232 A

Cash

	$		$
		Draft balance	1,240
		Bank charges	75
Revised balance	1,315		
	————		————
	1,315		1,315

	$
Balance per bank statement (β)	(1,005)
Unpresented cheques	(450)
Uncleared lodgements	140
	————
Revised balance = cash book balance	(1,315)
	————

233 C

An unrecorded difference is a transaction that is reflected in the bank statement but has not yet been entered into the cash book – usually because the accountant is not aware of the transaction until advised by the bank.

Examples include direct debits, standing orders, bank charges, bank interest, dishonoured cheques and direct credits. Uncleared lodgements and unpresented cheques are examples of timing differences – amounts which have been entered into the cash book but have not yet cleared the bank.

234 A

	$
Adjusted cash book balance per bank reconciliation	1,060
Outstanding lodgements	(5,000)
Unpresented cheques	2,800
	————
Balance overdrawn at the bank	(1,140)
	————

In the books of the bank and on the bank statement, an overdraft will appear as a debit balance.

CORRECTION OF ERRORS AND SUSPENSE ACCOUNTS

235   A

Suspense account

	$		$
Imbalance on TB (362,350 – 347,800)	14,550		
Disposals (2)	9,000		
Allowance for receivables (3)	2,600	Balance c/f	26,150
	26,150		26,150
Balance b/f	26,150		

The suspense account is only affected where the initial debit and credit were unequal:

(1)   An incorrect entry into the sales day book means that the subtotal of the day book is wrong and both sides of the double entry have been made for the wrong amount. This does not affect the suspense account.

(2)   An unequal entry has occurred:

		$
Entry was:	Dr Cash	9,000
	(Cr Suspense	9,000)
To correct:	Dr Suspense	9,000
	Cr Disposals	9,000

(Do not worry about the other journals required to record the disposal – they have not been recorded at all and so do not affect the suspense account.)

(3)   An unequal entry has occurred:

		$
Entry was:	Dr Irrecoverable debt expense	1,300
	Dr Allowance for receivables	1,300
	(Cr Suspense	2,600)
To correct:	Dr Suspense	2,600
	Cr Allowance for receivables	2,600

236   C

If the sales day book is undercast, then the debit and credit entries to the accounts are equal (although for the wrong amount).

Discounts received should be credited to the discounts received account. The credit entry has simply been made to the wrong account. It is assumed that the debit entry is correct and therefore an equal debit and credit entry have been made.

The omission of an opening accrual or prepayment will always result in an imbalance on the trial balance.

The undercasting of the debit side of the cash account will result in an incorrect balance for cash being extracted and shown on the trial balance. This will cause total debit balances to be unequal to total credit balances.

237 A

An extraction error arises when the balance on a particular account is not listed correctly in the trial balance. Therefore the trial balance does not balance.

An error of commission arises where an equal debit and credit have been recorded but one entry has been made to the wrong account.

An error of omission arises where a transaction has been completely omitted from the accounting records.

An error of original entry arises where an equal debit and credit have been made but for the wrong amount.

238 D

The suspense account initially has a credit balance in order to make the total debits equal to the total credits.

Where an opening accrual has been omitted, it should be recorded and the opposite entry made to the suspense account:

Dr Suspense account	$7,568
Cr Rental expense	$7,568

Suspense account

	$		$
Opening accrual	7,568	Per trial balance	7,568

Tutorial note:

Carriage inwards should be a debit in the trial balance of $3,784. If the account balance is wrongly shown as a credit, the total credits in the trial balance will exceed the total debits by 2 × $3,784.

Discounts received

Correct entry

		Actual entry	
Dr Payables ledger control account	$3,784	Cr Payables ledger control account	$3,784
Cr Discounts received.	$3,784	Cr Discounts received	$3,784
		(Dr Suspense account	$7,568)

The actual entry made was a double credit. This will result in a debit balance arising on the suspense account.

Sales day book

If the sales day book is undercast, the entries to the sales and receivables ledger control accounts will be equal, but for the wrong amount. This will not result in an imbalance on the trial balance.

---

239 C

The correct entry for sales commission is:

Dr Sales commission and Cr Cash

As the debit was made to the wages and salaries account in error, the amount need to be removed from that account and transferred to commission paid account.

Personal accounts are not maintained for the directors of an entity.

Where repairs are carried out by an entity's own staff using items of inventory, the correct journal to transfer the relevant costs to the repairs account is:

Dr Repairs and Cr Wages/purchases

If rent received is credited to the wrong account, no suspense account entry arises. The correction journal will involve debiting the account wrongly credited and crediting the rent receivable account.

240 B

(1)   A debit and credit are made for an equal amount (albeit to the wrong account in the case of the debit), and therefore the suspense account is not affected.

(2)   The undercasting of the debit side of the wages account will result in an incorrect balance being extracted. This will result in an imbalance on the trial balance and the creation of a suspense account.

(3)   The correct entry for discounts received is:

Dr Payables ledger control account

Cr Discounts received

The error made will therefore result in a double debit (correctly to the payables ledger control account, and incorrectly to purchases). When double entry recording of transactions breaks down, a suspense account will be created.

(4)   An equal debit and credit entry are made and therefore the suspense account is not affected.

241 C

Should do		Did do		To correct	
Dr Cash	13,000	Dr Cash	13,000	Dr Suspense	26,000
Cr Sales revenue	13,000	Dr Purchases	13,000	Cr Purchases	13,000
		(Cr Suspense	26,000)	Cr Sales revenue	13,000
Dr Plant and machinery	18,000	(Dr Suspense	18,000)	Dr Plant and machinery	18,000
Cr Cash	18,000	Cr Cash	18,000	Cr Suspense	18,000

242 B

(1) Double entry has been maintained (an equal debit and credit entry have been made). Therefore there is no effect on the suspense account.

| To correct: | Dr Plant account | $43,200 |
| | Cr Cash | $43,200 |

In addition, depreciation should have been charged at 10% × $48,000, i.e. $4,800.

| To record extra depreciation: | Dr Depreciation expense | $4,320 |
| | Cr Accumulated depreciation | $4,320 |

(2) This transaction has been omitted completely from the accounts therefore it has no effect on the suspense account.

| To correct: | Dr Bank charges | $440 |
| | Cr Cash | $440 |

(3) A debit entry has been made, but no credit entry. A suspense account entry will therefore be required to correct this error:

Should do		*Did do*		*To correct*	
Dr Payables		Dr Payables ledger		Dr Suspense	$800
ledger account	$800	account	$800	Cr Sundry	
Cr Sundry payables		(Cr suspense	$800)	payables	$800
(amount due to					
Director)	$800				

(4) The balance on the cash book will be $10,000 too high as a result of the understatement. Therefore the trial balance will not balance and a suspense account will arise.

| To correct: | Dr Suspense | $10,000 |
| | Cr Cash | $10,000 |

243 D

Correction journals only affect profit if one side is posted to an statement of profit or loss account and the other to a statement of financial position account. For this purpose, a suspense account is a statement of financial position account:

		Increase	Decrease
		$	$	$
Draft profit				630,000
(1)	Extra depreciation		4,320	
(2)	Bank charges		440	
(3)	No effect			
(4)	No effect			
			———	(4,760)
				———
				625,240
				———

244 C

Profit is only affected when one (but not both) side of the correction journal is posted to the statement of profit or loss.

Both entries in the journal to record cash drawings are to statement of financial position accounts.

The expense of $420 has already been recorded when the allowance was made during the year.

To correct the misclassification, interest receivable will be reduced and rental income increased by the same amount. Therefore there is no effect on profit.

Both entries in the journal to record the receipt are to statement of financial position accounts.

245 C

Should do		*Did do*		*To correct*	
Dr Purchases	$4,000	Dr Purchases	$4,700	Dr Suspense	$700
Dr Sales tax	$700	Dr Sales tax	$700	Cr Purchases	$700
Cr PLCA	$4,700	Cr PLCA	$4,700		
		(Cr Suspense	$700)		

Purchases (and sales) are recorded net of sales tax.

Payables (and receivables) are recorded gross of sales tax.

246 A

Suspense account			
	$		$
Balance per TB	500	Misrecording of decrease in allowance for receivables	840
Sales account undercast	150		
Balance c/f	190		–
	840		840
		Balance b/f	190

The misposting of rent received to the rent payable account does not affect the suspense account as double entry was maintained, despite the error.

247 C

An error of principle breaks the 'rules' of an accounting principle or concept, for example incorrectly treating revenue expenditure as capital expenditure. The purchase of a non-current asset should be debited to a non-current asset account, not to the purchases account.

248 B

Should do		Did do		To correct	
(1) Dr Motor expense	$4,600	Cr Cash	$4,600	Dr Motor expense	$4,600
Cr Cash	$4,600	Cr MV cost	$4,600	Dr MV cost	$4,600
		(Dr Suspense	$9,200)	Cr Suspense	$9,200
(2) Dr Cash	$360	Dr Cash	$360	Dr Green's account	$360
Cr Brown's account	$360	Cr Green's account	$360	Cr Brown's account	$360
(3) Dr Rent expense	$9,500	Dr Rent expense	$5,900	Dr Rent expense	$3,600
Cr Cash	$9,500	Cr Cash	$9,500	Cr Suspense	$3,600
		(Dr Suspense	$3,600)		
(4) Dr Payables control	$325	Dr Payables control	$325	Dr Purchases	$325
Cr Discount received	$325	Cr Purchases	$325	Cr Discounts received	$325
(5) Dr Cash	$100	–		Dr Cash	$100
Cr Sales	$100			Cr Sales	$100

249 B

Accounting for an expense should reduce profit. By crediting $40 to the Bank interest receivable account, when bank charges should have been debited to an expense account, has the effect of increasing profit by $40, rather than the proper outcome of reducing profit by $40. As a result of this error, profit has been overstated by 2 × $40 = $80.

250 A

Should do	Did do	To correct
(1) Dr Gas expense $420	Dr Gas expense $240	Dr Gas expense $180
Cr Cash $420	Cr Cash $420	Cr Suspense $180
	(Dr Suspense $180)	
(2) Dr Stationery $50	Cr Discounts received $50	Dr Stationery $50
Cr Cash $50	Cr Cash $50	Dr Discounts received $50
	(Dr Suspense $100)	Cr Suspense $100
(3) Dr Bank $70	Dr Bank $70	Dr Suspense $70
Cr Interest $70	(Cr Suspense $70)	Cr Interest $70

Suspense account

	$		$
Balance b/f (β)	210	Error (1)	180
Error (3)	70	Error (2)	100
	———		———
	280		280
	———		———

251 D

The error has been to debit the customer (receivable) account and credit the supplier (payable) account, instead of debiting the supplier account and crediting the customer account. As a result receivables are over-stated by 2 × $270 = $540, and payables are over-stated by $540. The error should be corrected, but sales and purchases are unaffected, so profit is unaffected. Total assets (receivables) and total liabilities (payables) are both $540 too high, so that net assets are unchanged.

252 D

Tutorial note:

The key to answering these types of questions correctly is to consider each option individually and establish if the error will cause a suspense account to be created. This will only occur if there has been a one-sided entry or both sides of a journal have been posted to the same side of the ledger.

In option A, there is a debit and a credit entry in the transaction so even though these are incorrect entries they will not cause the trial balance to be out of balance.

In option B, the sales day book total is posted to the Sales account and the Receivables account, so even though the total is incorrect, there will still be a journal that balances and this will not cause the trial balance to be out of balance.

In option C, Discounts received should be debited to the Payables ledger control account, which has happened, and should be credited to Discounts received. They have been incorrectly credited to Purchases, but as the transaction has a debit and credit entry of equal value it will not cause the trial balance to be out of balance.

Finally, in option D, purchases from the purchase day book should have been debited to Purchases and credited to Payables ledger control account. The credit entry has been dealt with correctly but instead of debiting purchases the entry has been made to credit sales. This journal entry has two credits and does not balance so the trial balance will not balance leading to a suspense account being required.

253 $1,160 Dr

The correct answer is calculated as follows:

	$
Balance b/f	1,820 Cr
(1) Sundry income	(180) Dr
(2) Sales ledger	(2,800) Dr
	————
Balance c/f	(1,160) Dr
	————

Transaction (1) requires an entry to the suspense account as too little sundry income has been recorded in the ledger account. The correcting journal entry is to Dr Suspense and Cr Sundry income with the difference of $180.

In Transaction (2) there has been a one-sided entry, so to correct it a post to Dr Suspense Cr Sales with $2,800 is required.

Transaction (3) does not require an entry to the suspense account as the incorrect total of the day book will be posted into the ledger accounts and will not cause the trial balance to be out of balance.

254 $1,860 Dr

The correct answer is calculated as follows:

	$
Balance b/f	1,250 Dr
(1) Purchase ledger control	160 Dr
(2) Receivables	450 Dr
	————
Balance c/f	1,860 Dr
	————

Transaction (1) – an addition error in a general ledger account will cause an imbalance. As a closing liability balance has been undercast this will have caused a credit entry to the suspense and will need correction by debiting the suspense account and crediting the purchase ledger control account with $160.

Transaction (2) – Again, an imbalance has occurred as there has been a one sided transaction. The only entry has been to debit cash and therefore the credit has been made to the suspense account. In order to clear this off the suspense account, the adjustment would be to debit the suspense account and credit receivables.

Transaction (3) – Does not require an entry to the suspense account as the incorrect total from the purchase returns day book has been posted into the ledger accounts and therefore will not need adjusting through the suspense account as no imbalance has occurred. The correction journal would be to debit purchase ledger control account and credit purchase returns.

255 C

	Current assets $	Current liabilities $
A – cash received and deferred income recognised	5,000	5,000
B – reduction in bank balance to pay premium	(5,000)	
B – insurance prepayment (3/6 × $5,000)	2,500	
C – Loan cash received	12,000	
C – interest accrual (5% × $12,000 × 6/12)		300
Current assets and current liabilities	14,500	5,300

Note that the liability to repay the loan is a non-current liability.

256 $72,200

Answer: $57,400 + $15,500 – ((($15,500 – $1,500)/10) × 6/12) = $72,200

PREPARING BASIC FINANCIAL STATEMENTS

STATEMENT OF FINANCIAL POSITION AND STATEMENT OF PROFIT OR LOSS AND OTHER COMPREHENSIVE INCOME

257 B

	$	$
Sales (β)		25,600
Cost of sales		
Opening inventory	1,500	
Purchases	12,950	
Inventory drawings	(75)	
Closing inventory	(900)	
		(13,475)
Gross profit		12,125

258 B

The profit or loss charge would be $500 underprovision b/fwd plus the charge for the current year of $8,000 = $8,500. The liability outstanding would be $8,000.

259 A

Opening net assets + capital injections + profit – drawings = closing net assets

Opening net assets + $9,800 + $8,000 – $4,200 = $19,000

Opening net assets = Opening capital = $5,400

260 D

Capital = net assets

If a supplier is paid by cheque, assets reduce as do liabilities, therefore there is no change to net assets.

If raw materials or non-current assets are purchased on credit, assets increase as do liabilities; again there is no change to net assets.

If wages are paid in cash, assets decrease (the other effect is to reduce profits which in turn reduces capital).

261 B

The loan was included as a current liability, but should be treated as a non-current liability. Correcting the error will reduce total current liabilities, and this will increase net current assets (= current assets minus current liabilities).

262 B

Profit is the increase in net assets between the beginning and end of the period, plus drawings taken out of the business, minus new equity introduced in the period (which is not profit).

263 C

The separate business entity concept means that accounting information should only relate to the business, not the owner of the business. Therefore goods taken by the owner must be treated as drawings and removed from the inventory of the business.

264 D

Current assets	$	Current liabilities	$
Receivables	23,800	Overdraft	3,250
Allowances for receivables	(1,500)	Payables	31,050
Inventory	12,560	Rent accrual	1,200
Petty cash	150	Loan	25,000
	35,010		60,500

The bank statement shows a debit balance, indicating an overdraft (from the bank's perspective, they are owed money by Andrew).

The first instalment of the loan (25%) is due within 12 months and so shown as a current liability.

265 A

Assets		=	Liabilities	+	Capital

At start of week:

15,700		=	11,200	+	4,500(β)

1 May

+300		+ 300	+ 1,400
+1,400			

3 May

−750			− 750

4 May

−400			− 400

7 May

+1,200			+ 1,200
−600			− 600

At end of week:

16,850		=	11,500	+	5,350

266 $70,000

Only the revaluation surplus arising in the year is included within other comprehensive income. The depreciation charge and the gain on disposal are accounted for in profit or loss.

267 $18,000

The development expenditure should be capitalised and should not, therefore be written off as an expense. The remaining items totalling $18,000 should be charged as an expense for the year.

268 $900

The original annual depreciation charge = $80,000/50 years = $1,600. The property has been depreciated for $16,000/$1,600 = 10 years, leaving a remaining estimated useful life of 40 years. The revised annual depreciation charge is ($100,000/40 years) = $2,500. The amount of the excess depreciation transfer is: $2,500 − $1,600 = $900.

269

Debit or Credit	Account	$
Debit	Non-current asset – property	40,000
Debit	Accumulated depreciation	40,000
Credit	Revaluation surplus	80,000

270 C

	Cost of sales $	Administrative expense $	Distribution costs $
Opening inventory	12,500		
Closing inventory	(17,900)		
Purchases	199,000		
Distribution costs			35,600
Administrative expenses		78,800	
Audit fee		15,200	
Carriage in	3,500		
Carriage out			7,700
Depreciation (70:30:0)	28,000	12,000	
	225,100	106,000	43,300

271 B

The first statement is false: the nominal value of the ordinary shares is 50c and therefore there are 200,000 in issue. The ordinary dividend paid is:

200,000 × 3c = $6,000

The second statement is true. A preference dividend is accounted for when it falls due and therefore the part of the dividend not yet paid must be accrued at the year end.

272 C

Share premium			
	$		$
		Balance b/f	30,000
Bonus issue (W2)	12,500	Rights issue (W1)	90,000
Balance c/f	107,500		
	120,000		120,000

(W1)	**Rights issue**	Existing number of shares	400,000
		New shares	100,000
	At $1.15 each	Dr Cash	$115,000
		Cr Share capital	$25,000
		Cr Share premium	$90,000
(W2)	**Bonus issue**	Existing shares	500,000
		New shares	50,000
		Dr Share premium	$12,500
		Cr Share capital	$12,500

273 D

Only dividend income is shown in the statement of profit or loss and other comprehensive income.

Only dividends payable in respect of preference shares are shown in the statement of financial position.

The statement of cash flows includes all dividends paid.

The statement of changes in equity includes dividends paid and dividends payable.

274 C

The tax charge is disclosed in the statement of profit or loss and other comprehensive income.

A revaluation surplus is not realised. However, in accordance with IAS 1 (revised) it is included in the statement of profit or loss and other comprehensive income and also shown in the statement of changes in equity.

275 D

Dividends are not shown in an entity's statement of profit or loss and other comprehensive income. Instead they are presented in the statement of changes to equity.

Unpaid ordinary dividends are only accrued at the year-end if they have been declared prior to the year end. In practise this is very rare.

276 A

A rights issue involves the issue of new shares for cash and therefore more equity capital will be raised.

The rights issue price will probably be above nominal value and therefore the share premium account will be increased by the amount of the premium. A bonus issue does not involve cash; when recording the transaction, the debit entry is normally made to the share premium account, therefore reducing it.

Both a rights and a bonus issue involve the potential issue of shares to existing shareholders. Therefore neither will increase the number of shareholders in an entity.

A bonus issue will result in more shares in issue without affecting the value of the entity as a whole. Therefore each share will be worth less, not more.

277 C

An overprovision from a previous year (i.e. credit balance) reduces the tax charge in the current year in the statement of profit or loss.

Tax payable is the full amount of the estimation of the charge for the year.

278 C

The credit sale is part of the entity's normal operating cycle and is therefore classified as a current asset.

The bank overdraft is repayable on demand and therefore classified as a current liability.

The shares have been purchased to sell and so are classified as a current asset investment.

279 D

	Share capital	Share premium	Revaluation surplus	Retained earnings	Total
	$	$	$	$	$
Share issue	2,000	3,000			5,000
Revaluation			230,000		230,000
Profit (178,000 – 45,000 – 5,600)				127,400	127,400
Dividends – ordinary				(12,000)	(12,000)
– preference				(8,000)	(8,000)
Total change	2,000	3,000	230,000	107,400	342,400

280 D

Preference shares do not generally carry voting rights. Preference dividends are fixed amounts, normally expressed as a percentage of their nominal value. Preference dividends are paid out in preference to ordinary dividends.

281 A

Accounting standards require that the commercial substance of a transaction is recorded rather than its legal form. Redeemable preference shares are repayable at a specified future date and therefore have the qualities of debt. They are therefore accounted for as liabilities.

282 B

Paid up share capital is the amount of the nominal value which have been paid currently. Issued share capital is the share capital which has actually been issued to shareholders. Authorised share capital is the nominal value of the maximum number of shares that an entity can have in issue at any one time.

283 B

Loan notes can be issued at a discount to their nominal value (unlike shares). Interest is always paid based on the nominal value. Interest accrued $8,000 (12% × $400,000 × 2/12).

284 A

A bonus share issue does not raise finance for an entity, as the shares are issued for no consideration (i.e. for free). Each share becomes worth less (as there are more shares in issue but the value of the entity as a whole remains the same), and so more marketable.

The reserves decreases when there is a bonus issue. The double entry is to debit the reserves and credit the share capital. Share capital increases (at the expense of other reserves) and so may seem more appropriate when compared to net assets.

285 D

Transfers between revenue reserves, as mentioned in A and B, have no effect on the overall total of revenue reserves; issuing shares at a premium increases capital reserves; the paying of dividends must be from revenue reserves, so these will decrease.

286

	Choice: A, B or C
Excess depreciation on revaluation	C
Increase in carrying amount of the property	B
Depreciation charge	A

Tutorial note:

Excess depreciation is accounted for in the statement of changes in equity. It is not accounted for in the statement of profit or loss and other comprehensive income.

287 D

288 B

When the charge in the statement of profit or loss is less than the year-end liability, this will be caused by an adjustment relating to an overprovision in an earlier year. If there had been an underprovision, the shortfall would need to be charged in the current year, thus increasing the income tax charge in the statement of profit or loss.

289 C

IFRS 15 Revenue From Contracts with Customers requires that revenue should recognised only when performance obligations have been complied with. As both transactions relate to the sale of goods, they would appear to be obligations satisfied at a point in time. Clooney has complied with the obligation to deliver the food processor on 28 August and transfers to control to Pitt on that date. Revenue can therefore be recognised on this transaction.

Similarly, it would appear the obligations to Damon were fulfilled on 26 August 20X7 when Damon collected the goods: control was transferred on that date. A receivable should be recognised for any amount due but not yet received on both transactions.

290 $16,000

The revenue relating to the course fees relate to goods and services to be provided in 20X9. Therefore, sales revenue on the study materials and lectures should not be recognised in the financial statements for the year ended 20 December 20X8. Revenue can be recognised in 20X9 as and when the separate performance obligations are fulfilled.

The course materials sold to students is a completed transaction as at 31 December 20X8 and sales revenue can be recognised on this transaction at a total amount of $16,000 (40 × $400). There is no further obligation other than to deliver the study material, which was complied with prior to 31 December 20X8.

291 $nil

Although customer orders have been received along with deposits, Vostok has not yet done anything to earn the revenue by 31 July 20X2. The deposits received should be accounted for as deferred income and treated as a current liability, rather than being recognised as revenue. It is only when the computer games have been despatched that Vostok will be able to regard the obligation as discharged and consequently recognise revenue.

292 $14,500

	$
Customers for a full year ((12 – 1) × $1,200)	13,200
Terminated contract to 31 August (5/12 × $1,200)	500
New contracts from 1 December (2 × 4/12 × $1,200)	800
	————
Revenue for the year ended 31 March 20X6	14,500

Note that, for revenue recognition in this situation, it is irrelevant when the cash is received for the services provided. Revenue can be recognised only when it has been earned – in the case of service provision, this will occur when services are provided over a period of time.

293 $437.50

	$
Total revenue from the servicing agreement	2,250
Therefore, revenue per annum is $2,250/3	750
Revenue for period 1 September X7 – 31 Mar X8 is:	**437.50**
7/12 × $750	

Provision of a service is normally regarded as giving rise to obligations that are satisfied over a period of time.

294 C

	P & L $	Liability $	Asset $
Balance b/fwd 1 Jan 20X8		(2,350)	
Cash paid – March 20X8		2,050	
Release overprovision to P/L	(300)	300	
Repayment due	(2,120)		2,120
	(2,420)	**Nil**	**2,120**

295 A

	P & L $	Liability $	Asset $
Balance b/fwd 1 July 20X5		(16,940)	
Cash paid		17,500	
Charge overprovision to P/L	560	(560)	
Repayment due	(4,500)		4,500
	(3,940)	**Nil**	**4,500**

DISCLOSURE NOTES

296 C

Tutorial note:

IAS 38 requires that development costs should only be capitalised when the directors are satisfied that those costs will be recovered at some future date.

If the directors are not satisfied on this point, such costs cannot be capitalised, – they must be written off as incurred.

297 B

Statement A is inappropriate as there are strict criteria for application of the valuation model to be applied, rather than arbitrary judgement of the directors. Normally intangible assets should be accounted for using a consistent valuation model. In addition, there is no indication of the amortisation rate or expected useful lives of the intangible assets.

Statement C is inappropriate as any increases in carrying amount should be accounted for in other comprehensive income and other components of equity. In addition, the valuation model will only be relevant intangible assets are traded on an active market.

298 C

Statement A is inappropriate as it implies that land is also depreciated over fifty years. Land should not be depreciated as it does not have a finite useful life.

Statement B is inappropriate as assets which have a finite useful life should be subject to depreciation to spread the cost over the estimated useful life to the business.

299 B

Statement A is inappropriate as compares the total cost of inventory with its total realisable value. This is likely to result in inventory being overvalued. Statement C would also result in an overvaluation of inventory.

300 B

The statement is false as, although non-adjusting events are not accounted for in the financial statements, if material, they must be disclosed in the notes to the financial statements.

301 D

302 D

Here is an example of a non-current asset disclosure note, which should demonstrate why items (1),(3) and (4) are all correct in this question as they would be disclosed within this note:

Asset	Land and buildings	Plant & equipment
	$	$
Balance b/fwd	X	X
Revaluation	X	X
Additions	X	X
Disposals	(X)	(X)
Balance c/fwd	X	X
Accumulated depreciation		
Balance b/fwd	X	X
Charge for year	X	X
Disposals	(X)	(X)
Balance c/fwd	X	X
CA at start of year (b/fwd)	X	X
CA at year end (c/fwd)	X	X

Don't forget that disclosures can be numerical and narrative. Hence Item (2) which is an example of a narrative note that would also be included, describing, in this example note, what the useful life or depreciation rates for land and buildings and plant and equipment would be.

303 **(1), (3) and (5)**

Item (2) is disclosed on the statement of financial position. Item (4) is disclosed in the statement of changes in equity. Item (6) is disclosed in the notes to the financial statements, rather than on the face of the statement of profit or loss.

304 **C**

Disclosure requirements may be monetary (e.g. the depreciation charge for the year) or narrative (e.g. a statement of accounting policies).

305 **False**

Disclosure is required of either the estimated useful lives, or the depreciation rates used. In effect, disclosure of the depreciation rates used provides information regarding the estimated useful lives of the assets, and vice versa.

306 **D**

307 **False**

In addition to stating he balance at the beginning and at the end of the year, the entity also needs to provide a reconciliation of the movement in the provision during the year.

308 **D**

There should be disclosure of depreciation and amortisation charges made during the year. In addition, in relation to revaluation of property, plant and equipment, the date of the valuation should be disclose, together with a statement of whether or not the valuer was a person independent of the entity.

309 **B**

EVENTS AFTER THE REPORTING PERIOD

310 **C**

The flood on 3 October does not provide additional information of conditions that existed at the year end and therefore is non-adjusting. The credit customer's insolvency is confirmed before the financial statements were approved and provides evidence of irrecoverability of the amount outstanding at 30 September and is therefore an adjusting event. The sale of inventory in November provides evidence of its net realisable value for the inventory valuation at 30 September 20X8 and is therefore an adjusting event. The declaration of the ordinary dividend is a non-adjusting event.

311 D

Details of adjusting events are not disclosed by note; instead, if material, the event is accounted for in the financial statements. The sale of inventory after the reporting date at a price lower than that at which it is valued in the statement of financial position is an adjusting event. A fall in the market value of property, plant and equipment after the reporting date is a non-adjusting event. It should therefore be disclosed if material. Statement (4) is a definition of an event after the reporting date.

312 B

Events 1, 2 and 4 occur between the reporting date and date of approval of the financial statements and each provides additional information of the situation as at the reporting date. Each of these is an adjusting event. Event 1 would initially be classed as a non-adjusting event as it occurred after the reporting date and does not provide additional information of the situation at that date. However, is it threatens the ability of Brakes Co to continue as a going concern, it is regarded as an adjusting event.

Event 3 is specifically identified in IAS 10 as non-adjusting.

313 A

314 B

Tutorial note:

IAS 10 specifically precludes adjusting for a dividend that was proposed before the year end and paid after the year end.

REVENUE FROM CONTRACTS WITH CUSTOMERS

315 $8,000

Rep Co has the obligation to arrange the sale and to collect the cash from the customer. Its obligations are therefore discharged on 28 September. Revenue of $8,000 (10% × $80,000) can be recognised in the year ended and 30 September 20X4. Note that as $80,000 was received from the customer, the balance of $72,000 ($80,000 – $8,000 commission earned) should be accounted for as a liability until it is paid to Zip Co.

316 $880

Loc Co should only recognise revenue when a performance obligation has been satisfied. The obligations to deliver and install the machine are satisfied at a point in time and were completed on 1 October 20X5, so revenue of $850 ($750 + $100) can be recognised. Revenue relating to the supply of the service support agreement is recognised over a period of time and, at the reporting date, three months of support service has been provided to the customer, so $30 ($120 × 3/12) can also be recognised as revenue in the year ended 31 December 20X5. Total revenue recognised on this transaction in the year is therefore $880.

317 C

Revenue on the contract with Far Co has been recognised appropriately. Revenue on the contract with Res Co should be only for commission earned, not the full contract price. Revenue on the contract with Cap Co should be spread evenly over the time period for the supply of the service, and only nine months of service has been provided, not a full year. Revenue on the contract with Ber Co should be $50,000, the cost of sales and gross profit would both be $25,000.

318 B

Contracts do not need to be in writing, although many business entities may prefer to have written contracts so that there is certainty as to what has been agreed with customers.

319 C

Revenue should be recognised when an obligation has been discharged, either at a point in time (usually for the sale of goods) or over a period of time (usually for provision of a service).

STATEMENTS OF CASH FLOWS

320 D

	$
Issue of shares (560,000 – 220,000)	340,000
Issue of loan notes	300,000
	───────
	640,000
	───────

Interest paid is included within the 'operating activities' heading of the cash flow statement.

321 B

Interest received = $13,000.

Interest and dividends paid are normally shown within cash from operating activities. An alternative presentation may place them within cash from financing activities.

322 C

Bonus issues do not involve the transfer of cash, whereas rights issues result in a cash inflow.

The revaluation of non-current assets does not involve the transfer of cash.

323   D

Depreciation is a non-cash expense and should therefore be added back to profit.

An increase in assets (inventory and receivables) means that less cash is available (as it has been used to fund assets), hence an increase in assets is shown as a deduction in the cash flow statement.

An increase in liabilities (payables) means that more cash is available (i.e. it has not been used to pay liabilities), hence an increase in liabilities is shown as an addition in the cash flow statement.

324   D

The carrying amount of non-current assets is shown in the statement of financial position.

Depreciation charged on non-current assets and any profit or loss on disposal is shown in the statement of profit or loss and other comprehensive income.

Revaluation surpluses relating to non-current assets are shown in the statement of changes in equity.

In relation to non-current assets, the indirect statement of cash flows will include:

- depreciation
- profit or loss on disposal
- proceeds of the disposal of non-current assets
- payments to acquire non-current assets.

325   D

	$	$
Cash generated from operations (β)	419,254	
Tax and dividends paid	(87,566)	
	———	
Net cash from operating activities (β)		331,688
Purchase of property, plant and equipment	(47,999)	
Proceeds from sale of property, plant and equipment	13,100	
	———	
Net cash from investing activities		(34,899)
Redemption of loans	(300,000)	
	———	
Net cash from financing activities		(300,000)
		———
Decrease in cash and cash equivalents		(3,211)
		———

326   A

	$000
Profit for the year (β)	**1,175**
Add back depreciation	100
Less: Increase in receivables & inventory	(575)
Cash flow from operating activities	700
Add: Cash from issue of shares	1,000
Less: Repayment of debentures	(750)
Less: Purchase of non-current assets	(200)
Increase in cash	750

327   B

Non-current assets at carrying amount

	$		$
Balance b/f	50,000	Disposals (4,000 – 1,500)	2,500
Additions (β)	7,500	Depreciation	9,000
		Balance c//f	46,000
	57,500		57,500

328   C

	$
Profit	8,000
Add: depreciation (not a cash expense)	12,000
Less: purchase of new non-current assets	(25,000)
Fall in cash balance	(5,000)

329 D

	$000
Profit for the year	18,750
Depreciation	1,250
Non-current asset purchases	(8,000)
Decrease in inventories	1,800
Increase in receivables	(1,000)
Increase in payables	350
Increase in cash and cash equivalents	13,150

330 D

Items added include the depreciation charge for the period, any losses on disposals of non-current assets, reductions in inventories and receivables (including prepayments) and any increase in trade payables (including accruals).

331 D

Statement (1)	is incorrect: net cash flow from operating activities is the same, whichever method of presentation is used.
Statement (2)	is incorrect. Companies with high profits can be cash-negative, due to high spending on new non-current assets and/or a large build-up of working capital.
Statement (3)	is incorrect. Profits and losses on non-current asset disposals are shown as an adjustment to net profit before tax.

332 D

New purchase (additions) are given in the question as $2,000.

The assets disposed of had a cost of $3,000 and accumulated depreciation at the time of disposal of $1,500. Their carrying amount at disposal was therefore $1,500. The profit on disposal was $500, so the cash received from the disposal was $2,000.

333 A

Major non-cash transactions are not highlighted within the statement of cash flows (although they are disclosed elsewhere in a set of accounts). These are of interest to the users of accounts as they may have an impact on future cash flows.

334 D

	$
Cash sales	212,500
Less:	
Cash purchases	(4,600)
Cash expenses	(11,200)
Cash paid to credit suppliers (W1)	(121,780)
Cash paid as wages and salaries (W2)	(33,800)
Cash generated from operations	41,120

(W1)

Payables

	$		$
		Balance b/f	12,300
Cash paid (β)	121,780	Purchases	123,780
Balance c/f	14,300		
	136,080		136,080

(W2)

Wages and salaries

	$		$
		Balance b/f	1,500
Cash paid (β)	33,800	Statement of profit or loss and other comprehensive income expense	34,600
Balance c/f	2,300		
	36,100		36,100

335 C

	$000
Retained profit for the year ($82,000 – $72,000)	10,000
Add back:	
Dividends payable (current year's)	1,600
Tax payable (current year's estimate)	15,000
Loan note interest payable (10% × $40,000)	4,000
Operating profit	30,600

The additional $10,000 loan notes were issued at the beginning of the year. Therefore, the total loan notes at the start of the year will be $40,000. The loan notes interest for the year will be $4,000 (i.e. 10% × $40,000).

336 $75,000 outflow

	$
Cash purchase of non-current assets	(140,000)
Disposal proceeds of non-current assets ($50,000 – $3,000)	47,000
Disposal proceeds of investments	18,000
Net cash outflow from investing activities	(75,000)

337 $10,000 inflow

	$
Proceeds of issue of share capital	60,000
Repayment of bank loan ($150 – $100)	(50,000)
Net cash inflow from financing activities	10,000

338 $1,395 outflow

	$000
Balance b/fwd	2,500
Revaluation in year ($1,700 – $1,200)	500
Depreciation charge for the year	(75)
Disposal removed at carrying amount	(120)
Cash paid for additions (bal fig)	1,395
Balance c/fwd	4,200

339 (1), (3) and (6)

Items (2) (4) and (5) are relevant only under the indirect method of preparation of the statement of cash flows. Item (6) is included within operating activities under both the direct and indirect method of preparation.

340 True

Using the direct or indirect method to prepare a statement of cash flows, there are no differences in the presentation of 'cash flows from investing activities' and 'cash flows from financing activities'. Only the presentation of 'cash flows from operating activities' will differ.

341 False

The depreciation charge for the year is disclosed as an adjustment to reported profit for the year within 'cash flows from operating activities' using the indirect method, rather than the direct method.

INCOMPLETE RECORDS

342 D

	$	$	%
Sales (100/70 × $756,000)		**1,080,000**	100
Cost of sales			
Opening Inventory	77,000		
Purchases	763,000		
Closing Inventory	(84,000)		
		(756,000)	70
		324,000	30

343 B

	$	$	%
Sales (174,825 – 1,146)		173,679	125%
Cost of goods sold			
Opening inventory	12,274		
Purchases (136,527 – 1,084)	135,443		
Closing inventory (β)	**(8,774)**		
$173,679 × 100/125		(138,943)	100%
Gross profit		34,736	25%

344 A

	$	$	%
Sales		650,000	100
Cost of sales			
Opening inventory	380,000		
Purchases	480,000		
Lost inventory (β)	**(185,000)**		
Closing inventory	(220,000)		
		(455,000)	70
Gross profit		195,000	30

345 D

	$	$	%
Sales		630,000	140
Cost of sales			
Opening Inventory	24,300		
Purchases (β)	458,450		
Closing Inventory	(32,750)		
	_____		
100/140 × $630,000		(450,000)	100
		_____	
		180,000	40

Payables ledger control account

	$		$
		Balance b/f	29,780
Cash paid to suppliers (β)	**453,630**	Purchases (cash and credit)	458,450
Balance c/f	34,600		
	_____		_____
	488,230		488,230
	_____		_____

346 C

	$
Inventory at 6 January 20X6	32,780
Sales at cost (β)	6,020
Purchases	(4,200)
	_____
Inventory at 31 December 20X5	34,600

Profit on sales: $8,600 − $6,020 = $2,580

Gross margin: $\dfrac{2,580}{8,600} = 30\%$

347 D

Cash

	$		$
Balance b/f	620		
Receipts from customers (β)	16,660	Payments	16,780
		Balance c/f	500
	_____		_____
	17,280		17,280
	_____		_____

Receivables

	$		$
Balance b/f	6,340		
Sales (β)	15,520	Cash receipts	16,660
		Balance c/f	5,200
	———		———
	21,860		21,860
	———		———

Gross profit: 25/125 × $15,520 = $3,104

348 B

	$	$
Sales		148,000
Opening inventory	34,000	
Purchases	100,000	
	———	
	134,000	
Closing inventory (β)	**(26,000)**	
	———	
Cost of sales (148,000 – 40,000)		108,000
		———
Gross profit		40,000
		———

349 C

You might need to answer this by testing each answer in turn.

$$\frac{\text{Gross profit}}{\text{Cost of sales}} \quad \frac{28,800}{72,000} = 40\%$$

	$
Sales	100,800
Cost of sales	(72,000)
	———
Gross profit	28,800
	———

350 C

	$	$	%
Sales		480,000	150
Cost of sales			
Opening inventory	36,420		
Purchases (β)	324,260		
Closing inventory	(40,680)		
100/150 × $480,000		(320,000)	100
		180,000	50

PLCA

	$		$
		Balance b/f	29,590
Cash paid (β)	319,975	Purchases	324,260
Balance c/f	33,875		
	353,850		353,850

351 B

Closing net assets	=	Opening net assets	+	Capital injections	−	Loss for the period	−	Drawings
($56,000 − $18,750)		($40,000 − $14,600)						($6,800 + $250)
$37,250	=	$25,400	+	$20,000	−	(β) $1,100	−	$7,050

352 D

As the inventory is insured, its cost (not selling price) is recoverable from the insurer. Therefore this amount is shown as a current asset.

The cost should also be taken out of cost of sales as these goods have not been sold.

PREPARING SIMPLE CONSOLIDATED FINANCIAL STATEMENTS

353   A

	$
Cost of investment	1,400,000
FV of NCI @ acquisition	525,000
Less fair value of net assets at acquisition –	
(600,000 × 0.50) + $50,000	(350,000)
	————
	1,575,000

354   C

	$
Reserves of Tom	400,000
Post-acquisition reserves of Jerry –	
($20,000 × 80%)	16,000
	————
	416,000

355   C

	$
Cost of investment	750,000
FV of NCI @ acquisition	150,000
Less fair value of net assets at acquisition –	
$20,000 + $10,000	(30,000)
	————
Goodwill	870,000

356   B

	$
FV of NCI @ acquisition	25,000
Post-acquisition reserves of Barlow	2,000
(15,000 – 10,000) × 40%	
	————
	27,000

357 A

	$
FV of NCI @ acquisition	50,000
Post-acquisition reserves of Barlow	5,250
(75,000 – 60,000) × 35%	
	————
	55,250
	————

358 A

Receivables = 540 + 160 – 40 =	$660,000
Payables = 320 + 180 – 40 =	$460,000

359 B

	$	
Sales value	1,044	120%
Cost value	870	100%
	————	————
Profit	174	20%
	————	————

Workings:

Mark-up means profit is based on cost, therefore cost represents 100%. If profit is 20%, the sales value must be worth 120%.

Total profit is $174 and 60% is still in stock = $104.40

360 B

Non-current assets = $1,800,000 + $2,200,000 + fair value adj 400,000 = $4,400,000

361 C

	$m	
Sales value	24	100%
Cost value	18	75%
	———	————
Total profit	6	25%
	———	————

Workings:

Profit is $6m and half of the amount is still in inventory i.e. $3m

362 D

Sales = 120 + 48 – 24 (intra-group) = $144m

Cost of sales = 84 + 40 – 24 + 3 (PURP) = $103m

363 A

Profit attributable to non-controlling interest should be $6,000,000 × 20% = $1,200,000

The PURP adjustment does not affect the NCI as the parent is selling to the subsidiary.

364 A

Non-current assets = $1,918,000 + $1,960,000 = $3,878,000

365 B

	$
Reserves of Really	2,464,000
Post-acquisition reserves –	
($1,204,000 + $112,000)) × 75%	987,000
	─────────
	3,451,000
	─────────

366 C

Ownership of more than 50% of the ordinary shares of another entity indicates a control relationship – such investments should be accounted for as a subsidiary. Ownership of less than 20% of the ordinary shares of another entity is not normally enough to indicate either significant influence or control relationships: such a shareholding should be accounted for as a trade investment.

367 D

The ability to exercise significant influence relates to an investment classified as an associate.

368 B

The ability of one entity to exercise significant influence over another is normally indicated by the ability to appoint at least one director to the board of that entity. If an entity was able to appoint the majority of the board of directors that would normally be regarded as having control of that other entity.

369 C

The ability of one entity to exercise control over another is normally indicated by the ability to appoint the majority of the board of directors of that other entity. Significant influence over another is normally indicated by the ability to appoint at least one director to the board of that entity.

370 A

The ability of one entity to exercise control over another is normally indicated by ownership of the majority of equity shares in that other entity.

371 D

The ability of one entity to exercise significant influence over another is normally indicated by ownership of between twenty per cent and fifty per cent of the equity shares of that other entity.

372 D

	$000
100,000 × 60% × 3/2 × $3.50	315

373 $1,020,000

	$000
250,000 × 80% × $3.00 cash	600
250,000 × 80% × 3/5 × $3.50	420
	———
	1,020
	———

374 A

	$000
S2m + ($1.5m × 3/12) − $0.1m	2,275

375 A

	$000
S5m + ($3m × 9/12) − $0.5m	6,750

376 C

	$000
10m + (9/12 × 4m)	13,000
Less: post-acq'n intra-group sales	(1,600)
Add: PURP re closing inventory	80
(1.6m × 25/125 × 1/4)	———
	11,480
	———

377 $10,300

	$000
10m + (4/12 × 6m)	12,000
Less: post-acq'n intra-group sales	(1,800)
Add: PURP re closing inventory	100
(1.8m × 20/120 × 1/3)	———
	10,300
	———

378 $7,000

		$000
Consideration paid		20,000
FV of NCI at acquisition		6,000
FV of net assets acquired:		
Equity share capital	8,000	
Retained earnings to I Jan X4	10,000	
Retained earnings to acquisition		
(6/12 × 2,000,000)	1,000	
	———	(19,000)
		———
Goodwill on acquisition		7,000
		———

379 B

		$000
Consideration paid		43,000
FV of NCI at acquisition		10,000
FV of net assets acquired:		
Equity share capital	25,000	
Retained earnings at I July X7	15,000	
Retained earnings to acquisition		
(8/12 × 6,000,000)	4,000	
Fair value adjustment	1,000	
	———	(45,000)
		———
Goodwill on acquisition		8,000
		———

380 C

		$000
Cash paid (10m × 60% × $3)		18,000
Shares (10m × 60% ×2/1 × $4.50)		54,000
FV of NCI at acquisition		14,000
FV of net assets acquired:		
Equity share capital	10,000	
Share premium	10,000	
Retained earnings	50,000	
	———	(70,000)
		———
Goodwill on acquisition		16,000
		———

381 A

		$000
Cash paid (15m × 75% × $4.50)		50,625
Shares (15m × 75% × 1 × $5.00)		56,250
FV of NCI at acquisition		27,000
FV of net assets acquired:		
Equity share capital	15,000	
Share premium	5,000	
Retained earnings	76,875	
FV adjustment	2,000	
		(98,875)
Goodwill on acquisition		35,000

382 $65,000

		$000
Cash paid (200 × 90% × $3)		540
Shares issued (200 × 90% × 1 × $2)		360
FV of NCI at acquisition		75
FV of net assets acquired:		
Equity share capital	200	
Share premium	100	
Retained earnings	590	
FV adjustment ($90 – $70)	20	
		(910)
Goodwill on acquisition		65

383 B

	$000
NCI share of group profit after tax	
(400 × 6/12 × 40%)	80

Note: Huyton made the intra-group sales and therefore bears all of the PURP adjustment. Only the post-acquisition element of Speke's profit after tax is taken into account.

384 D

	$
Ordinary share capital	1,000
Retained earnings	585
($710- (6/12 × $250)	1,585
Goodwill is calculated as:	$
Consideration transferred (75% × 1000) × $2 = $1,500	1,500
FV of NCI	300
	1,800
Less FV of NA at acquisition	(1,585)
Goodwill	215

The financial statement extracts are given at the year-end date of 30 September 20X3. Therefore, the net assets at the acquisition date (1 April 20X3) must be calculated by deducting the amount of retained earnings that was earned in the 6 months since the acquisition.

385 $114,667

The interest in Seal Co was acquired on 31 August 2012, which means that during the year ended 31 December 2012, Seal Co had only been a subsidiary for 4 months of the year, therefore only the post-acquisition results of the subsidiary should be consolidated.

Intra-group sales should also be eliminated, and as all these were made in October, they are all in the post-acquisition period and need to be cancelled. This means the consolidated revenue for Panther Group would be calculated as:

$100,000 + (4/12 × $62,000) – $6,000 = $114,667.

386 $22,900

The 70% holding was acquired on 1 March 20X2, which means that during the year ended 31 August 2012, Daffodil Co had only been a subsidiary for 6 months of the year. Only post-acquisition results of the subsidiary should be consolidated. This means the consolidated gross profit would be reported as:

Tulip $18,300 + Daffodil ($9,200 × 6/12) $4,600 = $22,900.

387 $147,750

	$
Fair value of consideration transferred:	
Cash paid 75% × 100,000 = 75,000 acquired × $2	150,000
Shares issued in Venus 75% × 100,000 = 75,000 × 1/1 × $1.75	131,250
	281,250
Plus: Fair value of the non-controlling interest at acquisition	82,000
	363,250
Less: Fair value of net assets at acquisition	(215,500)
Goodwill	147,750

388   B

An associate is often identified when between 20% and 50% of the equity shares of another entity are held as this is presumed to give significant influence over that entity. However, for an associate to exist, it is not a case of just a matter of the percentage of equity shares held, it also depends on whether the investing entity can exercise significant influence, which can be evidenced through the number of directors who can be appointed on the board and who participate in decision making. The investment in statement 3 is not equity accounted as the entity has appointed the majority of the board of directors, giving it control.

389   D

Statement (1) is incorrect. Firstly, if an investing entity holds 30% in another entity and has no other investments, consolidated accounts would not be produced and therefore equity accounting would not be used. Secondly, despite an investing entity having a 20% holding in another entity, significant influence may not exist. i.e. another entity may hold the remaining 80% of the shares and hence equity accounting would not be used in the investing entity books.

Statement (2) is incorrect. In the consolidated accounts, the basic principle of equity accounting is that the group's share of the associate's profit after tax is included, not the dividend income which would be shown in the investing entity's own statement of profit or loss.

INTERPRETATION OF FINANCIAL STATEMENTS

390 27.30% and 48.00%

ROCE: ((Operating profit/capital employed) × 100), where operating profit is defined as profit before interest and before tax. Capital employed is defined as shareholders' funds plus long-term loans.

20X4: ((340,995 − 161,450) /(596,165 + 61,600) × 100) = 27.30%

20X3: ((406,400 − 170,950/(407,420 + 83,100) × 100) = 48.00%

391 24.5% and 25.04%

Gross profit margin: ((Gross profit/Revenue) × 100)

20X4: ((340,995/1,391,820) × 100) = 24.50%

20X3: ((406,400/1,159,850) × 100) = 35.04%

392 12.9% and 20.30%

Operating profit margin: ((Operating profit/Revenue) × 100), where operating profit is defined as profit before interest and before tax.

20X4: (((340,995 − 161,450)/1,391,820) × 100) = 12.90%

20X3: (((406,400 − 170,950)/1,159,850) × 100) = 20.30%

393 2.12 and 2.36

Asset turnover: (Revenue/Capital employed)

20X4: (1,391,820/(596,165 + 61,600)) = 2.12

20X3: (1,159,850/(407,420 + 83,100)) = 2.36

394 1.23 and 1.62

Current ratio: (Current assets/Current liabilities)

20X4: ((528,855/430,680) = 1.23

20X3: ((390,710/241,590) = 1.62

395 0.97 and 1.25

Quick 'acid test' ratio: ((Current assets − inventory)/Current liabilities)

20X4: ((528,855 − 109,400)/430,680) = 0.97

20X3: ((390,710 − 88,760)/241,590) = 1.25

396 38 days and 43 days

Inventory holding period: ((Inventory/Cost of sales) × 365)

20X4 ((109,400/1,050,825) × 365) = 38 days

20X3 ((88,760/753,450) × 365) = 43 days

397   110 days and 65 days

Trade receivables collection period: ((Trade receivables/Credit sales) × 365)

20X4 ((419,455/1,391,820) × 365) = 110 days

20X3 ((206,550/1,159,850) × 365) = 65 days

398   120 days and 87 days

Trade payables payment period: ((Trade payables/Cost of sales) × 365)

20X4 ((345.480/1,050,825) × 365) = 120 days

20X3 ((179,590/753,450) × 365) = 87 days

399   10.33% and 20.40%

Debt-equity ratio: (Long-term loans/Shareholders' funds) × 100)

20X4 ((61,600/596,165) × 100) = 10.33%

20X3 ((83,100/407,420) × 100) = 20.40%

400   9.37% and 16.94%

Gearing ratio: (Long-term loans/(Shareholders' funds + long-term loans) × 100)

20X4: (((61,600/(596,165 + 61,600)) × 100) = 9.37%

20X3 (((83,100/(407,420 + 83,100)) × 100) = 16.94%

401   17.95 times and 16.82 times

Interest cover: ((Operating profit/Interest payable) × 100)

20X4 (((340,995 − 161,450)/10,000) × 100) = 17.95 times

20X3 (((406,400 − 170,950)/14,000) × 100) = 16.82 times

402   D

(4,600/20,000) × 100 = 23%

403   A

20X5 (2,140/20,000) × 100 = 10.7%

20X6 (2,180/26,000) × 100 = 8.38%

404   A

20X5 (4,400/20,000) × 365 = 80 days

20X6 (6,740/26,000) × 365 = 95 days

405   A

12,715/5,000 = 2.54 times

406 C

		$
Selling price (SP)	140	700
Cost of sales (COS)	100	???
Gross profit	40	???

Cost of sales × 140/100 = 700 Cost of sales = 700/1.4 = $500

407 D

Inventory turnover is found by dividing cost of goods sold by average inventory.

Average inventory is

$$\left(\frac{24,000 + 20,000}{2}\right) = \$22,000$$

$$\text{Inventory turnover} = \frac{\text{Cost of sales}}{\text{Average inventory}}$$

	$
Opening inventory	24,000
Purchases	160,000
	184,000
Less: Closing inventory	(20,000)
Cost of goods sold	164,000

Inventory holding period is therefore 22,000/164,000 × 365 = 49 days.

408 D

You need only know the correct formula here.

409 C

The current ratio is current assets divided by current liabilities: 5,800/2,200 = 2.64:1.

410 A

The gearing ratio is the proportion of long-term loans to shareholders' funds, thus it follows that if a decrease in long-term loans is less than a decrease in the shareholders' funds, the gearing ratio will rise.

411 B

The quick ratio is: current assets less inventory divided by current liabilities, that is 2,000:2,200 = 0.9:1.

412 A

The formula to calculate interest cover is: Profit before interest and tax/Finance cost

The complication in this question is that the profit before interest and tax is not given in the information and so must be calculated.

Profit before interest and tax (133 – 59)/26 = 2.85

413 29 days and 40 days

20X6: 4,400/52,000 × 365 = 29 days

20X5: 5,300/48,000 × 365 = 40 days

414 1.86 and 1.95

20X3: 38,595/20,750 = 1.86

20X2: 37,050/19,000 = 1.95

415 False

An issue of ordinary shares will reduce the gearing ratio.

416 False

Return on capital employed = Profit before interest and tax/Capital employed. An increase in long-term loans would increase capital employed which, in turn, would reduce return on capital employed.

417 True

The gross profit margin will increase if unit purchase or production costs fall whilst unit selling price remains unchanged.

418 5.0% and 7.0%

20X8: 4,500/90,000 = 5.0%

20X7: 5,600/80,000 = 7.0%

Note that this ratio excludes current liabilities.

419 C

If a significant discount is offered to credit customers, they are likely to take advantage of this, which will reduce the trade receivables collection period. Similarly, application of effective credit controls is likely to reduce the trade receivables collection period. The period taken to pay trade payables will not affect the trade receivables collection period. As an isolated factor, an increase in the volume of credit sales will not affect the trade receivables collection period.

420 B

Prompt payment of suppliers' invoices will reduce the trade payables payment period. Buying proportionately more, or proportionately fewer, goods on credit will not affect calculation of the trade payables payment period. Offering a discount to credit customers will not affect the trade payables payment period.

421 A

Option A would result in increased inventory levels, and therefore increase the inventory holding period. All other answers are likely to lead to a reduction in the inventory holding period.

422 43 days

365/8.49 = 43 days

423 C

The effect of a bonus issue of shares would be to increase issued share capital and reduce either share premium or retained earnings. There would be no change to either shareholders' funds or to long-term loans – the gearing ratio would remain unchanged.

424 D

An issue of shares would increase capital employed and would therefore lead to a reduction in the return on capital employed ratio. A reduction in long-term borrowings would reduce capital employed, and consequently increase the return on capital employed ratio. Similarly, an improved profit margin would increase profit, and therefore lead to an increase in the ratio.

425 C

A rights issue of shares will result in B Co receiving cash in exchange for the issue of shares, which will either reduce an overdraft or increase cash and bank balances. This will increase equity, and the gearing ratio will decrease.

426 C

If credit customers take advantage of extended credit periods, this will increase trade receivables. If all other factors remain unchanged, there will be an increase in current assets and, consequently, in the current ratio.

427 C

An issue of ordinary shares will increase equity, and the repayment of a non-current liability loan will decrease +-liabilities. These two factors will combine to reduce the debt/equity ratio.

428 A

There is an increase in payables days from 35 days in 20X8 to 45 days in 20X9.

429

	True/False
A statement of cash flows prepared using the direct method produces a different figure for investing activities in comparison with that produced if the indirect method is used	False
A bonus issue of shares does not feature in a statement of cash flows	True
The amortisation charge for the year on intangible assets will appear as an item under 'Cash flows from operating activities' in a statement of cash flows	True
Loss on the sale of a non-current asset will appear as an item under 'Cash flows from investing activities' in a statement of cash flows	False

430 A

Section 4

ANSWERS TO MULTI-TASK QUESTIONS

1 ICE

Key answer tips

This question tests s your knowledge of accounts preparation for a limited company.

As you need to prepare both a statement of profit or loss and a statement of financial position, you will experience time pressure. One good way to manage this effectively with this is to begin your answer by preparing well-spaced proformas for each statement. You can then insert information easily as you identify information from the question that does not need to be amended, or as you complete each working.

Statement of profit or loss for year ended 31 December 20X1

	$	*Marks*
Revenue ($600,000 – $500 (W1))	599,500	1.0
Cost of sales (W2)	(255,000)	2.0
Gross profit	344,500	
Administrative expenses (W3)	(236,000)	1.5
Distribution costs	(75,000)	0.5
Operating profit	33,500	
Finance costs ($100,000 × 6% × 9/12)	(4,500)	0.5
Profit before tax	29,000	
Income tax expense	(6,000)	1.0
Profit after taxation	23,000	6.5

Statement of financial position as at 31 December 20X1

	$	
Non-current assets		
Property, plant and equipment	84,000	1.5
($120,000 – $15,000 – $21,000 (W2))		
Current assets		
Inventories	30,000	1.0
Receivables (W4)	17,000	1.5
Cash and cash equivalents	130,000	0.5
	———	
Total assets	261,000	
	———	
EQUITY AND LIABILITIES	$	
Equity		
Ordinary share capital	5,000	0.5
Retained earnings ($43,500 + $23,000 (P/L)	66,500	1.0
Non-current liabilities		
Loan	100,000	0.5
Current liabilities		
Trade and other payables ($29,000 + $4,500 loan interest)	33,500	1.0
Tax payable	6,000	0.5
Provision	50,000	0.5
	———	
Total equity and liabilities	261,000	8.5
	———	———

Workings

(W1) Sales return

A sales return has not been accounted for. The correcting entry is:

Dr revenue $500

Cr receivables $500

(W2) Cost of sales

	$
Opening inventory	24,000
Purchases	240,000
Depreciation	21,000
(($120,000 – $15,000) × 20%)	
Closing inventory	(30,000)
	———
	255,000
	———

(W3) Administrative expenses

	$
Per trial balance	185,000
Irrecoverable debt	1,000
Provision	50,000
	————
	236,000
	————

(W4) Receivables

	$
Per trial balance	20,500
Allowance per trial balance	(2,000)
Irrecoverable debt	(1,000)
Sales return (W1)	(500)
	————
	17,000
	————

Marking scheme	
	Marks
Statement of profit or loss	6.5
Statement of financial position	8.5
	———
Total	**15.0**
	———

2 WILLOW

Key answer tips

Remember that, although it may be tempting to do a lot of work on your calculator, you should also include your workings as part of your submitted answers so that the marker can see what you have done. If you are not completely correct with your workings, you will be given credit for appropriate method, but the marker can only do this is they can see and understand what you have done.

Statement of profit or loss and other comprehensive income for the year ended 30 June 20X1

	$000	Marks
Revenue	100,926	0.5
Cost of sales (W1)	(67,051)	1.5
Gross profit	33,875	
Distribution costs (W2)	(7,826)	1.0
Administrative expenses (W3)	(11,761)	1.0
Profit from operations	14,288	
Finance costs (W4)	(1,000)	1.0
Profit before taxation	13,288	
Income tax expense	(2,700)	1.0
Profit for the year	10,588	
Other comprehensive income for the year		
Surplus on revaluation of land (W5)	14,000	1.0
Total comprehensive income for the year	24,588	7.0

Statement of financial position as at 30 June 20X1

	$000	
Non-current assets		
Property, plant and equipment (W6)	119,500	2.0
Current assets		
Inventories	9,420	0.5
Trade and other receivables (W7)	20,800	1.0
Cash and cash equivalents	2,213	0.5
Total assets	151,933	
Equity		
Share capital	50,000	0.5
Share premium	25,000	0.5
Retained earnings (W8)	20,508	
Revaluation reserve ($10,000 + $14,000 (W5))	24,000	1.0
Non-current liabilities		
5% bank loan	20,000	0.5
Current liabilities		
Trade and other payables (W9)	9,725	1.0
Tax payable	2,700	0.5
Equity and liabilities	151,933	8.0

Workings

(W1) Cost of sales

	$000
Opening inventories	7,280
Purchases	67,231
Less closing inventories	(9,420)
Dep'n P&M ($2,800 (W4) × 70%)	1,960
Total	67,051

(W2) Distribution costs

	$000
Distribution costs	8,326
Dep'n P&M ($2,800 (W4) × 20%)	560
Advertising prepayment ($2,120 × 6/12)	(1,060)
Total	7,826

(W3) Administrative expenses

	$000
Administrative expenses	7,741
Depreciation Buildings (W4)	3,200
Dep'n P&M ($2,800 (W4) × 10%)	280
Irrecoverable debt	540
Total	11,761

(W4) Finance costs

	$000
Finance costs	0
Accrual for loan interest ($20,000 × 5%)	1,000
Total	1,000

(W5) Revaluation

	$000
Revalued amount	54,000
CV	40,000
Revaluation gain	14,000

(W6) PPE

	$000
Land and buildings cost	120,000
Revaluation	14,000
Accumulated depreciation	(22,500)
Depreciation charge (($120,000 – $40,000) × 4%)	(3,200)
Plant and equipment cost	32,000
Accumulated depreciation	(18,000)
Depreciation charge ($32,000 – $18,000) × 20%)	(2,800)
Total	119,500

(W7) Trade and other receivables

	$000
Trade and other receivables	20,280
Irrecoverable debt w/off	(540)
Advertising prepayment (W2)	1,060
Total	20,800

(W8) Retained earnings

	$000
Retained earnings	12,920
Profit per P/L	10,588
Dividends	(3,000)
Total	20,508

(W9) Trade and other payables

	$000
Trade and other payables	8,725
Accrual for loan interest (W4)	1,000
Total	9,725

Marking scheme	
	Marks
Statement of profit or loss & OCI	7.0
Statement of financial position	8.0
Total	**15.0**

3   CLERC

Key answer tips

Remember that, these questions will test your accounting knowledge. In this question, you need to deal with calculation and accounting for depreciation, and also accounting for irrecoverable receivables. You need to ensure that you have a good working knowledge of all relevant areas of the syllabus.

Statement of profit or loss and other comprehensive income for the year ended 31 December 20X9

	$	Marks
Revenue	178,833	0.5
Cost of sales (W1)	(146,920)	2.0
Gross profit	31,913	
Distribution costs	(7,009)	0.5
Administrative expenses (W2)	(14,820)	1.0
Profit from operations	10,084	
Investment income	100	0.5
Finance costs (W3)	(2,000)	1.0
Profit before taxation	8,184	
Income tax expense	(7,162)	0.5
Profit for the year	1,022	
Other comprehensive income for the year		
Gain on revaluation of land (W4)	40,000	1.0
Total comprehensive income for the year	41,022	7.0

Statement of financial position as at 31 December 20X9

	$	
Non-current assets		
Property, plant and equipment (W5)	267,592	2.0
Current assets		
Inventories (W1)	19,371	1.0
Trade and other receivables (W6)	7,032	0.5
Cash and cash equivalents	6,993	0.5
Total assets	300,988	

EQUITY AND LIABILITIES	$	
Equity		
Share capital	100,000	0.5
Share premium	20,000	0.5
Retained earnings (W7)	24,915	
Revaluation reserve ($50,000 + $40,000 (W4))	90,000	1.0
Non-current liabilities		
Bank loans	40,000	0.5
Current liabilities		
Trade and other payables (W8)	18,911	1.0
Tax payable	7,162	0.5
Total equity and liabilities	300,988	8.0

Workings

(W1) Cost of sales

	$
Opening inventories	17,331
Purchases	130,562
Less closing inventories	(19,371)
(19,871 – (4,000 – 3,500))	
Dep'n – building ($10,000 (W5) × 40%)	4,000
Dep'n – plant (W5)	14,398
Total	146,920

(W2) Administrative expenses

	$
Administrative expenses	7,100
Dep'n – building ($10,000 (W5) × 60%)	6,000
Irrecoverable debt w/off	1,720
Total	14,820

(W3) Finance costs

	$
Finance costs	0
Accrual for loan interest ($40,000 × 5%)	2,000
Total	2,000

(W4) Revaluation of land

	$
Revalued amount	150,000
CV	110,000
Revaluation gain	40,000

(W5) PPE

	$
Land and buildings cost	210,000
Revaluation	40,000
Accumulated depreciation	(30,000)
Dep'n charge (($210,000 – $110,000) × 10%)	(10,000)
Plant and machinery cost	88,000
Accumulated depreciation	(16,010)
Dep'n charge (($88,000 – $16,010) × 20%)	(14,398)
Total	267,592

(W6) Trade and other receivables

	$
Trade and other receivables	8,752
Irrecoverable debt w/off	(1,720)
Total	7,032

(W7) Retained earnings

	$
Retained earnings	23,893
Profit	1,022
Total	24,915

(W8) Trade and other payables

	$
Trade and other payables	13,882
Accruals ($3,029 + $2,000 (W3))	5,029
Total	18,911

Marking scheme	
	Marks
Statement of profit or loss	7.0
Statement of financial position	8.0
Total	**15.0**

4 CARBON

Statement of profit or loss for the year ended 31 December 20X5

	$	Marks
Revenue ($450,000 – $1,000 (W1))	449,000	1.0
Cost of sales (W2)	(210,000)	2.0
	_____	
Gross profit	239,000	
Administrative expenses (W3)	(162,500)	1.5
Distribution costs	(56,000)	0.5
	_____	
Operating profit	20,500	
Finance costs ($50,000 × 8% × 3/12)	(1,000)	1.0
	_____	
Profit before tax	19,500	
Income tax charge	(5,000)	1.0
	_____	_____
Profit after taxation	14,500	7.0
	_____	_____

Statement of financial position as at 31 December 20X5

	$	
Non- current assets		
Property, plant and equipment	96,000	1.5
($150,000 – $30,000 – $24,000 (W2))		
Current assets		
Inventories	27,000	0.5
Receivables (W4)	30,000	1.5
Cash and cash equivalents	5,000	0.5
	_____	
Total assets	158,000	
	_____	
Equity		
Ordinary share capital	10,000	0.5
Retained earnings ($25,500 + $14,500 (P/L)	40,000	0.5
Non-current liabilities		
8% Loan	50,000	0.5
Current liabilities		
Trade and other payables ($32,000 + $1,000 loan interest)	33,000	1.0
Tax payable	5,000	0.5
Provision	20,000	1.0
	_____	_____
Total equity and liabilities	158,000	8.0
	_____	_____

Workings

(W1) Sales return

A sales return has not been accounted for. The correcting entry is:

Dr Revenue $1,000

Cr Receivables $1,000 (W4)

(W2) Cost of sales

	$
Opening inventory	33,000
Purchases	180,000
Depreciation	24,000
(($150,000 – $30,000) × 20%)	
Closing inventory	(27,000)
	210,000

(W3) Administrative expenses

	$
Per trial balance	140,000
Irrecoverable debt (W4)	1,500
Increase in allowance for receivables (W4)	1,000
Provision – defective goods claim	20,000
	162,500

(W4) Receivables

	$
Per trial balance	36,000
Allowance per trial balance	(2,500)
Increase in allowance required (W3)	(1,000)
Irrecoverable debt (W3)	(1,500)
Sales return (W1)	(1,000)
	30,000

Marking scheme	
	Marks
Statement of profit or loss	7.0
Statement of financial position	8.0
Total	**15.0**

5   MARKUS

Statement of profit or loss for the year ended 30 April 20X3

	$	Marks
Revenue	230,000	0.5
Cost of sales (W1)	(94,550)	2.0
Gross profit	135,450	
Administrative expenses (W2)	(65,500)	1.5
Distribution costs (W3)	(31,550)	1.0
Operating profit	38,400	
Finance costs ($300 + $135 (W4))	(435)	1.0
Profit for the year	37,965	6.0

Statement of financial position as at 30 April 20X3

	$	Marks
Non- current assets		
Property, plant and equipment	39,950	1.5
($72,000 − $25,000 − $7,050 (W1))		
Current assets		
Inventories (W1)	16,250	1.0
Trade receivables (W5)	16,750	1.5
Prepayment	400	0.5
Total assets	73,350	
Capital account		
Balance at 1 May 20X2	30,000	0.5
Profit for the year	37,965	
Less: Cash drawings	(18,000)	0.5
Goods for own use	(5,000)	1.0
	44,965	
Non-current liabilities		
6% Loan	3,000	0.5
Current liabilities		
Trade payables	17,500	0.5
Accruals ($135 (W4) + $350 (W3))	485	1.0
Bank overdraft	7,400	0.5
	73,350	9.0

Workings

(W1) Cost of sales

	$
Opening inventory	18,750
Purchases for resale ($90,000 – $5,000 own use)	85,000
Depreciation	7,050
(($72,000 – $25,000) × 15%)	
Closing inventory ($17,500 – ($5,000 – $3,750))	(16,250)
	94,550

(W2) Administrative expenses

	$
Per trial balance	65,800
Irrecoverable debt (W5)	600
Reduction in allowance for receivables (W5)	(500)
Less: Insurance prepaid	(400)
	65,500

(W3) Distribution costs

	$
Per trial balance	31,200
Freight and delivery accrual	350
	31,550

(W4) Loan interest accrual

	$
$3,000 × 6% × 9/12	135

(W5) Trade receivables

	$
Per trial balance	20,000
Allowance per trial balance	(3,150)
Reduction in allowance required	500
Irrecoverable debt (W2)	(600)
	16,750

Marking scheme	
	Marks
Statement of profit or loss	6.0
Statement of financial position	9.0
Total	**15.0**

6 FIREWORK

Key answer tips

Ensure that you remember the proforma presentation of a statement of cash flows – it will help you to complete relevant extracts in an examination question.

Firework – Statement of cash flows for the year ended 31 March 20X1

	$000	$000	Marks
Cash flows from operating activities			
Profit before tax	31,000		
Adjustments for:			
Depreciation charge	15,000		0.5
Loss on sale of plant and equipment	2,000		0.5
Interest payable	750		0.5
Increase in inventories ($36,000 – $30,000)	(6,000)		1.0
Increase in trade receivables ($40,000 – $35,000)	(5,000)		1.0
Increase in trade payables ($36,500 – $30,000)	6,500		1.0
	———		
Cash generated from operations	44,250		
Interest paid	(750)		0.5
Income taxes paid (W3)	(9,500)	34,000	1.0
	———		
Cash flows from investing activities			
Cash purchase of property, plant and equipment (W1)	(40,000)		1.0
Disposal proceeds of plant and equipment (W2)	8,000	(32,000)	1.0
	———		
Cash flows from financing activities			
Repayment of bank loan (W4)	(10,000)		1.0
Proceeds of share issue ($5,000 + $5,000) (W5)	10,000		2.0
Dividend paid (W6)	(14,000)	(14,000)	2.0
	———	———	
Increase in cash and cash equivalents ($10,000 + $2,000)		(12,000)	1.0
Cash and cash equivalents b/fwd		10,000	0.5
		———	
Cash and cash equivalents c/fwd (overdraft)		(2,000)	0.5
		———	
			15.0

Workings

(W1) PPE additions in the year

	$000
PPE CV bal b/fwd	93,000
Less: CV of disposals ($8,000 + $2,000 loss)	(10,000)
Less: depreciation charge	**(15,000)**
Revaluation in year	2,000
Cash paid for PPE additions	**40,000**
PPE CV bal c/fwd	110,000

(W2) Loss on disposal of plant and equipment

	$000
PPE CV of disposals ($8,000 + $2,000)	10,000
Less: loss on disposal in cost of sales	**(2,000)**
Disposal proceeds received	8,000

(W3) Income tax paid

	$000
Income tax liability b/fwd	10,000
Income tax charge for the year per P/L	6,000
Cash paid in year	**(9,500)**
Income tax liability c/fwd	6,500

(W4) Bank loan – amount repaid

	$000
Bank loan b/fwd	17,000
Cash paid	**(10,000)**
Bank loan c/fwd	7,000

(W5) Issue of shares in the year

	Share capital	Share premium
	$000	$000
Balance b/fwd	15,000	3,000
Proceeds of share issue in year	**5,000**	**5,000**
Balance c/fwd	20,000	8,000

(W6) Dividend paid

	$000
Retained earnings b/fwd	85,000
Profit after tax for the year	25,000
Cash paid	**(14,000)**
Bank loan c/fwd	96,000

Marking scheme	
	Marks
Statement of cash flows (per answer)	15
Total	**15**

7 CRACKER

Key answer tips

Ensure that you understand which items are classified under each of the standard headings in a statement of cash flows. It will help you to complete relevant parts of a question efficiently. Begin with cash flows from operating activities, with the first item as 'profit before tax' from the statement of profit or loss.

Cracker – Statement of cash flows for the year ended 31 March 20X1

	$000	$000	*Marks*
Cash flows from operating activities			
Profit before tax	11,650		
Adjustments for:			
Depreciation charge	500		0.5
Profit on sale of plant and equipment	(300)		0.5
Investment income	(320)		0.5
Interest payable	2,150		0.5
Increase in inventories ($27,500 – $25,500)	(2,000)		1.0
Increase in trade receivables ($37,500 – $33,000)	(4,500)		1.0
Decrease in trade payables ($31,900 – $29,450)	(2,450)		1.0
	———		
Cash generated from operations	4,730		
Interest paid	(2,150)		0.5
Income taxes paid (W3)	(2,310)		1.0
		270	

Cash flows from investing activities

Investment income	320	0.5
Cash purchase of property, plant and equipment (W1)	(3,800)	1.0
Disposal proceeds of plant and equipment (W2)	1,100	1.0
	(2,380)	

Cash flows from financing activities

Proceeds of loan raised (W4)	3,500	1.0
Proceeds of share issue ($1,000 + $610)(W5)	1,610	2.0
	5,110	
Net increase in cash and cash equivalents ($4,250 – $1,250)	3,000	1.0
Cash and cash equivalents b/fwd	1,250	1.0
Cash and cash equivalents c/fwd	4,250	1.0
		15.0

Workings

(W1) PPE additions in the year

	$000
PPE CV bal b/fwd	70,500
Less: CV of disposals	(800)
Less: depreciation charge	**(500)**
Cash paid for PPE additions	**3,800**
PPE CV bal c/fwd	73,000

(W2) Gain on disposal of plant and equipment

	$000
PPE CV of disposals	800
Add: profit on disposal per P/L	**300**
Disposal proceeds received	**1,100**

(W3) Income tax paid

	$000
Income tax liability b/fwd	2,310
Income tax charge for the year per P/L	2,900
Cash paid in year	**(2,310)**
Income tax liability c/fwd	2,900

(W4) Loan finance – additional loan finance raised

	$000
10% debenture Loan liability b/fwd	20,000
Cash received – additional loan finance	**3,500**
10% debenture Loan liability c/fwd	23,500

(W5) Issue of shares in the year

	Share capital $000	Share premium $000
Balance b/fwd	10,000	Nil
Proceeds of share issue in year	**1,000**	**610**
Balance c/fwd	11,000	610

Marking scheme	Marks
Statement of cash flows (per answer)	15
Total	**15**

8   SPARKLER

Key answer tips

You can include items under the classification of investing activities and financing activities respectively in any order – there is not a defend sequential order for these items as long as they have been correctly classified.

Sparkler – Statement of cash flows for the year ended 30 September 20X9

	$000	$000	Marks
Cash flows from operating activities			
Profit before tax	18,000		
Adjustments for:			
Depreciation charge (W1)	12,500		0.5
Profit on sale of plant and equipment	(500)		0.5
Interest payable	2,700		0.5
Decrease in inventories ($36,000 – $30,750)	5,250		1.0
Decrease in trade receivables ($45,000 – $39,250)	5,750		1.0
Decrease in trade payables ($38,500 – $35,000)	(3,500)		1.0
Cash generated from operations	40,200		
Interest paid (W7)	(2,575)		1.0
Income taxes paid (W3)	(4,000)		1.0
		33,625	
Cash flows from investing activities			
Cash purchase of property, plant and equipment (W1)	(21,000)		1.0
Disposal proceeds of plant and equipment (W2)	2,000		1.0
		(19,000)	

Cash flows from financing activities

Proceeds of loan raised (W4)	5,000	1.0
Proceeds of share issue ($6,000 + $2,000)(W5)	8,000	2.0
Dividend paid (W6)	(20,125)	1.0
	(7,125)	
Net increase in cash and cash equivalents ($4,500 + $3,000)	7,500	1.0
Cash and cash equivalents b/fwd	(4,500)	0.5
Cash and cash equivalents c/fwd	3,000	0.5
		15.0

Workings

(W1) PPE additions in the year

	$000
PPE CV bal b/fwd	85,000
Less: CV of disposals	(1,500)
Revaluation in year	3,000
Less: depreciation charge	**(12,500)**
Cash paid for PPE additions	**21,000**
PPE CV bal c/fwd	95,000

(W2) Gain on disposal of plant and equipment

	$000
PPE CV of disposals	1,500
Add: profit on disposal per P/L	**500**
Disposal proceeds received	**2,000**

(W3) Income tax paid

	$000
Income tax liability b/fwd	4,000
Income tax charge for the year per P/L	3,500
Cash paid in year	**(4,000)**
Income tax liability c/fwd	3,500

(W4) Loan finance – additional loan finance raised

	$000
10% debenture Loan liability b/fwd	20,000
Cash received – additional loan finance	**5,000**
10% debenture Loan liability c/fwd	25,000

(W5) Issue of shares in the year

	Share capital	Share premium
	$000	$000
Balance b/fwd	24,000	8,000
Proceeds of share issue in year	**6,000**	**2,000**
Balance c/fwd	30,000	10,000

(W6) Dividend paid in the year

	$000
Retained earnings b/fwd	66,500
Profit after tax for the year	14,500
Dividend paid in the year	**(20,125)**
Retained earnings c/fwd	60,875

(W7) Interest paid in the year

	$000
Interest payable b/fwd	500
P&L charge for the year	2,700
Interest paid in the year	**(2,575)**
Interest payable c/fwd	625

Marking scheme	
	Marks
Statement of cash flows per answer	15
Total	**15**

9 OUTFLOW

Outflow – Statement of cash flows for the year ended 30 April 20X2

	$000	$000	Marks
Cash flows from operating activities			
Loss before tax	(4,300)		1.0
Adjustments for:			
Depreciation charge (W2)	11,000		0.5
Loss on scrapped assets (W1)	1,000		0.5
Interest payable	1,000		1.0
Decrease in inventories ($33,000 – $30,000)	3,000		1.0
Decrease in trade receivables ($52,000 – $48,750)	3,250		1.0
Decrease in trade payables ($27,500 – $26,300)	(1,200)		1.0
	————		
Cash generated from operations	13,750		
Interest paid	(1,000)		1.0
Income taxes paid (W3)	(5,000)		1.0
	————	7,750	
Cash flows from investing activities			
Cash purchase of property, plant and equipment (W2)	(20,000)		1.0
	————	(20,000)	
Cash flows from financing activities			
Proceeds of loan raised (W4)	7,500		1.0
Proceeds of share issue ($4,000 + $1,000)(W5)	5,000		2.0
Dividend paid (W6)	(1,000)		1.0
	————	11,500	
Net decrease in cash and cash equivalents		(750)	1.0
Cash and cash equivalents b/fwd		(3,250)	0.5
		————	
Cash and cash equivalents c/fwd		(4,000)	0.5
		————	————
			15.0

Workings

(W1) Loss on disposal of scrapped assets

	$000
Disposal proceeds received	Nil
PPE CV of scrapped items (W1)	1,000
	————
Loss on disposal	**1,000**
	————

(W2) PPE additions in the year

	Cost or valuation	Accumulated depreciation
	$000	$000
Carrying amount b/fwd	245,000	145,000
Additions in year (bal fig)	**20,000**	
Charge for the year		11,000
Disposals in year (CV of $1,000)	(7,000)	(6,000)
Revaluation in year	2,000	
Carrying amount bal c/fwd	260,000	150,000

(W3) Income tax paid

	$000
Income tax liability b/fwd	5,000
Income tax recoverable per P/L	(500)
Cash paid in year (bal fig)	**(5,000)**
Income tax recoverable (asset) c/fwd	(500)

(W4) Bank loan – additional loan finance raised

	$000
Bank loan liability b/fwd	8,000
Cash received – additional loan finance (bal fig)	**7,500**
Bank loan liability c/fwd	15,500

(W5) Issue of shares in the year

	Share capital	Share premium
	$000	$000
Balance b/fwd	40,000	4,000
Proceeds of share issue in year (bal fig)	**4,000**	**1,000**
Balance c/fwd	44,000	5,000

(W6) Dividend paid in the year

	$000
Retained earnings b/fwd	77,250
Loss after tax for the year	(3,800)
Dividend paid in the year (bal fig)	**(1,000)**
Retained earnings c/fwd	72,450

Marking scheme	
	Marks
Statement of cash flows (per answer)	15
Total	**15**

10 PATTY AND SELMA

(a)   **Gross profit margin:**

Patty: (423/987) = 42.9%   Selma: (232/567) = 40.9%

Operating profit margin:

Patty: (200/987) = 20.3%   Selma: (110/567) = 19.4%

Interest cover:

Patty: (200/50) = 4.0   Selma: (110/30) = 3.7

(b)   **Consolidated statement of profit or loss and other comprehensive income for year ended 31 December 20X1**

	$000
Revenue ($987 + $567 − $120)	1,434
Cost of sales ($564 + $335 −$120 + $5 (W1))	(784)
Gross profit	650
Administrative expenses ($223 + $122)	(345)
Operating profit	305
Finance costs ($50 + $30)	(80)
Profit before taxation	225
Income tax expense ($40 + $25)	(65)
Profit after tax for the year	160
Profit after tax attributable to:	
Owners of Patty (bal fig)	145
Non-controlling interest (W2)	15
	160

Workings

(W1) PURP

$120k/120 × 20 = $20k

The proportion of this profit remaining in inventory must be eliminated:

$20 × 25% = $5k

The double entry to adjust for this is:

Dr Cost of sales (P/L)	$5k
Cr Inventory (SFP)	$5k

Tutorial note

Ensure that you can identify whether sales have been made on a 'cost plus' basis or based upon sales margin as this will affect your calculation of the provision for unrealised profit.

(W2) Non-controlling interest share of profit after tax

	$000
NCI % of S's PAT (30% × $55k)	16.5
NCI % of PURP (30% × $5k (W1))	(1.5)
	———
	15.0
	———

Marking scheme	
	Marks
Part (a) 2 marks per ratio calculated correctly	6
Part (b) Consolidated statement of profit or loss and OCI per answer	9
	——
Total	**15**
	——

11 CUBE AND PRISM

(a) **Quick ratio**

Cube: ($110 + $8)/$48 = 2.5   Prism: ($99 + $51)/$50 = 3.0

Gearing ratio

Cube: ($200/($100 + $435 + $200) = 27.2% Prism: ($70/($50 + $209 + $70) = 21.3%

(b) **Consolidated statement of financial position as at 31 December 20X1**

		$
Assets		
Non-current assets		
Property, plant and equipment ($270,000 + $179,000 + $70,000 FV uplift)		519,000
Goodwill (W3)		115,000
Current assets		
Inventories ($95,000 + $50,000 – $3,000 PURP (W6))		142,000
Trade and other receivables ($110,000 + $99,000)		209,000
Cash and cash equivalents ($8,000 + $51,000)		59,000
Total assets		1,044,000
Equity and liabilities		
Equity		
Share capital		80,000
Revaluation surplus		20,000
Retained earnings (W5)		498,750
Non-controlling interest (W4)		77,250
Non-current liabilities		
Loans ($200,000 + $70,000)		270,000
Current liabilities		
Trade and other payables ($48,000 + $50,000)		98,000
Total equity and liabilities		1,044,000

Workings

(W1) Group structure

Cube

75%

Prism

(W2) Net assets of Prism

	$ Reporting date	$ Acquisition	$ Post –acq
Share capital	40,000	40,000	
Revaluation surplus	10,000	10,000	
Retained earnings	209,000	120,000	
FV uplift ($170,000 – $100,000)	70,000	70,000	
	329,000	240,000	89,000

Tutorial note

Remember that in the net assets working, the issued share capital and share premium account (if there is one) should be the same value at the date of acquisition and at the reporting date. If there is a revaluation surplus, then like retained earnings, this may be different between the date of acquisition and the reporting date.

(W3) Goodwill

	$
Consideration	300,000
Less net assets at acquisition (W2)	(240,000)
Add NCI at acquisition	55,000
	115,000

(W4) Non-controlling interest

	$
NCI at acquisition	55,000
NCI % of Prism post-acquisition retained earnings	22,250
(25% × $89,000 (W2))	
	77,250

(W5) Retained earnings

	$
100% of Cube	435,000
PURP	(3,000)
75% of Prism post-acquisition retained earnings	66,750
(75% × $89,000 (W2))	
	498,750

(W6) PURP

Profit = $30,000 × 30% = $9,000

Profit remaining in group inventory = $9,000 × 1/3 = $3,000

The correcting entry is:

Dr Retained earnings (W5)	$3,000
Cr Inventories	$3,000

12   BRYSON AND STOPPARD

(a)   **Current ratio:**

Bryson: $5,760/$2,640 = 2.2

Stoppard: $5,010/$1,410 = 3.6

(b)   **Consolidated statement of financial position at 31 March 20X1**

	$000
ASSETS	
Goodwill (W3)	3,990
Non-current assets ($11,280 + $3,670 + $1,000 (FV adj))	15,950
Current assets ($5,760 + $5,010 – $40 PURP (W6) – $250 (W6))	10,480
Total assets	30,420
EQUITY AND LIABILITIES	
Equity	
Share capital	9,200
Retained earnings (W5)	12,560
Non-controlling interest (W4)	2,240
Non-current liabilities ($1,440 + $1,180)	2,620
Current liabilities ($2,640 + $1,410 – $250 (W6))	3,800
Total equity and liabilities	30,420

Workings

(W1) Group structure

Bryson

│
│   75%
│

Stoppard

(W2) Net assets of Stoppard

	$000 Acquisition date	$000 Reporting date	$000 Post –acq
Share capital	4,800	4,800	
Retained earnings (W2a)	1,130	1,290	
FV adjustment	1,000	1,000	
	6,930	7,090	160

(W2a) Retained earnings at acquisition

	$000
Retained earnings at reporting date:	1,290
Less: profit after tax for the year	(640)
Retained earnings at 31 March 20X0	650
Add: profit for period to 31 Dec X0	
9/12 × 640	480
Retained earnings at 1 January 20X1	1,130

(W3) Goodwill

	$000
Consideration	8,720
FV of NCI at acquisition	2,200
Net assets at acquisition (W2)	(6,930)
Total	3,990

Tutorial note

Remember that the value for non-controlling interest at the date of acquisition used in (W3) to help calculate goodwill will also be used in (W4) as the starting point to calculate non-controlling interest at the reporting date.

(W4) Non-controlling interest

	$000
NCI at acquisition	2,200
NCI % of Stoppard's post acquisition retained earnings	
((25% × $160) (W2))	40
Total	2,240

(W5) Retained earnings

	$000
Bryson	12,480
PURP (W6)	(40)
Bryson's % of Stoppard's post acquisition retained earnings (75% × $160 (W2))	120
Total	12,560

(W6) PURP & inter-company balance

Profit on intra-company sale = $50,000

Amount still in group inventory = $50,000 × 80% = $40,000.

The correcting entry is:

Dr Retained earnings (W5) $40,000

Cr Inventory $40,000

Inter-company receivable and payable to cancel at reporting date:

$500,000 × 50% = $250,000.

Reduce both group receivables and payables by $250,000.

13   PEN AND STAPLE

(a)   Gross profit margin:

Pen: (725/1,500) = 48.3%   Staple: (330/700) = 47.1%

Operating profit margin:

Pen: (408/1,500) = 27.2%   Staple: (195/700) = 27.8%

Interest cover:

Pen: (408/60) = 6.8 times   Staple: (195/35) = 5.6 times

(b)   Consolidated statement of profit or loss for year ended 31 December 20X4

	$000
Revenue ($1,500 + $700 – $150 inter-co)	2,050
Cost of sales ($775 + $370 –$150 inter-co + $5 (W1))	(1,000)
	___
Gross profit	1,050
Administrative expenses ($317 + $135)	(452)
	___
Operating profit	598
Finance costs ($60 + $35)	(95)
	___
Profit before taxation	503
Income tax expense ($96 + $45)	(141)
	___
Profit after tax	362
	___
Profit attributable to:	
Owners of Pen (bal fig)	329
Non-controlling interest (W2)	33
	___
	362
	___

Workings

(W1) PURP

$150,000 /120 × 20 = $25,000

The proportion of this profit remaining in inventory must be eliminated:

$25,000 × 1/5 = $5,000

The double entry to adjust for this is:

Dr Cost of sales (P/L) $5,000, Cr Inventory (SFP) $5,000

(W2) Non-controlling interest

	$000
NCI % of S's PAT (30% × $115,000)	34.5
NCI % of PURP (30% × $5,000 (W1))	(1.5)
	——
	33

14   PEBBLE AND STONE

(a)   Consolidated statement of financial position at 31 December 20X6

	$
Assets	
Non-current assets	
Property, plant & equip't ($300,000 + $225,000 + $30,000 FV adj)	555,000
Goodwill (W3)	230,000
Current assets	
Inventories ($80,000 + $75,000 – $5,000 PURP (W6))	150,000
Trade and other receivables ($60,000 + $140,000)	200,000
Cash and cash equivalents ($10,000 + $25,000)	35,000
	————
Total assets	1,170,000
	————
Equity and liabilities	
Equity	
Share capital	80,000
Share premium	20,000
Retained earnings (W5)	370,000
Non-controlling interest (W4)	100,000
	————
Total equity of the group	570,000
Non-current liabilities	
Loans ($300,000 + $85,000)	385,000
Current liabilities	
Trade and other payables ($155,000 + $60,000)	215,000
	————
Total equity and liabilities	1,170,000
	————

(b) Characteristics relevant to an investment in an associate are:

Significant influence over the activities of Archive.

Ownership of between 20% and 50% of the ordinary shares of archive.

Do not account for goodwill or recognise non-controlling interest as these are characteristics of accounting for a subsidiary where there is a relationship of control.

Workings

(W1) Group structure

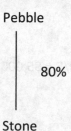

Pebble

80%

Stone

(W2) Net assets of Stone

	$ Reporting date	$ Acquisition	$ Post –acq
Share capital	60,000	60,000	
Share premium	10,000	10,000	
Retained earnings	250,000	150,000	
FV uplift ($180,000 – $150,000)	30,000	30,000	
	350,000	250,000	100,000

(W3) Goodwill

	$
Consideration	400,000
Add: NCI at acquisition	80,000
Less net assets at acquisition (W2)	(250,000)
	230,000

(W4) Non-controlling interest

	$
NCI at acquisition	80,000
NCI % of Stone post-acquisition retained earnings (20% × $100,000 (W2))	20,000
	100,000

(W5) Retained earnings

	$
100% of Pebble	295,000
PURP (W6)	(5,000)
80% of Stone post-acquisition retained earnings	80,000
(80% × $100,000 (W2))	
	370,000

(W6) PURP

Profit = $50,000 × 25% = $12,500

Profit remaining in group inventory = $12,500 × 2/5 = $5,000

The correcting entry is:

Dr Retained earnings (W5)	$5,000
Cr Inventories (SOFP)	$5,000

15   HELSINKI AND STOCKHOLM

(a)   Goodwill on acquisition of Stockholm

		$000
Fair value of consideration paid		25,000
FV of NCI at acquisition		7,000
Less: net assets of S at acquisition:		
Issued equity capital	4,000	
Retained earnings at acquisition	20,000	
		(24,000)
Goodwill on acquisition		8,000

(b)

Tutorial note

When dealing with a consolidated statement of profit or loss, always look to see whether the acquisition of the subsidiary was a mid-year acquisition during the year you are dealing with. If it was, remember to pro-rata each item of the subsidiary's income and expense so that your account only for the post-acquisition results in the group accounts.

Consolidated statement of profit or loss for the year ended 31 December 20X6

	$000
Revenue ($200,000 + (6/12 × $100,000) − $12,500 inter-co))	237,500
Cost of sales ($110,000 + (6/12 × $50,000) − $12,500 inter-co + $1,000 PURP (W1))	(123,500)
Gross profit	114,000
Distribution costs ($20,000 + (6/12 × $10,000))	(25,000)
Administrative expenses ($40,000 + (6/12 × $20,000))	(50,000)
Profit before tax	39,000
Income tax expense ($10,500 + (6/12 × $6,000))	(13,500)
Profit after tax	25,500
Profit attributable to:	
Owners of Pen (bal fig)	24,000
Non-controlling interest (W2)	1,500
	25,500

Workings

(W1) PURP and inter-company sales

Original cost plus 25% mark-up = $10m × 1.25 = $12,5m

This is the value of the inter-company sale and purchase which must be removed from both sales revenue and cost of sales.

Total profit on this sale = $12,5m − $10.0m = $2.5m

The proportion of this profit remaining in inventory must be eliminated:

40% × $2.5m = $1.0m

The double entry to adjust for this is:

Dr Cost of sales (P/L) $1m

Cr Inventory (SFP) $1m

(W2) Non-controlling interest

	$000
NCI % of (S's PAT − inter-co profit made by sub)	
(25% × ($7,000 − 1,000))	1,500

Marking scheme		
		Marks
(a)	Goodwill on acquisition	4
(b)	Group statement or profit or loss	11
	Total	**15**

16 PEDANTIC

(a) **Consolidated statement of profit or loss for the year ended 30 September 20X8**

	$000
Revenue (85,000 + 42,000 − 6,000 intra-group sales)	121,000
Cost of sales (w (i))	(89,250)
Gross profit	31,750
Distribution costs (4,000 + 3,500)	(7,500)
Administrative expenses (8,000 + 1,000)	(9,000)
Finance costs (600 + 400)	(1,000)
Profit before tax	14,250
Income tax expense (2,162 + 1,000)	(3,162)
Profit for the year	11,088
Attributable to:	
Equity holders of the parent	9,548
Non-controlling interest	
((4,100 − 250 PURP) × 40%)	1,540
	11,088

(b) **Consolidated statement of financial position as at 30 September 20X8**

	$000
Assets	
Non-current assets	
Property, plant and equipment	
(40,600 + 12,600)	53,200
Goodwill (W3)	9,100
	62,300
Current assets (W8)	21,350
Total assets	83,650
Equity and liabilities	
Equity attributable to owners of the parent	
Equity shares of $1 each (10, 000 + 1,600 (W3))	11,600
Share premium (W3)	8,000
Retained earnings (W5)	37,710
	57,310
Non-controlling interest (W4)	7,440
Total equity	64,750
Non-current liabilities	
10% loan notes (3,000 + 4,000)	7,000
Current liabilities (8,200 + 4,700 − 1,000 intra-group balance)	11,900
Total equity and liabilities	83,650

Workings (figures in brackets in $000)

(W1) Group structure

Pedantic

60%

Sophistic

Investment acquired on the first day of the accounting period – 1 October 20X7. Therefore Pedantic has exercised control over Sophistic for the full year.

(W2) Net assets of Sophistic

	At acquisition	At reporting date
	$000	$000
Share capital	4,000	4,000
Retained earnings	2,400	6,500
PURP on inventory (W6)		(250)
	6,400	10,250

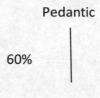

Tutorial note

As the parent gained control of the subsidiary on the first day of the accounting period, the profit after tax of the subsidiary must all be post-acquisition. Any retained earnings prior to that date must have been earned up to the date of acquisition.

	$000
Subsidiary retained earnings at reporting date	*6,500*
Less: profit after tax for the year (from P/L)	*4,100*
Retained earnings up to date of acquisition	*2,400*

(W3) Goodwill

	$000
Parent holding (investment) at fair value:	
Share exchange ((4,000 × 60%) × 2/3 × $6)	9,600
NCI value at acquisition (given)	5,900
	15,500
Less:	
Fair value of net assets at acquisition (W2)	(6,400)
	9,100

Tutorial note

The share consideration given on the acquisition of Sophistic has not been recorded. Therefore share capital should be increased by ((4,000 x 60%) × 2/3 × $1) $1,600 and share premium should be increased by ((4,000 × 60%) × 2/3 × $5) $8,000.

(W4) Non-controlling interest

	$000
NCI value at acquisition	5,900
NCI share of post-acquisition reserves	1,540
((10,250 – 6,400) (W2) × 40%)	
	7,440

(W5) Consolidated retained earnings

	$000
Pedantic	35,400
Sophistic ((10,250 – 6,400) × 60%)	2,310
	37,710

(W6) Provision for unrealised profit on inventory

The unrealised profit (PURP) in inventory is calculated as ($6 million/1.2 × 20% = $1 million. Unrealised profit = $1 million × 25% = $250,000.

(W7) Cost of sales

	$000
Pedantic	63,000
Sophistic	32,000
Intra-group sales	(6,000)
PURP in inventory (W6)	250
	89,250

(W8) Current assets

	$000
Pedantic	16,000
Sophistic	6,600
PURP in inventory (W6)	(250)
Intra-group balance	(1,000)
	21,350

Marking scheme		
		Marks
(a)	Statement of profit or loss	6
(b)	Statement of financial position	9
	Total	**15**

Section 5

SPECIMEN EXAM QUESTIONS

SECTION A

ALL 35 questions are compulsory and MUST be attempted

Please use the space provided on the inside cover of the Candidate Answer Booklet to indicate your chosen answer to each multiple choice question.

Each question is worth 2 marks.

1   Which of the following calculates a sole trader's net profit for a period?

    A   Closing net assets + drawings – capital introduced – opening net assets

    B   Closing net assets – drawings + capital introduced – opening net assets

    C   Closing net assets – drawings – capital introduced – opening net assets

    D   Closing net assets + drawings + capital introduced – opening net assets

2   Which of the following explains the imprest system of operating petty cash?

    A   Weekly expenditure cannot exceed a set amount

    B   The exact amount of expenditure is reimbursed at intervals to maintain a fixed float

    C   All expenditure out of the petty cash must be properly authorised

    D   Regular equal amounts of cash are transferred into petty cash at intervals

3   Which of the following statements are TRUE of limited liability companies?

    (1)   The company's exposure to debts and liability is limited.

    (2)   Financial statements must be produced.

    (3)   A company continues to exist regardless of the identity of its owners.

    A   (1) and (2) only

    B   (1) and (3) only

    C   (2) and (3) only

    D   (1), (2) and (3)

4   Annie is a sole trader who does not keep full accounting records. The following details relate to her transactions with credit customers and suppliers for the year ended 30 June 20X6:

	$
Trade receivables, 1 July 20X5	130,000
Trade payables, 1 July 20X5	60,000
Cash received from customers	687,800
Cash paid to suppliers	302,800
Discounts received	2,960
Contra between payables and receivables ledgers	2,000
Trade receivables, 30 June 20X6	181,000
Trade payables, 30 June 20X6	84,000

What figure should appear for purchases in Annie's statement of profit or loss for the year ended 30 June 20X6?

A $325,840

B $330,200

C $331,760

D $327,760

5   **Which TWO of the following errors would cause the total of the debit column and the total of the credit column of a trial balance not to agree?**

(1)   A transposition error was made when entering a sales invoice into the sales day book.

(2)   A cheque received from a customer was credited to cash and correctly recognised in receivables.

(3)   A purchase of non-current assets was omitted from the accounting records.

(4)   Rent received was included in the trial balance as a debit balance.

A   (1) and (2)

B   (1) and (3)

C   (2) and (3)

D   (2) and (4)

6   At 31 December 20X5 the following require inclusion in a company's financial statements:

(1)   On 1 January 20X5 the company made a loan of $12,000 to an employee, repayable on 1 January 20X6, charging interest at 2% per year. On the due date the employee repaid the loan and paid the whole of the interest due on the loan to that date.

(2)   The company paid an annual insurance premium of $9,000 in 20X5, covering the year ending 31 August 20X6.

(3)   In January 20X6 the company received rent from a tenant of $4,000 covering the six months to 31 December 20X5.

For these items, what total figures should be included in the company's statement of financial position as at 31 December 20X5?

A   Current assets $10,000   Current liabilities $12,240

B   Current assets $22,240   Current liabilities $nil

C   Current assets $10,240   Current liabilities $nil

D   Current assets $16,240   Current liabilities $6,000

7   A company's statement of profit or loss for the year ended 31 December 20X5 showed a net profit of $83,600. It was later found that $18,000 paid for the purchase of a motor van had been debited to the motor expenses account. It is the company's policy to depreciate motor vans at 25% per year on the straight line basis, with a full year's charge in the year of acquisition.

What would the net profit be after adjusting for this error?

A $106,100

B $70,100

C $97,100

D $101,600

8   Xena has the following working capital ratios:

	20X9	20X8
Current ratio	1·2:1	1·5:1
Receivables days	75 days	50 days
Payables days	30 days	45 days
Inventory turnover	42 days	35 days

Which of the following statements is correct?

A   Xena's liquidity and working capital has improved in 20X9

B   Xena is receiving cash from customers more quickly in 20X9 than in 20X8

C   Xena is suffering from a worsening liquidity position in 20X9

D   Xena is taking longer to pay suppliers in 20X9 than in 20X8

9 **Which of the following statements is/are correct?**

(1) A statement of cash flows prepared using the direct method produces a different figure to net cash from operating activities from that produced if the indirect method is used.

(2) Rights issues of shares do not feature in a statement of cash flows.

(3) A surplus on revaluation of a non-current asset will not appear as an item in a statement of cash flows.

(4) A profit on the sale of a non-current asset will appear as an item under cash flows from investing activities in the statement of cash flows.

A (1) and (3) only

B (3) and (4) only

C (2) and (4) only

D (3) only

10 A company receives rent from a large number of properties. The total received in the year ended 30 April 20X6 was $481,200.

The following were the amounts of rent in advance and in arrears at 30 April 20X5 and 20X6:

	30 April 20X5	30 April 20X6
	$	$
Rent received in advance	28,700	31,200
Rent in arrears (all subsequently received)	21,200	18,400

What amount of rental income should appear in the company's statement of profit or loss for the year ended 30 April 20X6?

A $486,500

B $460,900

C $501,500

D $475,900

11 **Which of the following statements is true?**

A The interpretation of an entity's financial statements using ratios is only useful for potential investors.

B Ratios based on historical data can predict the future performance of an entity.

C The analysis of financial statements using ratios provides useful information when compared with previous performance or industry averages.

D An entity's management will not assess an entity's performance using financial ratios.

12 Which of the following are differences between sole traders and limited liability companies?

(1) A sole trader's financial statements are private and never made available to third parties; a company's financial statements are sent to shareholders and may be publicly filed.

(2) Only companies have share capital.

(3) A sole trader is fully and personally liable for any losses that the business might make.

(4) Drawings would only appear in the financial statements of a sole trader.

A (1) and (4) only

B (2), (3) and (4)

C (2) and (3) only

D (1), (3) and (4)

13 A company's motor vehicles cost account at 30 June 20X6 is as follows:

Motor vehicles – cost

	$		$
Balance b/f	35,800	Disposal	12,000
Additions	12,950	Balance c/f	36,750
	———		———
	48,750		48,750
	———		———

What opening balance should be included in the following period's trial balance for Motor vehicles – cost at 1 July 20X6?

A $36,750 Dr

B $48,750 Dr

C $36,750 Cr

D $48,750 Cr

14 Which TWO of the following items must be disclosed in the note to the financial statements for intangible assets?

(1) The useful lives of intangible assets capitalised in the financial statements.

(2) A description of the development projects that have been undertaken during the period.

(3) A list of all intangible assets purchased or developed in the period.

(4) Impairment losses written off intangible assets during the period.

A (1) and (4)

B (2) and (3)

C (3) and (4)

D (1) and (2)

15   **Which of the following statements are correct?**

(1)   Capitalised development expenditure must be amortised over a period not exceeding five years.

(2)   Capitalised development costs are shown in the statement of financial position under the heading of non-current assets.

(3)   If certain criteria are met, research expenditure must be recognised as an intangible asset.

A   (2) only

B   (2) and (3)

C   (1) only

D   (1) and (3)

16   The following transactions relate to Rashid's electricity expense ledger account for the year ended 30 June 20X9

	$
Prepayment brought forward	550
Cash paid	5,400
Accrual carried forward	650

What amount should be charged to the statement of profit or loss in the year ended 30 June 20X9 for electricity?

A $6,600

B $5,400

C $5,500

D $5,300

17   At 30 June 20X5 a company's allowance for receivables was $39,000. At 30 June 20X6 trade receivables totalled $517,000. It was decided to write off debts totalling $37,000 and, based upon a review of amounts outstanding, it was decided to adjust the allowance for receivables to the equivalent of 5% of the trade receivables.

What figure should appear in the statement of profit or loss for the year ended 30 June 20X6 for receivables expense?

A $61,000

B $52,000

C $22,000

D $37,000

18   The total of the list of balances in Valley's payables ledger was $438,900 at 30 June 20X6. This balance did not agree with Valley's payables ledger control account balance. The following errors were discovered:

(1)   A contra entry of $980 was recorded in the payables ledger control account, but not in the payables ledger.

(2)   The total of the purchase returns day book was undercast by $1,000.

(3)   An invoice for $4,344 was posted to the supplier's account as $4,434.

What amount should Valley report in its statement of financial position for accounts payable at 30 June 20X6?

A $436,830

B $438,010

C $439,790

D $437,830

19   **According to IAS 2 Inventories, which TWO of the following costs should be included in valuing the inventories of a manufacturing company?**

(1)   Carriage inwards

(2)   Carriage outwards

(3)   Depreciation of factory plant

(4)   General administrative overheads

A   (1) and (4)

B   (1) and (3)

C   (3) and (4)

D   (2) and (3)

20   Prisha has not kept accurate accounting records during the financial year. She had opening inventory of $6,700 and purchased goods costing $84,000 during the year. At the year-end she had $5,400 left in inventory. All sales are made at a mark-up on cost of 20%.

What is Prisha's gross profit for the year?

A $13,750

B $17,060

C $16,540

D $20,675

21 At 31 December 20X4 a company's capital structure was as follows:

	$
Ordinary share capital (500,000 shares of 25c each)	125,000
Share premium account	100,000

In the year ended 31 December 20X5 the company made a rights issue of 1 share for every 2 held at $1 per share and this was taken up in full. Later in the year the company made a bonus issue of 1 share for every 5 held, using the share premium account for the purpose.

What was the company's capital structure at 31 December 20X5?

	Ordinary share capital	Share premium account
A	$450,000	$25,000
B	$225,000	$250,000
C	$225,000	$325,000
D	$212,500	$262,500

22 Which of the following should appear in a company's statement of changes in equity?

(1)   Total comprehensive income for the year.

(2)   Amortisation of capitalised development costs.

(3)   Surplus on revaluation of non-current assets.

A   (1), (2) and (3)

B   (2) and (3) only

C   (1) and (3) only

D   (1) and (2) only

23 The plant and machinery account (at cost) of a business for the year ended 31 December 20X5 was as follows:

Plant and machinery – cost

20X5	$	20X5	$
1 Jan Balance b/f	240,000	31 Mar Transfer to disposal account	60,000
30 Jun Cash purchase of plant	160,000	31 Dec Balance c/f	340,000
	400,000		400,000

The company's policy is to charge depreciation at 20% per year on the straight line basis, with proportionate depreciation in the years of purchase and disposal.

What should be the depreciation charge for the year ended 31 December 20X5?

A $68,000

B $64,000

C $61,000

D $55,000

24 The following extracts are from Hassan's financial statements:

	$
Profit before interest and tax	10,200
Interest	(1,600)
Tax	(3,300)
Profit after tax	5,300

	$
Share capital	20,000
Reserves	15,600
	35,600
Loan liability	6,900
	42,500

What is Hassan's return on capital employed?

A 15%

B 29%

C 24%

D 12%

25 **Which of the following statements about sales tax is/are true?**

(1) Sales tax is an expense to the ultimate consumer of the goods purchased.

(2) Sales tax is recorded as income in the accounts of the entity selling the goods.

A (1) only

B (2) only

C Both (1) and (2)

D Neither (1) nor (2)

26 Q's trial balance failed to agree and a suspense account was opened for the difference. Q does not keep receivables and payables control accounts. The following errors were found in Q's accounting records:

(1) In recording an issue of shares at par, cash received of $333,000 was credited to the ordinary share capital account as $330,000.

(2) Cash of $2,800 paid for plant repairs was correctly accounted for in the cash book but was credited to the plant asset account.

(3) The petty cash book balance of $500 had been omitted from the trial balance.

(4) A cheque for $78,400 paid for the purchase of a motor car was debited to the motor vehicles account as $87,400.

Which of the errors will require an entry to the suspense account to correct them?

A   (1), (2) and (4) only

B   (1), (2), (3) and (4)

C   (1) and (4) only

D   (2) and (3) only

27 Prior to the financial year end of 31 July 20X9, Cannon Co has received a claim of $100,000 from a supplier for providing poor quality goods which have damaged the supplier's plant and equipment. Cannon Co's lawyers have stated that there is a 20% chance that Cannon will successfully defend the claim.

Which of the following is the correct accounting treatment for the claim in the financial statements for the year ended 31 July 20X9?

A   Cannon should neither provide for nor disclose the claim

B   Cannon should disclose a contingent liability of $100,000

C   Cannon should provide for the expected cost of the claim of $100,000

D   Cannon should provide for an expected cost of $20,000

28 Amy is a sole trader and had assets of $569,400 and liabilities of $412,840 on 1 January 20X8. During the year ended 31 December 20X8 she paid $65,000 capital into the business and she paid herself wages of $800 per month.

At 31 December 20X8, Amy had assets of $614,130 and liabilities of $369,770.

What is Amy's profit for the year ended 31 December 20X8?

A $32,400

B $23,600

C $22,800

D $87,800

29 Gareth, a sales tax registered trader purchased a computer for use in his business. The invoice for the computer showed the following costs related to the purchase:

	$
Computer	890
Additional memory	95
Delivery	10
Installation	20
Maintenance (1 year)	25
	1,040
Sales tax (17.5%)	182
	———
Total	1,222

How much should Gareth capitalise as a non-current asset in relation to the purchase?

A $1,193

B $1,040

C $1,222

D $1,015

30 The following bank reconciliation statement has been prepared by a trainee accountant:

	$
Overdraft per bank statement	3,860
Less: unpresented cheques	9,160
	———
	5,300
Add: outstanding lodgements	16,690
	———
Cash at bank	21,990
	———

What should be the correct balance per the cash book?

A $21,990 balance at bank as stated

B $3,670 balance at bank

C $11,390 balance at bank

D $3,670 overdrawn

31 The IASB's Conceptual Framework for Financial Reporting (the Framework) identifies characteristics which make financial information faithfully represent what it purports to represent.

Which of the following are examples of these characteristics?

(1) Accruals

(2) Completeness

(3) Going concern

(4) Neutrality

A (1) and (2)

B (2) and (4)

C (2) and (3)

D (1) and (4)

32 The following control account has been prepared by a trainee accountant:

Receivables ledger control account

	$		$
Opening balance	308,600	Cash	148,600
Credit sales	154,200	Interest charges on overdue debts	2,400
Cash sales	88,100	Irrecoverable debts	4,900
Contras	4,600	Allowance for receivables	2,800
		Closing balance	396,800
	555,500		555,500

What should the closing balance be when all the errors made in preparing the receivables ledger control account have been corrected?

A $395,200

B $304,300

C $309,500

D $307,100

33 **Which of the following material events after the reporting date and before the financial statements are approved are adjusting events?**

(1)   A valuation of property providing evidence of impairment in value at the reporting date.

(2)   Sale of inventory held at the reporting date for less than cost.

(3)   Discovery of fraud or error affecting the financial statements.

(4)   The insolvency of a customer with a debt owing at the reporting date which is still outstanding.

A   (1), (2) and (4) only

B   (1), (2), (3) and (4)

C   (1) and (4) only

D   (2) and (3) only

34 A company values its inventory using the FIFO method. At 1 May 20X5 the company had 700 engines in inventory, valued at $190 each. During the year ended 30 April 20X6 the following transactions took place:

20X5

1 July   Purchased 500 engines at $220 each

1 November   Sold 400 engines for $160,000

20X6

1 February   Purchased 300 engines at $230 each

15 April   Sold 250 engines for $125,000

What is the value of the company's closing inventory of engines at 30 April 20X6?

A $188,500

B $195,500

C $166,000

D $106,000

35 Bumbly Co extracted the trial balance for the year ended 31 December 20X7. The total of the debits exceeded the credits by $300.

Which of the following could explain the imbalance?

A   Sales of $300 were omitted from the sales day book

B   Returns inward of $150 were extracted to the debit column of the trial balance

C   Discounts received of $150 were extracted to the debit column of the trial balance

D   The bank ledger account did not agree with the bank statement by a debit of $300

(Total 70 marks)

SECTION B

BOTH questions are compulsory and MUST be attempted

Please write your answer within the answer booklet in accordance with the detailed instructions provided within each of the questions in this section of the exam paper.

1   Keswick Co acquired 80% of the share capital of Derwent Co on 1 June 20X5. The summarised draft statements of profit or loss for Keswick Co and Derwent Co for the year ended 31 May 20X6 are shown below:

	Keswick Co	Derwent Co
	$000	$000
Revenue	8,400	3,200
Cost of sales	(4,600)	(1,700)
Gross profit	3,800	1,500
Operating expenses	(2,200)	(960)
Profit before tax	1,600	540
Tax	(600)	(140)
Profit for the year	1,000	400

During the year Keswick Co sold goods costing $1,000,000 to Derwent Co for $1,500,000. At 31 May 20X6, 30% of these goods remained in Derwent Co's inventory.

Required:

(a)   **Prepare the Keswick group consolidated statement of profit or loss for the year ended 31 May 20X6.**

   Note: The statement should stop once the consolidated profit for the year has been determined. The amounts attributable to the non-controlling interest and equity owners of Keswick are not required. Show all workings as credit will be given to these as appropriate.   **(7 marks)**

(b)   **Which of the following formulas describes the amount to be entered in the consolidated statement of profit or loss 'Profit attributable to: Equity owners of Keswick Co?**

   A   Group profit after tax – non-controlling interest

   B   Group profit after tax + non-controlling interest

   C   Keswick Co's profit after tax

   D   Group profit after tax   **(2 marks)**

(c)   **What amount should be shown in the consolidated statement of profit or loss for the non-controlling interest?**   **(2 marks)**

(d) The following table shows factors to be considered when determining whether a parent–subsidiary relationship exists.

Factor	Description
A	Significant influence
B	Control
C	Non-controlling interest
D	Greater than 50% of the equity shares being held by an investor
E	100% of the equity shares being held by an investor
F	Greater than 50% of the preference shares being held by an investor
G	50% of all shares and all debt being held by an investor
H	Greater than 50% of preference shares and debt being held by an investor

Which of the above factors A to H illustrate the existence of a parent–subsidiary relationship? (4 marks)

(Total 15 marks)

2 Malright, a limited liability company, has an accounting year end of 31 October. The accountant is preparing the financial statements as at 31 October 20X7 and requires your assistance. The following trial balance has been extracted from the general ledger.

	Dr	Cr
	$000	$000
Buildings at cost	740	
Buildings accumulated depreciation 1 November 20X6		60
Plant at cost	220	
Plant accumulated depreciation at 1 November 20X6		110
Bank balance		70
Revenue		1,800
Net purchases	1,140	
Inventory at 1 November 20X6	160	
Cash	20	
Trade payables		250
Trade receivables	320	
Administrative expenses	325	
Allowance for receivables at 1 November 20X6		10
Retained earnings at 1 November 20X6		130
Equity shares, $1		415
Share premium account		80
	2,925	2,925

The following additional information is also available:

(i) The allowance for receivables is to be increased to 5% of trade receivables. The allowance for receivables is treated as an administrative expense.

(ii) Plant is depreciated at 20% per annum using the reducing balance method and buildings are depreciated at 5% per annum on their original cost. Depreciation is treated as a cost of sales expense.

(iii) Closing inventory has been counted and is valued at $75,000.

(iv) An invoice of $15,000 for energy costs relating to the quarter ended 30 November 20X7 was received on 2 December 20X7. Energy costs are included in administrative expenses.

Required:

Prepare the statement of profit or loss and the statement of financial position of Malright Co as at 31 October 20X7. **(Total: 15 marks)**

Section 6

ANSWERS TO SPECIMEN EXAM QUESTIONS

SECTION A

1   A

2   B

3   C

4   C

Payables	$
Balance b/f	60,000
Cash paid to suppliers	(302,800)
Discounts received	(2,960)
Contra	(2,000)
Balance c/f	(84,000)
	———
Purchases	331,760
	———

5   D

6   B

Current assets	$
Loan asset	12,000
Interest (12,000 × 12%)	240
Prepayment (8/12 × 9,000)	6,000
Accrued rent	4,000
	———
	22,240
	———

7   C

	$
Profit	83,600
Purchase of van	18,000
Depreciation (25% × 18,000)	(4,500)
	97,100

8   C

9   D

10   D

	$
Balance b/f (advance)	28,700
Balance b/f (arrears)	(21,200)
Cash received	481,200
Balance c/f (advance)	(31,200)
Balance c/f (arrears)	18,400
	475,900

11   C

12   B

13   A

14   A

15   A

16   A

	$
Balance b/f	550
Expense incurred (cash)	5,400
Accrual c/f	650
	6,600

17 C

	$	$
Debts written off		37,000
Movement in allowance	24,000	
(517 – 37) × 5%		
Less: opening allowance	39,000	
		(15,000)
Receivables expense		22,000

18 D

	$
Balance per ledger	438,900
Less: contra	(980)
Posting error	(90)
Corrected balance	437,830

19 B

20 B

(6,700 + 84,000 – 5,400) × 20% = $17,060

21 B

	Share capital	Share premium
	$	$
Balance /f	125,000	100,000
Rights issue	62,500	187,500
Bonus issue	37,500	(37,500)
Balance c/f	225,000	250,000

22 C

23 D

Depreciation	$	
Jan – Mar	12,000	(240,000 × 20% × 3/12
Apr – Jun	9,000	(240,000 – 60,000) × 20% × 3/12
Jul – Dec	34,000	(180,000 + 160,000) × 20% × 6/12
	55,000	

24 C

10,200/42,500

25 A

26 B

27 C

28 A

	$	
Opening assets	569,400	
Opening liabilities	(412,840)	
Capital introduced	65,000	
Drawings (12 × $800)	(9,600)	
	211,960	
Profit (bal fig)	32,400	
Closing net assets	244,360	(614,130 – 369,770)

29 D

1,040 – 25 = $1,015

30 B

	$
Overdraft per bank statement	(3,860)
Less: unpresented cheques	(9,160)
Add: outstanding lodgements	16,690
Cash at bank	3,670

31   B

32   D

Receivables ledger control account

	$		$
Opening balance	308,600	Cash	148,600
Credit sales	154,200	Contras	4,600
Interest charged on overdue accounts	2,400	Irrecoverable debts	4,900
		Closing balance	307,100
	_____		_____
	465,200		465,200
	_____		_____

33   B

34   A

Closing inventory	$
50 × $190	9,500
500 × $220	110,000
300 × $230	69,000
	_____
	188,500
	_____

35   C

SECTION B

1 KESWICK

(a) Consolidated statement of profit or loss for the year ended 31 May 20X6

	$
Revenue (W1)	10,100
Cost of sales (W1)	(4,950)
Gross profit	5,150
Operating expenses (W1)	(3,160)
Profit before tax	1,990
Tax (W1)	(740)
Profit for the year	1,250

(b) A

(c) Non-controlling interest = $80,000 ($400,000 (W1) × 20%)

(d) The following factors illustrate the existence of a parent-subsidiary relationship:

B, C, D and E

(W1)

	Keswick Co	Derwent Co	Adjustments	Consolidated
	$000	$000	$000	$000
Revenue	8,400	3,200	(1,500)	10,100
Cost of sales	(4,600)	(1,700)	1,500	(4,950)
Unrealised profit	(150)			
Operating expenses	(2,200)	(960)		(3,160)
Tax	(600)	(140)		(740)
	850	400		

Marking scheme		
		Marks
(a)	Statement of profit or loss	
	Format	1.0
	Revenue	2.0
	Cost of sales	2.0
	Operating expenses	1.0
	Tax expense	1.0
	Maximum	7.0
(b)	Profit attributable to equity owners	2.0
(c)	Non-controlling interest	2.0
(d)	Parent-subsidiary relationship	4.0
Total		**15.0**

2 MALRIGHT

Statement of profit or loss for the year ended 31October 20X7

	$000
Revenue	1,800
Cost of sales (W1)	(1,284)
Gross profit	516
Administrative expenses (325 +10(W4)+16(W3)−100)	(341)
Profit for the year	175

Statement of financial position as at 31 October 20X7

	$000
Assets	
Non-current assets (W2)	731
Current assets	
Inventories	75
Trade receivables (W3)	304
Cash	20
Total assets	1,130
Equity and liabilities	
Equity	
Share capital	415
Share premium	80
Retained earnings (130 + 175 (W4))	305
	800
Current liabilities	
Trade and other payables (250 + 10 (W4))	260
Bank overdraft	70
Total equity and liabilities	1,130

Workings

(W1) Cost of sales

	$000
Opening inventory	160
Purchases	1,140
Closing inventory	(75)
Depreciation (W2)	59
	1,284

(W2) Depreciation

	Property $000	Plant $000	Total $000
Cost	740	220	960
Depreciation b/f	(60)	(110)	(170)
Expense (740 × 5%)	(37)		
Expense (220 – 110) × 20%		(22)	(59)
Carrying amount 31 October 20X7	643	88	731

(W3) Trade receivables

	$
Allowance = 320,000 × 5%	16,000
Receivables 320,000 – 16,000	304,000

(W4) Energy cost accrual

	$
15,000 × 2/3	10,000
	119,885

Section 7

REFERENCES

The Board (2016) *Conceptual Framework for Financial Reporting*. London: IFRS Foundation.

The Board (2015) *ED/2015/3: Conceptual Framework for Financial Reporting*. London: IFRS Foundation.

The Board (2015) *ED/2015/8: IFRS Practice Statement: Application of Materiality to Financial Statements*. London: IFRS Foundation.

The Board (2016) *IAS 1 Presentation of Financial Statements*. London: IFRS Foundation.

The Board (2016) *IAS 2 Inventories*. London: IFRS Foundation.

The Board (2016) *IAS 7 Statement of Cash Flows*. London: IFRS Foundation.

The Board (2016) *IAS 16 Property, Plant and Equipment*. London: IFRS Foundation.

The Board (2016) *IAS 27 Separate Financial Statements*. London: IFRS Foundation.

The Board (2016) *IAS 28 Investments in Associates and Joint Ventures*. London: IFRS Foundation.

The Board (2016) *IAS 37 Provisions, Contingent Liabilities and Contingent Assets*. London: IFRS Foundation.

The Board (2016) *IAS 38 Intangible Assets*. London: IFRS Foundation.

The Board (2016) *IFRS 3 Business Combinations*. London: IFRS Foundation.

The Board (2016) *IFRS 10 Consolidated Financial Statements*. London: IFRS Foundation.

The Board (2016) *IFRS 15 Revenue from Contracts with Customers*. London: IFRS Foundation.

Kaplan Publishing are constantly finding new ways to make a difference to your studies and our exciting online resources really do offer something different to students looking for exam success.

This book comes with free MyKaplan online resources so that you can study anytime, anywhere. This free online resource is not sold separately and is included in the price of the book.

Having purchased this book, you have access to the following online study materials:

CONTENT	ACCA (including FFA,FAB,FMA)		FIA (excluding FFA,FAB,FMA)	
	Text	Kit	Text	Kit
Eletronic version of the book	✓	✓	✓	✓
Check Your Understanding Test with instant answers	✓			
Material updates	✓	✓	✓	✓
Latest official ACCA exam questions*		✓		
Extra question assistance using the signpost icon**		✓		
Timed questions with an online tutor debrief using clock icon***		✓		
Interim assessment including questions and answers	✓		✓	
Technical answers	✓	✓	✓	✓

*   Excludes F1, F2, F3, F4, FAB, FMA and FFA; for all other papers includes a selection of questions, as released by ACCA

**   For ACCA P1-P7 only

*** Excludes F1, F2, F3, F4, FAB, FMA and FFA

How to access your online resources

Kaplan Financial students will already have a MyKaplan account and these extra resources will be available to you online. You do not need to register again, as this process was completed when you enrolled. If you are having problems accessing online materials, please ask your course administrator.

If you are not studying with Kaplan and did not purchase your book via a Kaplan website, to unlock your extra online resources please go to www.mykaplan.co.uk/addabook (even if you have set up an account and registered books previously). You will then need to enter the ISBN number (on the title page and back cover) and the unique pass key number contained in the scratch panel below to gain access.

You will also be required to enter additional information during this process to set up or confirm your account details.

If you purchased through Kaplan Flexible Learning or via the Kaplan Publishing website you will automatically receive an e-mail invitation to MyKaplan. Please register your details using this email to gain access to your content. If you do not receive the e-mail or book content, please contact Kaplan Publishing.

Your Code and Information

This code can only be used once for the registration of one book online. This registration and your online content will expire when the final sittings for the examinations covered by this book have taken place. Please allow one hour from the time you submit your book details for us to process your request.

Please scratch the film to access your MyKaplan code.

Please be aware that this code is case-sensitive and you will need to include the dashes within the passcode, but not when entering the ISBN. For further technical support, please visit www.MyKaplan.co.uk